Vegan Richa's
Everyday Kitchen

Epic Anytime Recipes
with a World of Flavor

Richa Hingle

Best-selling author of
Vegan Richa's Indian Kitchen

VEGAN HERITAGE PRESS, LLC

Woodstock • Virginia

Vegan Richa's Everyday Kitchen: Epic Anytime Recipes with a World of Flavor by Richa Hingle (Copyright © 2017 by Richa Hingle)

ISBN: 978-1-941252-39-0

First Edition, September 2017

10 9 8 7 6 5 4 3 2

Vegan Heritage Press, LLC books are available at quantity discounts. For information, please visit our website at www.veganheritagepress.com or write the publisher at Vegan Heritage Press, P.O. Box 628, Woodstock, VA 22664-0628.

Library of Congress Cataloging-in-Publication Data

Hingle, Richa.
Vegan Richa's everyday kitchen : epic anytime recipes with a world of
    flavor / Richa Hingle.
Woodstock, Virginia : Vegan Heritage Press, 2017.
LCCN 2017029423 (print) | LCCN 2017035682 (ebook) | ISBN
    9781941252406 (epub) | ISBN 9781941252413 (prc) | ISBN 9781941252390
    (paperback)
LCSH: Vegan cooking. | BISAC: COOKING / Vegetarian & Vegan.
    LCGFT: Cookbooks.
LCC TX837 (ebook) | LCC TX837 .H55 2017 (print) | DDC
    641.5/636--dc23
LC record available at https://lccn.loc.gov/2017029423

Photo Credits: Cover and interior photography by Richa Hingle. Front cover: Buffalo Chickpea Tacos (page 91). Back Cover: Marble Pumpkin Chocolate Loaf (page 225). Cover design based on a concept by Kat Marshello.

Disclaimer: The information provided in this book should not be taken as medical advice. If you require a medical diagnosis or prescription, or if you are contemplating any major dietary change, please consult a qualified health-care professional. You should always seek an expert medical opinion before making changes in your diet or supplementation regimen.

Publisher's Note: The information in this book was correct and complete to the best of our knowledge. Website addresses and contact information were correct at the time of publication. The publisher is not responsible for specific health or allergy issues or adverse reactions to recipes contained in this book.

Vegan Heritage Press books are distributed by Andrews McMeel Publishing.

Printed in the United States of America

Vegan Richa's Everyday Kitchen so celebrates flavor that simply reading these recipes is a feast. And their skillful juxtaposition of color and texture and spice makes preparing them in your own kitchen an adventure not to miss. – Victoria Moran, author of *Main Street Vegan*

You don't have to be vegan or a culinary beginner to enjoy this excellent follow-up to Richa Hingle's successful first book. With her easy-to-follow recipes and suggestions for personalizing for taste and dietary consideration (most are gluten-free), you will feel as if you have Richa herself in the kitchen guiding you. – Fran Costigan, author of *Vegan Chocolate*

Throughout history, human societies around the globe have flourished eating mainly plant foods. In this wonderful book, Richa draws on diverse traditions and shares amazing recipes that show how varied and tasty vegan food can be. – Gene Baur, president and co-founder of Farm Sanctuary and author of *Farm Sanctuary: Changing Hearts and Minds about Animals and Food*

One flavor-rich, thoughtful meal at a time, Richa shows us that everyday vegan eating can be an experience to savor. – Terry Hope Romero, author of *Salad Samurai*, *Vegan Eats World*, and co-author of *Veganomicon*

Richa Hingle has your next meal covered! Super easy recipes–from Teriyaki Lentil Balls and Peanut-Sauce Fried Rice to Tiramisu Fudge Bars and Chocolate Peanut Butter Ganache Cake–are right here in this truly delicious vegan cookbook. Yum! – Chloe Coscarelli, author of *Chloe's Kitchen*

Richa has an innate sense for spice combinations and a flair for flavor. From simple dishes that pack a punch to layered, complex meals that delight all senses, Richa's cookbook is a culinary treasure trove. Katie Hay, *T.O.F.U. Magazine*

Vegan Richa's Everyday Kitchen is a perfect expression of Richa Hingle's bold, creative, and flavor-driven approach to food. The recipes are vibrant and healthful, and the book is a clever primer in using flavors and spices to guide one's home cooking. This is an invaluable addition to any plant-based kitchen! – Gena Hamshaw, co-author of *Food52 Vegan* and creator of the *Full Helping* blog

Every vegan knows Richa is the go-to source for a plant-based Indian cuisine that's bursting with flavor and creativity. This new book is a beautiful collection of uniquely reimagined staples that perfectly showcase what Vegan Richa does best! – Lauren Toyota, creator of *Hot for Food* blog and YouTube series

In Richa's new cookbook, she presents inventive recipes with international flavors that are somehow accessible and exotic at the same time. I love how the recipes are grouped by master sauces and similar concepts, so the cook can develop a deeper understanding of the underlying flavors and techniques. I want to make every recipe in this book. – Kathryne Taylor, author of *Love Real Food*

Also by Richa Hingle

Vegan Richa's Indian Kitchen

Dedication

To you, blog readers, the people who inspire me every day to do more.

Contents

Preface

Many years ago, I was in the tech industry working on multiple projects, running from meeting to meeting, and spending countless hours on a computer. Due to a health issue, all of that suddenly changed, and I was not able to return to that work. After years of recovery and acceptance, I started cooking and experimenting in the kitchen to make use of my time. I started my food blog, *Vegan Richa* (www.veganricha.com), and began baking breads. The blog had a different name when I started as I was not vegan. Around the same time, my husband, Vivek, and I adopted Chewie, our Pomeranian, and started fostering other dogs. Food blogging and an online presence in the rescue community came together for me when I started reading other vegan blogs, and I finally made the connection that all animals deserve love. I couldn't continue to eat animals while I was caring for one as a member of my family. I also educated myself about the cruelties in the meat and dairy industries. My heart ached with every new discovery about the pain and suffering farmed animals experience. Gradually, I went vegan, and my husband followed me.

Richa's parents, Tripti and Tribhuvan Hingle, and Chewie

My transition to a vegan diet at home was not very difficult, because everyday Indian food is already vegetable-rich, generally vegetarian, and not dependent on cheese or meat. Soon, because of the success of my blog, I started trying my hand at other cuisines and vegan baking. The blog was, in a way, a journey of learning on the job. While I do not have formal culinary training, after making similar things repeatedly, I often discover a shorter method or learn how to adjust recipes to achieve authenticity and desirable results. But that's the thing that keeps me excited about my cooking: my blog readers and I are all learning together as a community.

I grew up eating seasonal, local, and freshly made food with tons of flavor from spices and herbs. At home, our food celebrated lentils, beans, vegetables, and fresh fruits. Most of what I cook comes from Mom, as well as what I learned cooking for myself after I moved out of my parents' home—I had to feed myself while living with roommates, and then I had to feed myself and my husband. I am also inspired by other cookbook authors, websites, and bloggers. I admit that I am a fussy eater. I guess that is what helps me develop a balance of flavors and textures that I enjoy. Thankfully, my readers love my creations too, judging by the success of my first book, *Vegan Richa's Indian Kitchen*.

My first book established that Indian cuisine can be veganized well. This book expands on that idea and veganizes recipes from many more cuisines. Hopefully, you will find a recipe for whatever you have in the refrigerator and pantry, as this book has many recipes that turn everyday staples into delicious meals. While *Vegan Richa's Indian Kitchen* was about introducing my Indian food to America, this one is about applying my Indian roots to everyday food.

Many of the recipes can be made with variations, so you can enjoy months and months of easy, satisfying vegan meals. I have filled this book with a new collection of incredible recipes that have been tested and loved by all who have tried them.

This book is an extension of my own vegan lifestyle that combines my love of complex flavors, enjoyment of the time in the kitchen, and compassion for the animals. Let's cook!

Richa Hingle with her mother, Tripti Hingle

Introduction

It can be a challenge providing everyday meals that are wholesome, delicious, simple to make, and fun to eat. If you want to put out the most amazing vegan food, you need this book.

When I am developing recipes, I follow a few simple rules. I strongly believe that vegan food should be easy to make, flavorful, and inclusive. This means that my recipes tend to have a lot of flavor, offer allergy-friendly variations, and provide multiple substitutions. At times, this requires a longer list of herbs and spices. The recipes in this book are no exception, but please don't let long ingredient lists deter you. The recipes themselves are quite simple to prepare.

Many of my readers request to see my blog recipes in printed form. So, in this book, I have included a number of recipes that have become popular on VeganRicha.com. However, more than half the recipes are new and were created exclusively for this book, including recipes for Thai and other Asian dishes, pizza, curries, bowls, burgers, and casseroles. There is also a big chapter on desserts and one dedicated to DIY recipes.

Defying the misconception that everyday vegan meals consist mostly of salads, today's vegan dishes go way beyond. Some days, it's all about stir-fries, which can include vegetables paired with amazing sauces: Kung Pao Sauce (page 35), Peanut Butter Sauce (page 2), or Makhani Sauce or Tikka Masala Sauce (page 54). On other days, when you want to eat with your fingers, Lentil-Walnut Burgers (page 97) and Chickpea Jackfruit Burgers (page 104) have you covered. Pizzas are no longer a weekend fix with my twenty-minute pizza crust. Chapter 6, with the Buddha Bowl with Nacho-Spiced Sweet Potatoes (page 136), will surprise you. A weekend lasagna meal can be topped off with a simple crisp cookie, fudgy blondie, or decadent pie. So many options!

I have worked hard to develop these recipes and I hope you will enjoy this book as much as I loved writing it for you.

The "Awesome Sauce" Way

The most important element to a great dish is the sauce. In my kitchen as well as in this book, the sauce is the driving force behind any recipe. The flavors, herbs, and spices (as well as all the love) you put into your cooking are reflected in the sauce.

One of the things that sets this book apart from others is that many of the chapters are organized according to the sauces that are integral to the recipes. In my own kitchen, I often make the sauce in advance of making dinner, so that I have it ready to go and can get dinner on the table faster.

> "One of the things that sets this book apart from others is that many of the chapters are organized according to the sauces that are integral to the recipes."

Many people simply do not take advantage of all the amazing flavor options available to them when provided with a given set of recipes, so this book shares its recipes in a new way: the "awesome sauce" way. If you plan your meals thinking "sauce first," then you can create a new meal every day.

The sauces in these chapters can also be used in many different ways. I feature a few of my favorite recipes with each sauce in this book, but you can also use the various sauces in other recipes and have several weeks of menus planned.

One way to do this is to make batches of a few different sauces at the beginning of the week and use them in different ways throughout your week. For example, you can make the Manchurian Sauce (page 44) and toss in some vegetables and noodles for a one-pot noodle meal, or add cooked rice instead of noodles for a fried rice dish. You could also combine some crisped cauliflower with the sauce for crispy Manchurian cauliflower, or combine the sauce with chickpeas or tofu and vegetables for a stir-fry. See? The same sauce, but many different meals.

If you don't generally plan your meals, that can work just fine, too. Pick a recipe you like and cook the sauce and the meal in parallel. If you have help, then divide the sauce and meal preparation, and dinner will be served within a short time.

In addition to the chapters based on sauces, such as chapter 1 and chapter 2, there are chapters organized according to how the meal is cooked and served, such as chapter 7, which is about casseroles, lasagna, and pizza. So, whether you're in the mood for a particular flavor or form, you can choose a chapter and choose a recipe.

Awesome Sauces

Here are the sauces, dressings, pastes, and other flavor-makers used in this book, listed in alphabetical order with their page numbers. Feel free to mix and match these sauces with your favorite ingredients, or whatever you have on hand, to make an almost limitless variety of meal combinations.

Almond-Sriracha Sauce, 100

Barbecue Sauce, 241

Berbere Paste, 68

Buffalo Sauce, 84

Butter Masala Sauce, 54

Cauliflower Alfredo Sauce, 147

Celery Ranch Sauce, 87

Chipotle Ranch Sauce, 87

Creamy White Masala Sauce, 52

Date-Sweetened Teriyaki Sauce, 29

Firecracker Sauce, 78

Green Curry Paste, 13

Hoisin Sauce, 40

Jalapeño Popper Cream, 139

Kung Pao Sauce, 35

Laksa Curry Paste, 129

Makhani Sauce, 54

Manchurian Sauce, 44

Mint-Cilantro Herb Sauce, 183

Orange Sauce, 42

Peanut Butter Sauce, 2

Peanut-Free Peanut Sauce, 3

Ranch Dressing, 87

Ranch Dressing, Nut-Free, 86

Red Curry Paste, 17

Red Pizza Sauce, 146

Smoky Cheese Sauce, 171

Spinach Curry Sauce, 62

Sweet and Sour Sauce, 24

Tahini Garlic Sauce, 123

Tamarind Chutney, 240

Teriyaki Sauce, 28

Tikka Masala Sauce, 54

Tinga Sauce, 122

White Garlic Sauce, 85

White Garlic Sauce, Nut-Free, 86

Times and Timing Used In the Recipes

Once you decide on a recipe, read through the complete recipe first, including the headnote and variations. This allows you to be ready with substitutions, the kitchen utensils needed, and the time the recipe requires. Some components of the recipe can also be made while other elements are cooking. Keep the times and ingredients for those components in mind when planning.

Often, all the ingredients are not used at the same time, so use the inactive time (see the following section) to reduce your overall preparation time. And, as in the case of sauces, grains, or beans, various components can be made well in advance.

Most of the recipes use several vegetables, which may need chopping, shredding, or slicing. A food processor can be helpful to speed things up.

If you don't have all the ingredients for a recipe, no worries. Many of the recipes can also be mixed and matched with components from other recipes. You can always adjust the meal depending on your pantry.

Recipe Cooking Times

Each recipe indicates the time it takes to make from start to finish. Here is an explanation of them and how they can help you manage your time.

Prep time: This is the time needed to chop, slice, dice, or mince the ingredients and get the spices ready. It also includes the soaking time (such as for nuts and beans) and other steps needed before you start to actively cook. I generally need 5 to 10 minutes to prep the first few steps as the rest can be done during the inactive cooking time. The ingredients are added in order and generally there are some minutes between each step of the process. However, you may require longer prep times if you haven't cooked from this book or my blog before.

Need Something Quick?

For those times when you're in a hurry to get dinner on the table, refer to the Index of Recipe Groups (page 258) for a list of recipes that can be ready in 30 minutes or less.

Active time: The active time is the time you spend doing the hands-on cooking. This cooking time is in addition to the prep time. Active time begins once the cooking starts and includes stirring, tossing, adding vegetables, prepping baking sheets or pans, and so on.

Inactive time: Inactive time is the time the food is cooking or baking without the need for your attention or presence. It is the time that elapses while the sauce or beans cook, for instance, or the baking time while food is in the oven.

The total time for a finished dish is **prep time** + **active time** + **inactive time**, if none of the steps are done simultaneously.

Adjust Seasonings to Your Taste

The seasonings used in the recipes are written to be flexible to your taste, especially regarding salt and heat preferences. Taste as you go and adjust to your preference. Start out using lower levels of saltiness, tanginess, and spiciness and increase them as you see fit. Hearty vegetables and beans don't absorb much salt when added at the end of cooking, so add the salt in stages.

Light, heat, air and time affect the spices and herbs and the flavor payoff might be different accordingly. Adjust the flavor by adding more of the spices and herbs later in the recipe.

Adjusting for Dietary Preferences

Like my blog, this book offers gluten-free, soy-free, and nut-free options wherever possible. As you read the chapter introductions and recipe headnotes, you'll find suggestions for substitutions. If the recipe cannot be substituted without a major change, there is an alternate recipe for the same dish. For example, there is a gluten-free pizza crust to use for pizzas, a cashew-free white sauce, and a nut-free peanut sauce. (See the Index of Recipe Groups on page 258 for a complete list of gluten-free, soy-free, nut-free recipes.)

When considering each recipe, look for the following notations regarding dietary substitutions:

Soy-Free or Soy-Free Option: This indicates recipes that are soy-free or can be made soy-free. Soy sauce, when used as a minor flavor component, can be substituted with soy-free coconut aminos. When used as a major flavor component, soy sauce is difficult to completely replace with a soy-free option. (If you also need to ensure that your food is gluten-free, use tamari or gluten-free soy sauce in the recipe.) Tofu and tempeh are used in some recipes. They can be substituted in most of the recipes with chickpea (Burmese) tofu, cooked chickpeas, beans, or more vegetables.

Gluten-Free or Gluten-Free Option: This indicates that the recipe is gluten-free or has an option to make it gluten-free. Most meals in the book are inherently gluten-free or have gluten-free options, or you will find a similar recipe in the book that is gluten-free. For example, there is a gluten-free pizza crust and gluten-free crispy cauliflower.

Nut-Free or Nut-Free Option: These recipes are nut-free or have an option mentioned. Most of the recipes do well with substituting seeds (e.g., sunflower, pumpkin, or hemp) for the nuts or using cauliflower, nondairy yogurt, coconut milk, blended silken tofu, or beans. There are some nut-free corresponding recipes in the book like the Nut-Free White Garlic Sauce (page 86) and Peanut-Free Peanut Sauce (page 3).

About the Nutritional Information

This book provides nutritional information as a support tool. The calculations were done using online tools, such as Cronometer.com, but these figures should be considered as estimates only. Varying factors (such as product types or brands, natural fluctuations in fresh produce, substitutions, serving sizes, and the way ingredients are processed) can alter the information in any given recipe. An ingredient change (such as using a different nondairy milk or a sweetened version) will change the data as well. Different online calculators provide varying figures, depending on their own nutrition-fact sources and algorithms. To obtain the most accurate representation of the nutritional information in a given recipe, calculate the nutritional information with the actual ingredients and amounts used, using your preferred nutrition calculator.

Metric Values

This book has metric measures as well as standard US measures. The recipes were cooked and tested with US measurements by volume (cups). Most of the metric values were calculated using online conversion tools. We have tried to keep the conversions correct to the best of our efforts, but there might be inaccuracies due to the conversion tool being used. Such differences in the conversion should not matter much in meals as they can adjusted during cooking, but they might matter in baking recipes. If in doubt, refer to the recipe notes about the expected consistency of the batter, and check the Metric Conversions and Equivalents chart on page 272, or recalculate with your favorite online conversion tool. For questions, you can contact me through my social media details on page 263.

Oil-Free Cooking

I cook with some oil on my website as well as in this book. Some recipes in this book have oil-free alternatives mentioned with the recipe. The same steps can be used to make other similar recipes without oil. Many other recipes in this book can be adjusted to be oil-free. There are no deep-fried recipes in the book. The baked recipes can often be made without oil by substituting oil with applesauce, aquafaba, or nut butter. Savory baked recipes can be made without oil by just omitting it.

To cook recipes that use whole spices, lightly toast the ground spices in a dry skillet before using. Then cook in water or broth and continue with the next step. Whole spices can also be substituted with ground spices later in the recipe.

Use water or vegetable broth to sauté the onions or vegetables until translucent or golden as the recipe needs. Depending on the pan used, the onions and vegetables will have a tendency to stick or burn. Add additional water or broth to help reduce the sticking. Also see the sidebar on page 67.

Everyday Kitchen Basics

For those of you who are new to cooking or would like some basic information about cooking techniques, equipment, and ingredients, please refer to chapter 11 (page 249), entitled "My Everyday Kitchen." There you will find pantry lists, cooking charts for lentils, peas, and beans, and much more. But for now, let's dig into the recipes!

Vivek, Richa, and Chewie

1
Peanut Butter & Coconut

This chapter is all about peanut butter-based sauces and coconut milk curries. Everyone loves a good nut butter sauce, and peanut butter-based sauces have been big hits on my blog. There is something about the combination of sweet, sour, and creamy that makes them irresistible.

Here you'll find one-pot meals, stir-fries, and other simple meals that can be made with your favorite protein, along with some new flavors and combinations to try, including Thai curries and Asian fusion dishes. If you love green curry, you will love my from-scratch Green Curry Paste (page 13) which makes a vibrant coconut milk curry, and Green Curry Fried Rice (page 14). The general formula for the fabulous fried rice recipes in this chapter is: chop up all the vegetables that you want to use, have cooked rice on hand, cook the vegetables and toast the paste or sauce you plan to use, then toss in the rice. And you're done!

I recommend you start this chapter with the One-Pot Peanut Butter Noodles (page 10), then try the Chickpeas in Peanut Butter Sauce (page 8). Note that I use smooth almond butter or peanut butter in these dishes interchangeably with equally good results. If you cannot consume peanuts, use other nuts or use the Peanut-Free Peanut Sauce (page 3) in the recipes.

One-Pot Peanut Butter Noodles (page 10)

Peanut Butter Sauce

Yes, there are a million recipes for peanut butter sauce online and in cookbooks. But believe me, you will want to make this version and give it to everyone! I used this sauce with lentils on the blog and that is now one of my top ten posts. This sauce has a deep flavor profile that comes out stronger when the sauce is cooked with noodles, lentils, or tofu. For variation, use almond butter or another nut butter.

Prep time: 15 minutes
Active time: 5 minutes
soy-free option, gluten-free
Makes 2 cups (480ml)

1/2 cup (130g) smooth peanut butter
1 (2 1/2-inch [6cm]) knob fresh ginger, peeled and coarsely chopped
3 to 4 cloves garlic
2 tablespoons (30ml) soy sauce (or coconut aminos to make soy-free)
1 tablespoon fresh lime juice
Zest of 1 lime
2 teaspoons rice vinegar
1 tablespoon sriracha sauce or Asian chile sauce, or more to taste
1/2 teaspoon cayenne
1/2 teaspoon salt
2 1/2 tablespoons (30g) sugar, or more to taste
1/2 teaspoon toasted sesame oil
1 (13.5-ounce [400ml]) can full-fat coconut milk
2 tablespoons (6g) chopped fresh cilantro (optional)
1/2 teaspoon tamarind concentrate (optional)

1. Combine the peanut butter, ginger, garlic, soy sauce, lime juice, lime zest, vinegar, sriracha, cayenne, salt, sugar, oil, milk, cilantro, and tamarind concentrate (if using) in a blender and blend until smooth.

2. Use the sauce immediately or transfer it to a tightly covered container and refrigerate for up to 4 days. Freeze for up to 2 months. After reheating the sauce, taste it and adjust the seasonings, if needed.

Variations: For a quicker dipping sauce, see the peanut sauce from Firecracker Chickpea Salad with Peanut Dressing on page 80. For a nut-free option, see the Peanut-Free Peanut Sauce on page 3 or use soy nut butter in this recipe. Use this sauce with lentils and vegetables (page 4), in fried rice (page 7), in stir-fries with Crisped Tofu (page 243) and vegetables, or add some noodles of your choice. And don't forget you can use it as a dip or a dressing for salads and burgers.

Per 1/2 cup: Calories 397, Total Fat 31g, Saturated Fat 16g, Sodium 721mg, Total Carbs 21g, Fiber 2g, Sugars 15g, Protein 10g

Peanut-Free Peanut Sauce

Awesome Sauce

Use this sauce wherever you want to use the Peanut Butter Sauce on page 2. Sunflower seed butter is a good substitute for peanut butter. Sunflower seeds can leave a bit of bitter aftertaste, though; adjust the sauce flavors with additional sugar, salt, and cayenne, if needed. This sauce can also be made with soy nut butter.

Prep time: 15 minutes
Active time: 5 minutes
soy-free option, gluten-free, nut-free
Makes 2 cups (480ml)

- 1/3 cup (87g) smooth toasted sunflower seed butter
- 1 (2 1/2-inch [6cm]) knob fresh ginger, peeled and coarsely chopped
- 3 to 4 cloves garlic
- 2 tablespoons (30ml) soy sauce (or coconut aminos to make soy-free)
- 1 tablespoon fresh lime juice
- Zest of 1 lime
- 2 teaspoons rice vinegar
- 1 tablespoon sriracha sauce or Asian chile sauce
- 1/2 teaspoon cayenne, or to taste
- 1/2 teaspoon salt
- 2 1/2 tablespoons (30g) raw sugar
- 1 teaspoon toasted sesame oil
- 1 (13.5-ounce [400ml]) can full-fat coconut milk
- 2 tablespoons (6g) chopped fresh cilantro (optional)
- 1/2 teaspoon tamarind concentrate (optional)

1. Combine the sunflower seed butter, ginger, garlic, soy sauce, lime juice, lime zest, vinegar, sriracha, cayenne, salt, sugar, oil, milk, cilantro (if using), and tamarind concentrate (if using) in a blender and blend until smooth. Use the sauce immediately or transfer it to an airtight container and store it in the refrigerator until needed.

2. Reheat the sauce over low heat in a small saucepan. Taste the reheated sauce and adjust the salt, sugar, and cayenne, if needed.

Note: You can also make this sauce with ground raw sunflower seeds if you don't have sunflower seed butter. Toast 3/4 cup (90g) raw shelled sunflower seeds in a medium skillet over medium-low heat for 10 minutes, stirring occasionally. Alternatively, spread the seeds on a medium baking sheet and bake at 325°F (160°C) for 10 minutes, stirring halfway through the cooking time. After the seeds are cool, put them in a blender with 1 teaspoon cornstarch or arrowroot starch. Pulse the blender to create a powder and use 1/3 cup (87g) in the recipe.

Per 1/2 cup: Calories 352, Total Fat 29g, Saturated Fat 15g, Sodium 744mg, Total Carbs 83g, Fiber 7g, Sugars 12g, Protein 6g

Red Lentils
in Peanut Butter Sauce

This is a favorite recipe for everyone who makes it. The peanut butter sauce packs a flavor punch. The lentils combine well with the sauce and vegetables, and the lime and fresh basil add a bright note. I use quick-cooking red lentils in this recipe as they do not taste as earthy as brown lentils. Serve this recipe over cooked rice, grains, vermicelli, or other noodles of your choice. Make this nut-free with Peanut-Free Peanut Sauce (page 3).

Prep time: 10 minutes + Peanut Butter Sauce

Active time: 30 minutes

Inactive time: 15 minutes

soy-free option, gluten-free, nut-free option

Serves 4

---

1 cup (190g) red lentils, picked over, rinsed, and drained (see sidebar)

3 1/4 cups (780ml) water, divided

2 teaspoons organic safflower or other neutral oil

1/2 cup (100g) thinly sliced red or white onion

1 1/4 cups (120g) thinly sliced red bell pepper

3/4 cup (90g) thinly sliced carrots

1 medium zucchini, sliced paper thin

1 recipe Peanut Butter Sauce (page 2)

2 tablespoons (6g) tightly packed fresh basil leaves, finely chopped

1 1/2 cups (45g) baby spinach or other baby greens

1/4 teaspoon red pepper flakes or cayenne

1. Combine the lentils with 3 cups (720ml) of the water and a good pinch salt in a large saucepan over medium heat. Cook for 13 to 15 minutes or until the lentils are nearly tender, stirring once. Drain the lentils and set aside.

2. Heat the oil in a large skillet over medium-high heat. Add the onion and cook until translucent, 3 to 4 minutes. Add the bell pepper and carrots and cook for 2 minutes. Add the zucchini.

3. Add the peanut butter sauce and the remaining 1/4 cup (60ml) water and mix well. Stir in the drained lentils. Reduce the heat to medium and bring the sauce to a boil. Taste and adjust the salt, sugar, and spices, if needed. Fold in the basil and spinach. Check the lentils for doneness, cooking 1 to 2 minutes longer, if needed. Remove the skillet from the heat. Cover the skillet and let it sit for 2 minutes. Garnish the lentils with the red pepper flakes and serve hot.

Note: This dish is freezer friendly. Freeze it in an airtight container that is just big enough to hold it (this prevents extra air in the container, which can dry out the food). Thaw the lentils and reheat them on the stove. Add some water and fresh lemon juice to refresh the lentils.

Per serving: Calories 634, Total Fat 35g, Saturated Fat 16g, Sodium 918mg, Total Carbs 61g, Fiber 10g, Sugars 20g, Protein 23g

Red Lentils

In Indian cuisine, red lentils are known as masoor dal. If you go to an Indian market to purchase your red lentils, look for that name on the packaging.

Peanut-Sauce Fried Rice

We do love peanut sauce, don't we? You know what else you can do with that delicious sauce? Make fried rice. Time to whip out the sauce from the freezer. For any of the fried rice dishes, use white or brown rice that cooks to a nonsticky, fluffy state. I prefer medium-grain white rice or any jasmine rice, or a combination with medium-grain brown rice, or brown basmati. Make this nut-free with Peanut-Free Peanut Sauce (page 3).

Prep time: 10 minutes + Peanut Butter Sauce
Active time: 20 minutes
soy-free option, gluten-free, nut-free option
Serves 4

2 teaspoons organic safflower or other neutral oil
1/2 medium red onion, thinly sliced
4 cloves garlic, finely chopped
3/4 cup (90g) thinly sliced carrots
1 medium red bell pepper, thinly sliced
7 ounces (200g) firm tofu, drained, pressed (page 243), and cubed or 1 cup (200g) additional vegetables
1 cup (90g) loosely packed chopped cabbage or broccoli
1/2 recipe Peanut Butter Sauce (page 2)
3 cups (600g) cooked and cooled rice (or other grain of choice)
Salt, to taste (if using unsalted rice)
Red pepper flakes or cayenne, as needed
1 teaspoon fresh lime or lemon juice, or more to taste
1/4 cup (10g) loosely packed finely chopped fresh cilantro or Thai basil, for garnish
Sriracha sauce, for garnish

1. Heat the oil in a large skillet over medium-high heat. Add the onion and a pinch salt. Toss and cook the onion for 2 to 3 minutes. Add the garlic, carrots, and bell pepper. Toss well and cook for 2 minutes. Add the tofu and cabbage, toss well, and cook for 2 to 3 minutes. Add the peanut butter sauce and mix well. Reduce the heat to medium. Cover the skillet and cook for 3 minutes or until the sauce bubbles and thickens slightly.

2. Add the rice and salt (if using unsalted rice). Mix well to incorporate the sauce. Cover the skillet and cook for 2 minutes. Taste and adjust the saltiness and spiciness. Add the red pepper flakes to taste. If the rice seems too dry, add some nondairy milk or water and mix well. Cover the skillet and cook for 1 minute. Let the rice sit, covered, for a few more minutes. Add the lime juice. Garnish with the cilantro and additional red pepper flakes or sriracha and serve.

Per serving: Calories 488, Total Fat 22g, Saturated Fat 9g, Sodium 476 mg, Total Carbs 59g, Fiber 6g, Sugars 11g, Protein 16g

Chickpeas in Peanut Butter Sauce

I discovered this dish when I combined some vegetables and chickpeas and added turmeric, because gold is "in" this year. I also wanted something to thicken it and make it interesting. So, I added peanut butter, adjusted the flavor, and *boom*: the blog post went viral. This recipe is very flexible—serve it over cooked grains, vegetables, or baked potatoes.

Prep time: 10 minutes
Active time: 30 minutes
Inactive time: 10 minutes
soy-free, gluten-free
Serves 6

1/2 cup (60g) coarsely chopped onion

6 cloves garlic

1 (1 1/2-inch [4cm]) knob fresh ginger

1 teaspoon organic safflower or other neutral oil

1 teaspoon ground cumin

1 teaspoon ground coriander

1/2 teaspoon ground cinnamon

1/2 teaspoon ground cardamom (optional)

1/2 teaspoon cayenne, or to taste

1/4 teaspoon black pepper

1 teaspoon ground turmeric

6 to 8 tablespoons (100 to 130g) smooth peanut butter

1 1/2 cups (360ml) almond milk (see note)

1 medium red bell pepper, thinly sliced

1 cup (120g) thinly sliced carrots

1 1/2 cups (225g) thinly sliced zucchini or summer squash

2 (15-ounce [425g]) cans chickpeas or 3 cups (500g) cooked chickpeas, drained and rinsed

3/4 to 1 1/4 teaspoons salt

2 teaspoons sugar, or more to taste

1 teaspoon fresh lime juice, or to taste

1/4 cup (10g) chopped fresh cilantro or 2 tablespoons (6g) chopped fresh Thai basil

1/4 teaspoon red pepper flakes

1. Combine the onion, garlic, and ginger in a small blender with a few tablespoons water. Blend until smooth and set aside. Alternatively, mince the onion, garlic, and ginger.

2. Heat the oil in a large skillet over medium heat. Add the cumin, coriander, cinnamon, cardamom (if using), cayenne, and black pepper and cook until fragrant, 15 to 30 seconds. Add the onion puree (or minced onion, garlic, and ginger) to the skillet and stir to combine. Add the turmeric and cook until the mixture is well roasted and the raw-onion smell dissipates, 7 to 9 minutes, stirring occasionally. (If using minced onion, garlic, and ginger, cook over medium-low heat.)

3. Add the peanut butter and milk, stirring for 30 seconds to combine. (Alternatively, you can use a blender to blend the peanut butter and milk before adding the puree to the skillet.) Add the bell pepper, carrots, zucchini, chickpeas, salt (beginning with 3/4 teaspoon and adding up to 1 1/4 teaspoons, depending on how salty the chickpeas and peanut butter are), and sugar. Cover the skillet and bring the mixture to a boil. Reduce the heat to medium-low and continue cooking for 5 minutes. Add the lime juice and cilantro. Taste and adjust the seasonings, adding more salt or sugar, if needed. Stir in the red pepper flakes.

4. Continue simmering for another 3 to 4 minutes, until the sauce thickens to your preference. (Add more milk for a thinner sauce or cook it longer, uncovered, for a thicker sauce while being careful to not overcook the vegetables.)

Note: For a creamier sauce, use coconut milk.

Variations: Add 1/2 teaspoon Garam Masala (page 244) or 1/4 teaspoon ground cloves for a deeper spice profile. Omit the turmeric if you are not fond of the flavor. Add other vegetables of your choosing, such as broccoli or mushrooms. Use cooked lentils or other cooked beans for variation. Add chunks of juicy mango, pineapple, or lychees. Add 2 packed cups (60g) baby greens a few minutes before serving.

Per serving: Calories 399, Total Fat 23g, Saturated Fat 11g, Sodium 479mg, Total Carbs 39g, Fiber 10g, Sugars 11g, Protein 13g

One-Pot Peanut Butter Noodles

This weeknight meal uses one pot and is very easy. Chop the vegetables, gather the spices and other ingredients, combine everything in the pot, and bring it to a boil. That's it. Sometimes I wonder why I order similar food from restaurants when the delivery often takes an hour! This dish is fresh and hits all the right flavor notes. Adjust the cooking time depending on the noodles used. For noodles with a longer cooking time, you might want to cook them separately to al dente and add them to the pot so the vegetables do not overcook.

Prep time: 10 minutes
Active time: 10 minutes
Inactive time: 10 minutes
gluten-free, nut-free option
Serves 4

8 to 10 ounces (230 to 280g) **brown rice noodles, vermicelli, or angel hair pasta**
4 cups (960ml) **water, or as needed**
7 ounces (200g) **firm tofu, drained and cut into 1/2-inch (1cm) dice**
3/4 cup (90g) **thinly sliced carrots**
1 large **red bell pepper, sliced paper thin**
1/2 cup (75g) **thinly sliced zucchini, green bell pepper, or broccoli**
2 tablespoons (6g) **chopped scallions (optional)**
1 tablespoon **ginger paste or minced fresh ginger**
2 teaspoons **minced garlic**
1 teaspoon **garlic powder**
1 to 1 1/2 tablespoons **sriracha**
2 tablespoons (30ml) **soy sauce (or tamari to make gluten-free)**
6 tablespoons (100g) **smooth peanut butter, almond butter, or sun butter**
2 teaspoons **fresh lime or lemon juice, plus more for serving**
2 teaspoons **distilled white vinegar or apple cider vinegar**
1 1/2 to 2 tablespoons **sugar**
1/2 teaspoon **salt, or to taste**
1/4 teaspoon **cayenne, or to taste**
3/4 cup (80g) **chopped celery or bok choy**
2 tablespoons (6g) **chopped fresh cilantro or basil (or both)**
2 tablespoons (20g) **chopped roasted peanuts for garnish (optional)**

1. Add the noodles and water to a large saucepan and push down the noodles so they are covered in water. Arrange the tofu, carrots, bell pepper, and zucchini among the noodles. Add the scallions (if using), ginger paste, garlic, garlic powder, sriracha, soy sauce, peanut butter, lime juice, vinegar, sugar, salt, and cayenne.

2. Bring to a boil over medium heat. The noodles will start to soften at the 4- to 5-minute mark. The peanut butter might clump up, so stir for a few seconds so the peanut butter mixes in and the noodles cook evenly.

3. Once the mixture is boiling, add the celery. Cook for 2 minutes or longer (depending on the noodles used). Check the noodles for doneness, then taste and adjust the seasonings, adding more sugar, cayenne, or lime juice, if needed. Fold in the cilantro and basil. Let the noodles sit for another minute before serving. Garnish with the peanuts, if using.

Variations: Add the zest of a lime to the pot. Instead of 4 cups (960ml) water, add 1 cup (240ml) coconut milk plus 3 cups (720ml) water for a creamier consistency.

Per serving: Calories 488, Total Fat 19g, Saturated Fat 3.5g, Sodium 819mg, Total Carbs 70g, Fiber 7g, Sugars 15g, Protein 18g

Green Curry Paste

I have always loved green curry from Thai restaurants. However, the store-bought and restaurant versions might contain shrimp paste or other fish ingredients. This easy paste comes in handy when I want a quick green curry for dinner. This paste is fragrant, vibrant, and so fresh. Simply blend the ingredients, add some vegetables, tofu or beans, and coconut milk and you're done. Use it to make the Green Curry Chickpeas and Eggplant (page 16) or toss it up in Green Curry Fried Rice (page 14).

Prep time: 15 minutes
Active time: 10 minutes
soy-free, gluten-free, nut-free
Makes 3/4 cup (180g)

1/2 teaspoon ground cumin (preferably freshly ground from roasted cumin seeds)

2 teaspoons ground coriander

4 to 6 small serrano or other green chiles, seeded if desired

1 (8-inch [20cm]) stalk fresh lemongrass, outer skin removed and finely chopped

1/4 cup (30g) coarsely chopped red onion or shallot

4 to 5 cloves garlic

1 (1 1/2-inch [4cm]) knob fresh galangal or ginger

1/2 cup (20g) tightly packed fresh cilantro with tender stems

1/4 cup (10g) tightly packed fresh basil leaves

Dash black pepper

2 teaspoons soy sauce (or coconut aminos to make soy-free)

1 tablespoon fresh lime juice

Zest of 1 lime or 2 kaffir lime leaves

1 teaspoon raw sugar

2 to 3 tablespoons (30 to 45ml) coconut milk

In a small blender or spice grinder (see note), process the cumin, coriander, chiles, lemongrass, onion, garlic, galangal, cilantro, basil, pepper, soy sauce, lime juice, lime zest, sugar, and milk until well combined. Refrigerate the paste for up to 4 days or freeze it in 3 (4-tablespoon [60g]) portions for up to 1 month.

Note: If you don't have a small blender or spice grinder, use a mortar and pestle and press the ingredients at an angle with the pestle. Keep working on the mixture for a few minutes. It takes a while for the ingredients to become a paste.

Per 3/4 cup: Calories 191, Total Fat 9g, Saturated Fat 6g, Sodium 410mg, Total Carbs 28g, Fiber 5g, Sugars 9g, Protein 5g

Green Curry Fried Rice

This fried rice is a great way to use up some vibrant Green Curry Paste. This rice and vegetable dish, without the soupy coconut milk found in traditional curry, lets the curry paste shine.

Prep time: 10 minutes + Green Curry Paste

Active time: 20 minutes

soy-free option, gluten-free, nut-free

Serves 4

---

2 teaspoons organic safflower or other neutral oil, divided

3/4 cup (150g) thinly sliced red onion

7 ounces (200g) firm tofu, drained, pressed (page 243), and cubed or 1 cup (200g) additional vegetables

3/4 cup (90g) thinly sliced carrots

1 cup (150g) thinly sliced zucchini, or more to taste

1 medium red bell pepper, sliced paper thin

1/2 cup (70g) canned bamboo shoots, drained and sliced paper thin

1 to 2 cups (100 to 200g) finely chopped mushrooms or broccoli or thinly sliced green cabbage (optional)

4 to 8 tablespoons (60 to 120g) Green Curry Paste (page 13)

1/2 cup (120ml) unsweetened coconut milk

1/4 teaspoon salt, plus more to taste, divided

2 teaspoons raw sugar or other sweetener

1/4 cup (10g) fresh Thai basil leaves

3 cups (600g) cooked and cooled rice (see note)

Red pepper flakes or cayenne, to taste

Fresh lime or lemon juice, to taste

1. Heat 1 teaspoon of the oil in a large skillet over medium-high heat. When the oil is hot, add the onion and a pinch salt. Toss and cook for 2 to 3 minutes.

2. Add the tofu and toss well. Cook for 2 to 3 minutes. Add the carrots, zucchini, bell pepper, bamboo shoots, and mushrooms (if using). Toss well, cover the skillet, and cook for 3 minutes.

3. Move the vegetables to make space for the green curry paste in the center of the pan. Add the green curry paste and the remaining 1 teaspoon oil and cook for 1 minute. Add the milk, 1/4 teaspoon of the salt, sugar, and Thai basil leaves and mix well. Cover and cook for 3 minutes or until the mixture is bubbling.

4. Add the rice and remaining salt (if using unsalted rice). Toss for about 30 seconds to incorporate the sauce. Cover and cook for 2 minutes. Add the red pepper flakes and lime juice. Taste and adjust the seasonings as desired. If the rice feels too dry, sprinkle in some additional milk or water and mix well. Let the rice sit, covered, another 3 to 5 minutes. Add additional lime juice, garnish with more red pepper flakes, and serve.

Note: Quinoa or another grain may be used instead of rice.

Variation: This fried rice can also be made with red curry paste. Add 1/2 teaspoon tamarind paste and 1 to 2 tablespoons peanut butter or almond butter along with the coconut milk when using red curry paste.

Tip: If you use store-bought green curry paste, it might be quite mild. Use more paste or add cayenne and lime juice according to your preferences.

Per serving: Calories 385, Total Fat 12g, Saturated Fat 6g, Sodium 403mg, Total Carbs 58g, Fiber 9g, Sugars 9g, Protein 13g

Green Curry Chickpeas and Eggplant

When I make green curry at home, I add chickpeas, tofu, or lentils. This recipe features chickpeas along with eggplant and your choice of zucchini, red bell pepper, or broccoli. If you are using a quick-cooking vegetable, like zucchini, add it in the last 5 minutes of simmering. Serve this delicious curry over cooked rice or other grain.

Prep time: 10 minutes
Active time: 30 minutes
Inactive time: 15 minutes
soy-free, gluten-free, nut-free
Serves 4

1 teaspoon organic safflower or other neutral oil

4 tablespoons (60g) Green Curry Paste (page 13)

2 dried red chiles or red pepper flakes, to taste

1 cup (80g) finely chopped or thinly sliced eggplant (preferably Japanese eggplant)

1 (15-ounce [425g]) can chickpeas, 1 1/2 cups (250g) cooked chickpeas, drained and rinsed, or 14 ounces (400g) diced firm tofu

1 cup (100g) coarsely chopped zucchini, red bell pepper, or broccoli

1 (13.5-ounce [400ml]) can full-fat coconut milk

1/2 cup (120ml) water

1/2 teaspoon lime zest or fresh lime juice, to taste

1/4 teaspoon salt

2 teaspoons coconut sugar or other sweetener

1/2 cup (20g) loosely packed fresh basil leaves

1. Heat the oil in a large skillet or saucepan over medium heat. Add the green curry paste and cook until fragrant, 1 to 2 minutes. Add the chiles and eggplant, mix them with the paste, and cook for 3 minutes.

2. Add the chickpeas, zucchini, milk, water, lime zest, salt, and sugar and stir to combine. Cover the skillet and cook for 15 minutes, stirring once halfway through the cooking time. Taste and adjust the seasonings, adding more green curry paste and milk to your preference. Add the basil leaves. Simmer for a few more minutes, until the eggplant is tender but not over-cooked. Serve hot.

Variation: Add 2 or 3 kaffir lime leaves along with the vegetables.

Per serving: Calories 238, Total Fat 11g, Saturated Fat 8g, Sodium 231mg, Total Carbs 27g, Fiber 9g, Sugars 8g, Protein 7g

Red Curry Paste

Red curry paste is easily available, but it's also great to make some at home—especially considering bottled pastes sometimes contain animal ingredients. You can adjust the heat and other flavors to your preference, and it freezes well. Make a batch of Red Curry Soup with Lentils (page 18) or Massaman Curry Vegetables (page 20) using this flavorful homemade paste. (Note that if you choose to use a mortar and pestle to make the paste, it's best to finely chop the ingredients.)

Prep time: 5 minutes
Active time: 10 minutes
Inactive time: 15 minutes
soy-free, gluten-free, nut-free
Makes about 1/2 cup (120g)

5 to 6 dried hot red chiles or 1 1/2
   tablespoons (11g) red pepper flakes
2 dried mild red chiles
2 teaspoons coriander seeds
1 teaspoon cumin seeds
1/2 teaspoon whole black peppercorns
   or ground black pepper
1 teaspoon paprika
1/4 to 1 teaspoon cayenne
2 medium shallots, chopped, or 1/4 cup
   (30g) coarsely chopped onion
1 (1 1/2-inch [4cm]) knob fresh ginger,
   coarsely chopped
1 (1/2-inch [1cm]) knob fresh galangal,
   coarsely chopped (optional)
6 cloves garlic, coarsely chopped
2 tablespoons (19g) coarsely chopped
   fresh lemongrass (see note)
2 tablespoons (6g) coarsely chopped
   cilantro stems or roots (see note)
Zest of 1 lime
2 teaspoons fresh lime juice
1/4 teaspoon salt
1/4 teaspoon sugar

1. Remove the stems from the chiles. Remove the seeds for a milder paste, if desired, and coarsely chop the chiles. Soak the chiles in warm water for 15 minutes.

2. Grind the coriander, cumin, peppercorns, paprika, and cayenne to a powder in a spice grinder or small blender. Set aside. Drain the chiles using a strainer.

3. Add the ground spices, chiles, shallots, ginger, galangal (if using), garlic, lemongrass, cilantro stems, lime zest, lime juice, salt, and sugar to a mortar. With the pestle at an angle, pound the ingredients, drag the pestle to grind the ingredients, and repeat. Alternatively, use a small blender to blend the ingredients with as little water as possible.

4. Store the red curry paste in the refrigerator for 1 week or freeze it in 2-tablespoon (30g) portions for up to 1 month.

Note: To prepare lemongrass, peel the outer thick layer and chop off the hard root end. Chop the lemongrass into small pieces and use. This paste traditionally uses cilantro root, which can be difficult to find in stores. Thankfully, cilantro stems work equally well.

Per 1/2 cup: Calories 185, Total Fat 3g, Saturated Fat 0g, Sodium 616mg, Total Carbs 41g, Fiber 8g, Sugars 12g, Protein 6g

Red Curry Soup with Lentils

This soup is very slurp-able. Serve it with large soup spoons. Add more coconut milk or water for brothy soup. I like this soup very brothy, somewhat like a red curry ramen.

Prep time: 10 minutes
Active time: 20 minutes
Inactive time: 15 to 20 minutes
soy-free, gluten-free, nut-free
Serves 4

1/2 cup (95g) red lentils, picked over, rinsed, and drained
3 1/4 cups (780ml) water, divided
1 teaspoon organic safflower or other neutral oil
3/4 cup (90g) coarsely chopped onion
4 cloves garlic, finely chopped
1 (1/2-inch [1cm]) knob fresh ginger, peeled and minced or grated
3 tablespoons (45g) Red Curry Paste (page 17)
2 1/2 to 3 1/2 cups (250 to 350g) thinly sliced bell pepper (any color), carrots, or zucchini (or small cauliflower or broccoli florets)
1 (13.5-ounce [400ml]) can full-fat coconut milk
1 teaspoon salt
1 1/2 tablespoons (18g) raw sugar or other sweetener
1/4 teaspoon cayenne
Zest of 1 lime
1 teaspoon fresh lime or lemon juice
1/2 cup (20g) loosely packed fresh Thai basil or sweet basil
1/4 cup (10g) coarsely chopped fresh cilantro, divided (optional)
Fresh lemon wedges, for garnish

1. Combine the lentils with 2 1/2 cups (600ml) of the water in a small saucepan over medium heat. Cook the lentils for 13 to 15 minutes, or until they are al dente, stirring once halfway through the cooking time. Drain the lentils and set aside.

2. Meanwhile, heat the oil in a large saucepan over medium heat. Add the onion, garlic, and a pinch salt and cook until the onion is translucent, about 4 minutes. Add the ginger and red curry paste and stir to combine. Cook the mixture for 1 to 2 minutes, until the paste is fragrant. Add the bell pepper and a splash of water and cook for 5 minutes.

3. Add the milk, remaining 3/4 cup (180ml) water, salt, sugar, cayenne, lime zest, and lime juice and stir to combine. Add the cooked lentils and bring the mixture to a rolling boil, 6 to 7 minutes. Taste and adjust the seasonings. Reduce the heat to low. Add the Thai basil and 2 tablespoons (6g) of the cilantro (if using) and stir to combine. Cover the saucepan and simmer for a few minutes, until the vegetables are cooked through and the flavors meld. Garnish with the remaining cilantro and lemon wedges and serve.

Variation: Add some smooth peanut butter and curry powder for a Massaman-style soup. Add 10 ounces (284g) cubed firm or extra-firm tofu instead of cooked lentils.

Per serving: Calories 324, Total Fat 16g, Saturated Fat 14g, Sodium 713mg, Total Carbs 34g, Fiber 6g, Sugars 10g, Protein 11g

Massaman Curry Vegetables

This Thai Malay curry is a favorite. The combination of curry paste, nut butter, spices, and tamarind make for a burst of many flavors in every bite. If you use vegetables that require a longer cooking time, blanch them until they are cooked al dente, then add them to the simmering sauce. You can add a variety of spices (or omit a few) for many flavor variations. For a heartier meal, add some Crisped Tofu or cooked red lentils. To substitute tamarind paste, use vegan Worcestershire sauce or lime juice to taste. Serve these veggies over rice or rice noodles.

Prep time: 15 minutes
Active time: 30 minutes
Inactive time: 10 minutes
soy-free, gluten-free
Serves 4

2 teaspoons coconut oil or organic safflower oil, divided

1/2 cup (100g) thinly sliced red or white onion

2 teaspoons minced fresh ginger

4 cloves garlic, minced

2 cups (210g) coarsely chopped cauliflower florets

1 medium red or green bell pepper, sliced paper thin

3/4 cup (75g) chopped green beans

1/2 cup (60g) thinly sliced carrots

1 cup (90g) chopped vegetables of choice or Crisped Tofu (page 243)

3/4 teaspoon salt, divided

2 to 3 tablespoons (30 to 45g) Red Curry Paste (page 17)

1/4 teaspoon ground cumin

1/4 teaspoon ground cinnamon

1/4 teaspoon ground cardamom

1/8 teaspoon ground cloves

1/4 teaspoon cayenne

1/4 teaspoon crushed fennel seeds or ground star anise

3 tablespoons (48g) peanut butter

1 tablespoon sugar

1/2 teaspoon tamarind paste

1 (13.5-ounce [400ml]) can full-fat coconut milk

1/4 to 1/2 cup (60 to 120ml) water

2 tablespoons (6g) finely chopped fresh basil

1. Heat 1 teaspoon of the oil in a large skillet over medium heat. Add the onion, ginger, and garlic and cook for 4 minutes, stirring occasionally. Add the cauliflower, bell pepper, green beans, carrots, additional vegetables, and 1/4 teaspoon of the salt and mix well. Cover the skillet and cook for 4 minutes.

2. Move the vegetables to the side to make some space in the middle of the skillet. Add the red curry paste, cumin, cinnamon, cardamom, cloves, cayenne, fennel, and the remaining 1 teaspoon oil and cook for 2 minutes to roast the spices and paste. Add the peanut butter, sugar, 1/4 teaspoon of the salt, tamarind paste, milk, and water and stir for 30 seconds, or until the peanut butter is incorporated.

3. Cover the skillet and cook for 8 minutes, or until the curry thickens a bit. Taste and add the remaining 1/4 teaspoon salt and additional cayenne, if needed. Cook for a few minutes longer, until the vegetables are cooked to your liking. Garnish with the basil. Serve hot.

Per serving: Calories 349, Total Fat 26g, Saturated Fat 18g, Sodium 583mg, Total Carbs 26g, Fiber 5g, Sugars 13g, Protein 8g

2
Sweet & Sour

Whenever I go out to Chinese or Asian fusion restaurants, I love their strongly flavored, simple sauces. For most meals, deep-fried tofu or fake meats can often make up the bulk of the dish. However, I prefer my versions with abundant vegetables and whole proteins, like chickpeas, lentils, or baked tofu or tempeh. The recipes in this chapter feature sweet and sour flavors and some heat. Chinese takeout can now be made at home.

The "Awesome Sauces" used in this chapter are simple to make from scratch and very flexible when it comes to adjusting the sweetness, saltiness, and oil content to your preference. Orange Sauce (page 42), Sweet and Sour Sauce (page 24), Kung Pao Sauce (page 35), and Hoisin Sauce (page 40) will help you make quick stir-fries, fried rice, or noodles. Once you eat crunchy baked broccoli (page 246) with the orange sauce, you might never again eat it blanched.

Start with Sweet and Sour Chickpeas (page 25) and Kung Pao Lentils (page 36) to get into the groove. Then make the cauliflower from the Crispy Kung Pao Cauliflower (page 38) and pair it with Manchurian Sauce (page 44) or Orange Sauce (page 42). For quick one-pot meals, Manchurian Sauce Noodles (page 46) or Black Pepper Tofu (page 48) seem to please everyone.

Hoisin Mushroom and Tofu Stir-Fry (page 41)

Sweet and Sour Sauce

This is a simple sweet and sour sauce that I use in many ways to satisfy the sweet and sour craving. The flavors are flexible and you can use a combination of sugar and stevia or other sweeteners. This sauce goes well in a stir-fry or as a dipping sauce (see note). Thicken this sauce to use over Crisped Tofu (page 243) or Crunchy Baked Cauliflower (page 246).

Prep time: 5 minutes
Active time: 5 minutes
gluten-free option, nut-free
Makes about 1 cup (240ml)

- 1/4 cup (50g) plus 1 to 2 tablespoons raw sugar
- 1/4 cup (60ml) water
- 3 tablespoons (45ml) distilled white vinegar or apple cider vinegar
- 1/4 cup (60ml) rice vinegar
- 2 tablespoons (30ml) ketchup or 1 1/2 tablespoons tomato paste
- 1 1/2 to 2 tablespoons soy sauce (or tamari to make gluten-free)
- 3 cloves garlic, minced
- 3/4 teaspoon garlic powder
- 1/4 teaspoon ground black or white pepper

In a medium bowl, whisk together the sugar, water, distilled white vinegar, rice vinegar, ketchup, soy sauce, garlic, garlic powder, and pepper. Store in the refrigerator for up to 2 weeks.

Note: To make a sweet and sour dipping sauce, whisk 2 teaspoons cornstarch into the 1/4 cup (60ml) water. Add the cornstarch mixture to a small saucepan over medium-high heat. Add the rest of the ingredients and whisk to combine. Bring the mixture to a boil and simmer for 1 minute or so to thicken. Taste and adjust the seasoning, adding more sugar or vinegar if needed.

Variation: Add 1/2 teaspoon grated fresh ginger. Add 1 teaspoon Asian chile sauce or red pepper flakes, to taste, for heat.

Per 1/2 cup: Calories 318, Total Fat 0g, Saturated Fat 0g, Sodium 873mg, Total Carbs 77g, Fiber 1g, Sugars 69g, Protein 3g

Sweet and Sour Chickpeas

Chickpeas and lentils work beautifully as a tofu or meat substitute in flavorful Asian sauces. This one-pot, protein-filled meal takes just twenty minutes of active kitchen time. A dash black pepper and cayenne brings out the strong sweet and sour flavors even more. Serve these chickpeas over cooked rice or a grain of your choice.

Prep time: 10 minutes + Sweet and
    Sour Sauce
Active time: 20 minutes
gluten-free, nut-free
Serves 4

1 teaspoon organic safflower or other
    neutral oil
4 cloves garlic, finely chopped
1 large red bell pepper, thinly sliced
1 large green bell pepper, thinly sliced
1 1/2 cups (130g) small broccoli florets
2 to 2 1/2 cups (330 to 415g) cooked
    chickpeas, drained and rinsed
1 recipe Sweet and Sour Sauce (page 24)
1/4 teaspoon salt
Dash black pepper
Dash cayenne
2 1/2 teaspoons cornstarch or other
    starch
2 tablespoons (30ml) cold water
1 teaspoon sesame seeds
2 tablespoons (6g) finely chopped scal-
    lions

1. Heat the oil in a large skillet over medium-high heat. Add the garlic and cook for 2 minutes, stirring frequently to avoid burning, or until the garlic is fragrant. Add the red and green bell peppers. Cover the skillet and cook for 2 minutes. Add the broccoli, cover the skillet, and cook for 1 minute. Add the chickpeas, sweet and sour sauce, salt, pepper, and cayenne. Reduce the heat to medium. Cover the skillet and cook for 10 minutes. Taste the sauce and adjust the seasonings, adding more vinegar, sugar, or salt if needed.

2. Whisk the cornstarch into the cold water and add the mixture to the skillet, stirring to combine. Cover the skillet and bring the sauce to a boil. Simmer over medium heat for another minute, or until the sauce thickens. Garnish with the sesame seeds and scallions and serve.

Per serving: Calories 300, Total Fat 5g, Saturated Fat 0.6g, Sodium 433mg, Total Carbs 56g, Fiber 10g, Sugars 27g, Protein 12g

Crispy Sweet and Sour Tofu

This super crispy tofu, glazed in my Sweet and Sour Sauce, will remind you of a deep-fried, sticky takeout version. But there is no deep-frying involved in this recipe. The tofu is coated in rice flour, pan-fried, and drizzled with sauce. Toss in vegetables with the sauce if you like, and serve it over cooked rice or grains. You can also substitute the Sweet and Sour Sauce with other sauces, such as Kung Pao Sauce (page 35), Orange Sauce (page 42), or Manchurian Sauce (page 44). Note that you might need additional cornstarch to thicken the sauces to your preference.

Prep time: 10 minutes + Sweet and
   Sour Sauce
Active time: 35 minutes
Inactive time: 15 minutes
gluten-free, nut-free
Serves 4

Marinade

3 tablespoons (45ml) tamari
1/2 teaspoon garlic powder
21 ounces (596g) firm or extra-firm
   tofu, drained

Coating

1/2 cup (80g) rice flour (preferably
   white rice flour), divided
1/2 cup (76g) cornstarch, divided
1/2 teaspoon salt, divided
1/2 teaspoon garlic powder, divided
1/2 teaspoon black pepper, divided
1 tablespoon organic safflower or
   other neutral oil, plus more as
   needed

Sauce

1 tablespoon cornstarch or other
   starch
1/4 cup (60ml) cold water
1 recipe Sweet and Sour Sauce (page
   24)
Optional Garnish: finely chopped scallions, red pepper flakes
Blanched vegetables, for serving
   (optional)

1. Marinade: In a large, shallow bowl, combine the tamari and garlic powder. Lightly press the tofu in a paper towel to remove some of the excess moisture. Cut the tofu into 1/2-inch (1cm) pieces and add them to the bowl. Toss to coat with the marinade, and let the tofu chill in the refrigerator for at least 15 minutes (longer is better).

2. Coating: In a large zip-top bag, combine 1/4 cup (40g) of the flour, 1/4 cup (38g) of the cornstarch, 1/4 teaspoon of the salt, 1/4 teaspoon of the garlic powder, and 1/4 teaspoon of the pepper. Shake the bag to mix the ingredients. Lightly drain the marinated tofu using a strainer or large spoon. Add half of the tofu cubes to the zip-top bag. Seal the bag and shake well to coat the tofu. Remove the coated cubes from the flour mixture and set aside. Add the remaining 1/4 cup (40g) flour, 1/4 cup (38g) cornstarch, 1/4 teaspoon salt, 1/4 teaspoon garlic powder, and 1/4 teaspoon pepper to the bag and shake to combine. Add the remaining drained tofu and shake well to coat the cubes.

3. Heat the oil in a large skillet over medium-high heat. Add the tofu cubes. Do not crowd the skillet, and cook in batches if needed. Cook the tofu for 6 to 8 minutes. Stir or flip the cubes every 2 to 3 minutes, until they are crispy.

4. Sauce: Whisk the cornstarch into the water to make a slurry. In a small saucepan, combine the sweet and sour sauce and the slurry. Bring the sauce to a boil and simmer for 1 minute or so to thicken. Pour the sauce over the tofu and toss well to coat. Garnish with the scallions or red pepper flakes (if using). At this point, you can also toss in hot blanched vegetables (if using) and toss to coat with sauce.

Per serving: Calories 435, Total Fat 15g, Saturated Fat 2g, Sodium 961mg, Total Carbs 53g, Fiber 2g, Sugars 18g, Protein 23g

Teriyaki Sauce

This teriyaki sauce is amazing drizzled over Crisped Tofu (page 243), slathered on burger patties, or tossed with salads. It became a favorite of recipe testers who previously disliked teriyaki! Try it with the lentil balls on page 31. If you don't have molasses, use brown sugar instead.

Prep time: 5 minutes
Active time: 10 minutes
gluten-free option, nut-free
Makes about 3/4 cup (180ml)

1/4 cup (60ml) soy sauce (or tamari to make gluten-free)
1/3 cup (66g) sugar
2 teaspoons minced fresh ginger
2 teaspoons minced fresh garlic
1 tablespoon rice wine vinegar
1 teaspoon blackstrap molasses
1/2 cup (120ml) water, divided
1 tablespoon cornstarch
1 tablespoon sesame seeds (optional)

1. Combine the soy sauce, sugar, ginger, garlic, vinegar, and molasses in a medium saucepan over medium heat. Add 1/4 cup (60ml) of the water. Stir well to dissolve the sugar and bring the mixture to a simmer, 3 to 4 minutes.

2. Combine the cornstarch with the remaining 1/4 cup (60ml) water and add the mixture to the saucepan. Fold in the sesame seeds (if using). Bring the sauce to a boil to thicken, 3 to 4 minutes. Let the sauce cool, and refrigerate it for up to 1 week or freeze it for up to 1 month.

Per 3/4 cup: Calories 316, Total Fat 6g, Saturated Fat 1g, Sodium 2315mg, Total Carbs 60g, Fiber 2g, Sugars 47g, Protein 7g

Date-Sweetened Teriyaki Sauce

I like teriyaki for its extreme flavors, but often the bottled versions have additives or way too much sugar and sodium. This version uses dates and the flavor can be adjusted to taste. This sauce thickens up, so thin it out depending on the application. Use it to bake up the Teriyaki Tempeh with Butternut and Cauliflower (page 32).

Prep time: 15 minutes
Active time: 10 minutes
gluten-free option, nut-free
Makes about 1 cup (240ml)

9 to 10 large Medjool dates, soaked in hot water for 15 minutes

1/4 cup (60ml) low-sodium soy sauce (or tamari to make gluten-free)

3/4 cup (180ml) water or vegetable broth

2 teaspoons rice vinegar, or to taste

1 teaspoon molasses

3/4 teaspoon garlic powder

1/4 teaspoon onion powder

1/4 teaspoon cayenne, or to taste

1 teaspoon grated fresh ginger, or to taste

1 teaspoon sesame oil

1 tablespoon maple syrup or coconut sugar, or to taste (optional)

1. Combine the dates, soy sauce, water, vinegar, molasses, garlic powder, onion powder, cayenne, ginger, oil, and maple syrup (if using) in a blender and blend until smooth.

2. Pour the sauce into a small saucepan over medium heat. Bring the sauce to a boil and cook about 5 minutes, stirring occasionally. Let the sauce cool and refrigerate it for up to 1 week.

Per 1 cup: Calories 826, Total Fat 0g, Saturated Fat 0g, Sodium 2303mg, Total Carbs 204g, Fiber 17g, Sugars 176g, Protein 11g

Teriyaki Lentil Balls

If you are wondering why lentil balls appear in this chapter, you have to try them with teriyaki sauce. I prefer these balls with the traditional Teriyaki Sauce (page 28), but they also go well with the Date-Sweetened Teriyaki Sauce (page 29). These lentil balls also work with Orange Sauce (page 42), Kung Pao Sauce (page 35), and Manchurian Sauce (page 44).

Prep time: 10 minutes + Teriyaki Sauce
Active time: 20 minutes
Inactive time: 20 minutes
gluten-free, nut-free
Serves 3 to 4

3/4 cup (90g) baby carrots
1 (1 to 1 1/2-inch [3 to 4cm]) knob fresh ginger, peeled
2 tablespoons (20g) coarsely chopped celery or onion
1/4 cup (20g) old fashioned oats
3/4 teaspoon garlic powder
1 to 1 1/2 tablespoons tamari
1/4 to 1/2 teaspoon cayenne
1/8 teaspoon salt
1 teaspoon toasted sesame oil, plus more as needed
1 tablespoon ground flaxseed (optional)
1 1/2 cups (300g) cooked lentils, drained and rinsed, divided
2 to 3 tablespoons (16 to 24g) unbleached all-purpose flour or oat flour
1 recipe Teriyaki Sauce (page 28) or Date-Sweetened Teriyaki Sauce (page 29)
Garnish: scallions, sesame seeds

1. Preheat the oven to 400°F (200°C). Pulse the carrots, ginger, celery, and oats in a food processor. Add the garlic powder, tamari, cayenne, salt, oil, ground flaxseed (if using), and 3/4 cup (150g) of the cooked lentils and pulse a few times to combine and mash most of the lentils.

2. Transfer the lentil mixture to a large bowl and add the remaining 3/4 cup (150g) lentils, stirring and mashing to combine. Add the flour to help reduce the moisture in the mixture if needed. You want the mixture to still be moist but not dripping liquid. Taste and adjust the salt if needed. Use a tablespoon scoop to pack and scoop balls. Place each meatball on a medium baking sheet lined with parchment paper and tap the scoop to release the meatball. (Dip the scoop in water before every scoop for easier release.)

3. Spray additional oil on the lentil balls. Bake for 20 minutes. If the balls are soft or squishy to the touch, bake them for another 2 to 3 minutes. The balls do harden and set during cooling, so be careful not to overbake them. Remove the baking sheet from the oven and let the lentil balls cool slightly. When you are ready to serve, dress the balls liberally with the heated teriyaki sauce. Garnish with the scallions and sesame seeds.

Per serving: Calories 223, Total Fat 4g, Saturated Fat 0.5g, Sodium 894mg, Total Carbs 41g, Fiber 7g, Sugars 14g, Protein 11g

Teriyaki Tempeh
with Butternut and Cauliflower

This is a simple casserole with tempeh, cauliflower, and squash. The teriyaki sauces work beautifully with these three ingredients. Don't like teriyaki? Try this with Peanut Butter Sauce (page 2) or Kung Pao Sauce (page 35). To keep this gluten-free, make sure to use gluten-free tempeh and gluten-free tamari in your teriyaki sauce.

Prep time: 10 minutes + Teriyaki Sauce
Active time: 15 minutes
Inactive time: 25 minutes
gluten-free, nut-free
Serves 3 to 4

8 ounces (227g) tempeh, cubed, or Crisped Tofu (page 243)

1/2 head small cauliflower, chopped into small florets, about 2 heaping cups (220g)

2 cups (410g) cubed butternut squash (see note)

Organic safflower or other neutral oil, as needed

1 recipe Teriyaki Sauce (page 28) or Date-Sweetened Teriyaki Sauce (page 29)

2 teaspoons toasted sesame seeds, for garnish

2 tablespoons (6g) finely chopped scallions, for garnish

Red pepper flakes, for garnish (optional)

1. Preheat the oven to 425°F (220°C). In a shallow baking dish, arrange the tempeh, cauliflower, and butternut squash in a single layer. Spray the oil on the tempeh and vegetables and bake for 12 minutes.

2. Drizzle the prepared teriyaki sauce over the tempeh and vegetables, stirring to coat. Bake for 15 to 17 minutes, or until the vegetables are done to your preference and the sauce has thickened. Let the tempeh and vegetables sit for 5 minutes before serving. Garnish with the sesame seeds, scallions, and red pepper flakes (if using). Serve over rice or another grain of your choice.

Note: If you prefer not to use butternut squash, substitute it with an equal amount of pumpkin or sweet potato.

Per serving: Calories 254, Total Fat 8g, Saturated Fat 1g, Sodium 609mg, Total Carbs 34g, Fiber 7g, Sugars 15g, Protein 14g

Kung Pao Sauce

Awesome Sauce

This sauce can be mild or super hot. Break one or two of the chiles for extra heat. Szechuan peppercorns are easily available in Asian stores or online. You can use the peppercorns in other Szechuanese dishes. If you can't get a hold of the peppercorns, you can get a good-quality chile oil to finish the dish where you are using this sauce. You can make this sauce with just red pepper flakes and black pepper as well. Try this sauce with Crispy Kung Pao Cauliflower (page 38), with noodles, or the Kung Pao Tofu and Vegetable Stir-Fry (page 37).

Prep time: 10 minutes
Active time: 15 minutes
Inactive time: 10 minutes
gluten-free
Makes 1 cup (240ml)

1 teaspoon organic safflower or other neutral oil

10 to 12 dried hot red chiles (or California chiles for a milder version)

1/2 teaspoon crushed Szechuan peppercorns (see note)

1/3 to 1/2 cup (40 to 60g) chopped cashews or peanuts

5 cloves garlic, finely chopped

1 (1-inch [3cm]) knob fresh ginger, peeled and finely chopped

2 tablespoons (6g) coarsely chopped scallions

1/4 cup (40g) finely chopped red or green bell pepper, celery, or onion (or a combination)

1/3 cup (80ml) soy sauce

2 1/2 to 3 tablespoons (38 to 45ml) rice vinegar

2 to 2 1/2 tablespoons (24 to 30g) raw sugar

1/4 teaspoon salt (optional)

1 1/4 cups (300ml) water, divided

1 1/2 to 2 teaspoons cornstarch

1. Heat the oil in a large skillet over medium-high heat. Add the red chiles and cook until the chiles are fragrant, but not overly brown, about 1 minute. (For more heat, break some of the chiles in half before adding them to the skillet.)

2. Add the peppercorns and cashews and stir for 30 seconds. Add the garlic and ginger, reduce the heat to medium low, and continue cooking until the garlic and cashews are golden, 4 to 5 minutes, stirring occasionally.

3. Add the scallions and bell pepper, stirring to combine. Increase the heat to medium and cook for 1 minute. Add the soy sauce, vinegar, sugar, salt (if using), and 1 cup (240ml) of the water and bring to a boil, about 4 minutes.

4. Whisk the cornstarch together with the remaining 1/4 cup (60ml) water and add the mixture to the boiling sauce. Cook until the sauce thickens slightly, 3 to 4 minutes. Carefully taste and adjust the seasonings. If you need more heat, break open a few of the chiles or add some red pepper flakes. Refrigerate the sauce for up to 3 days, or freeze it for up to 1 month.

Note: If you cannot find Szechuan peppercorns, substitute a mixture of red pepper flakes and crushed black peppercorns.

Por 1 cup: Calories 722, Total Fat 41g, Saturated Fat 5g, Sodium 2793mg, Total Carbs 68g, Fiber 11g, Sugars 40g, Protein 28g

Kung Pao Lentils

Lentils make a great substitute for tofu in this easy weeknight dinner. The hot Kung Pao Sauce with the earthy lentils works really well. Use precooked lentils or other cooked beans, such as green mung beans or chickpeas. With precooked lentils and made-ahead Kung Pao Sauce, this dish comes together in twenty minutes (see note). Serve it with cooked rice or grains of your choice.

Prep time: 20 minutes + Kung Pao Sauce
Active time: 35 minutes
Inactive time: 10 minutes
gluten-free
Serves 4

1 cup (200g) dried lentils, picked over, rinsed, and drained (see variation)
3 cups (720ml) water
1/4 teaspoon salt
1 teaspoon organic safflower or other neutral oil
1 medium red bell pepper, thinly sliced
1 medium green bell pepper, thinly sliced
1 cup (85g) finely chopped broccoli, snow peas, or zucchini
3/4 cup (80g) chopped celery
1 recipe Kung Pao Sauce (page 35)
Red pepper flakes, for garnish

1. Combine the lentils, water, and salt in a medium saucepan. Cover the saucepan and bring the lentils to a boil over medium-high heat. Reduce the heat to medium and cook for 20 to 25 minutes, or until the lentils are tender to your preference. Let the lentils sit for 5 minutes, drain any excess water, and set aside.

2. Heat the oil in a large skillet over medium-high heat. Add the red bell pepper, green bell pepper, broccoli, and celery and cook until the vegetables are golden on some of their edges, 3 to 4 minutes. Add the kung pao sauce and the cooked lentils to the skillet and mix well. Add some more water for a saucier result if desired. Reduce the heat to medium and cook for 5 to 7 minutes, or until the sauce thickens and glazes the lentils. Taste and adjust the seasonings. Garnish with the red pepper flakes.

Note: To reduce the cooking time and use only one skillet, while you are making the Kung Pao Sauce, add the bell peppers and celery at the third step of the Kung Pao Sauce recipe (page 35). Add the cooked lentils to the sauce once it has started to thicken and simmer for a few minutes.

Variation: If you would prefer not to use dried lentils, you can use 2 to 2 1/2 cups (400 to 500g) cooked lentils or 2 1/2 cups (415g) cooked chickpeas.

Per serving: Calories 333, Total Fat 12g, Saturated Fat 1.5g, Sodium 725mg, Total Carbs 42g, Fiber 11g, Sugars 13g, Protein 17g

Kung Pao Tofu and Vegetable Stir-Fry

This is another template recipe. Crisp up the tofu, choose some vegetables, add one of the sauces used in this chapter, and simmer. Serve this tasty stir-fry over rice or vermicelli noodles. I love this stir-fry with Kung Sao Sauce, Sweet and Sour Sauce, and Manchurian Sauce.

Prep time: 10 minutes + Kung Pao
   Sauce
Active time: 20 minutes
gluten-free
Serves 4

14 ounces (400g) firm tofu, drained and pressed (page 243)

3 teaspoons organic safflower or other neutral oil, divided

3 to 4 ounces (85 to 113g) sliced white or cremini mushrooms

2 to 3 cups (240 to 360g) thinly sliced carrots, bell peppers, zucchini, broccoli, or cabbage

Salt and black pepper, as needed

1 recipe Kung Pao Sauce (page 35), Manchurian Sauce (page 44), or Orange Sauce (page 42)

2 tablespoons (6g) scallions or bean sprouts

1. Slice the tofu into 1/2-inch (1cm) cubes. Heat 2 teaspoons of the oil in a large skillet over medium heat. Add the tofu and cook for 10 minutes, or until some sides are golden, stirring occasionally. Transfer the tofu to a shallow bowl.

2. Add the remaining 1 teaspoon oil and the mushrooms to the skillet over medium heat. Cook until some edges of the mushrooms are golden, 3 to 4 minutes, stirring occasionally. Add the carrots and a dash salt and pepper and cook for 3 minutes.

3. Add the kung pao sauce and tofu to the skillet and bring the mixture to a boil. Taste and adjust the seasonings. If the sauce isn't thick enough, mix 2 teaspoons cornstarch in 2 tablespoons (30ml) cold water and add the mixture to the skillet. Bring the sauce to a boil and simmer for 1 to 2 minutes to thicken. Garnish with the scallions or sprouts.

Per serving (with Kung Pao Sauce): Calories 320, Total Fat 20g, Saturated Fat 3g, Sodium 730mg, Total Carbs 21g, Fiber 6g, Sugars 12g, Protein 20g

Crispy Kung Pao Cauliflower

There's something about crisp, hearty vegetables glazed with sauce that always makes them a crowd pleaser. The strong sauces mask the plants' vegetable-ness, and florets also make great finger food. This is a template recipe. Choose a vegetable (the cauliflower can be substituted with broccoli, for example) and a crispy coating (you can make the coating gluten-free), bake the vegetable, and choose a sauce to drizzle all over the crispy florets. Make your own combination and serve it as is or over cooked rice.

Prep time: 45 minutes
Active time: 10 minutes
soy-free option, gluten-free option, nut-free option
Serves 4

1 recipe **Crunchy Baked Cauliflower (page 246) or Gluten-Free Crunchy Baked Cauliflower (page 246)**
1 recipe **Kung Pao Sauce (page 35), Manchurian Sauce (page 44), or Orange Sauce (page 42) (see note)**
Finely chopped scallions, for garnish

1. Bake the cauliflower florets according to instructions.

2. Meanwhile, make the sauce you plan to use.

3. Place the prepared cauliflower florets in a serving bowl. Drizzle the sauce all over the cauliflower. Flip or toss the florets to coat if you like. Garnish with the scallions.

Note: If your sauce of choice isn't thick enough to coat the cauliflower, mix 1 tablespoon cornstarch or arrowroot starch in 1/4 cup (60ml) cold water. (It takes a few seconds for the cornstarch to thoroughly combine with the water.) Add the cornstarch mixture to the simmering sauce. Stir and bring to a boil, cooking until the sauce has thickened to your liking.

Per serving (with Kung Pao Sauce): Calories 452, Total Fat 13g, Saturated Fat 2g, Sodium 1333mg, Total Carbs 71g, Fiber 6g, Sugars 13g, Protein 15g

Hoisin Sauce

This easy, from-scratch hoisin sauce makes a great accompaniment to stir-fries, and it makes a sensational dip. Toss in some noodles or rice for a one-pot meal—use hoisin sauce instead of Manchurian sauce in the Manchurian Sauce Noodles on page 46, add mushrooms and tofu or vegetables for a stir-fry, or marinate tofu or vegetables in it and bake them. This sauce also stores well.

Prep time: 10 minutes
Active time: 5 minutes
gluten-free, nut-free option
Makes about 1 cup (240ml)

1/2 cup (120ml) soy sauce (or tamari to make gluten-free)

2 to 3 teaspoons molasses

1/4 cup (65g) smooth almond butter or peanut butter (see note)

1 1/2 tablespoons rice vinegar

1 teaspoon toasted sesame oil

1 1/2 teaspoons garlic powder

1/2 teaspoon grated fresh ginger or 1/4 teaspoon ground ginger

2 1/2 tablespoons (30g) sugar

1/4 teaspoon ground black pepper

Combine the soy sauce, molasses, almond butter, vinegar, oil, garlic powder, ginger, sugar, and pepper in a blender and blend until smooth. Taste and adjust the seasonings. Store the sauce in the refrigerator for up to 1 week if using fresh ginger and 1 month if using ground ginger (see variation).

Note: The uncooked sauce tastes very nutty—especially with peanut butter, which mellows during cooking in stir-fries. Use almond butter for a less nutty flavor profile. To make nut-free, use sunflower seed butter or soy nut butter.

Variation: For an addition of pungent flavor, add 1/2 teaspoon miso to the sauce if you plan to use the sauce within a few days. Omit the miso if you plan to store it longer.

Per 1 cup: Calories 683, Total Fat 38g, Saturated Fat 4g, Sodium 4600mg, Total Carbs 65g, Fiber 8g, Sugars 46g, Protein 27g

Hoisin Mushroom and Tofu Stir-Fry

Mushrooms and tofu glazed in homemade hoisin sauce is a great weekday meal. The strong flavors from the hoisin sauce and the earthy mushrooms work well together in this one-pot stir-fry. The hoisin sauce takes five minutes to make, and if needed you can do it while the tofu or the mushrooms cook. Serve this stir-fry over rice or other grains.

Prep time: 15 minutes + Hoisin Sauce
Active time: 30 minutes
Inactive time: 10 minutes
gluten-free
Serves 4

2 teaspoons organic safflower or other neutral oil

21 ounces (596g) firm tofu, pressed (page 243) and cut into 1/2-inch (1cm) dice

8 ounces (227g) sliced cremini or white mushrooms

5 cloves garlic, finely chopped

Salt, as needed

1/2 teaspoon red pepper flakes

1 1/2 cups (150g) thinly sliced bell peppers, broccoli, or zucchini

1/2 recipe Hoisin Sauce (page 40)

1/2 teaspoon sugar, or to taste

1 1/2 teaspoons cornstarch

1 1/2 cups (360ml) water, divided

Heat the oil in a large skillet over medium heat. Add the tofu and cook until it is golden on most sides, 5 to 7 minutes. Remove the tofu from the skillet. Add the mushrooms, garlic, a pinch salt, and the red pepper flakes and cook until the mushrooms are golden on some sides, 6 to 8 minutes. Add the bell peppers and stir to combine. Cook for 2 minutes. Add the hoisin sauce and sugar. Add the tofu to the skillet and stir to combine. Whisk together the cornstarch and water and add the mixture to the skillet. Bring the sauce to a boil, 3 to 4 minutes. Taste and adjust the seasonings. Simmer for 1 minute or so, until the sauce thickens to your preference.

Variation: Add 2 to 3 tablespoons (14 to 21g) raw cashews with the mushrooms for a Thai-style cashew stir-fry.

Per serving: Calories 302, Total Fat 15g, Saturated Fat 2g, Sodium 653mg, Total Carbs 23g, Fiber 7g, Sugars 9g, Protein 24g

Orange Sauce

Orange sauce is a tangy, sweet sauce that works in many ways. The most perfect way is, of course, dunking Crunchy Baked Cauliflower (page 246) in it. Additionally, you can add it to vegetables and tofu or chickpeas for a stir-fry. Or you can use this sauce as a dressing over fresh lettuce or a Chinese cabbage salad.

Prep time: 5 minutes
Active time: 15 minutes
soy-free option, gluten-free, nut-free
Makes 1 1/2 cups (360ml)

2 teaspoons organic safflower or other neutral oil

7 to 8 cloves garlic, finely chopped

1 (1-inch [3cm]) knob fresh ginger, peeled and minced, or 1 tablespoon grated fresh ginger

2 to 3 tablespoons (30 to 45ml) soy sauce or tamari (or coconut aminos to make soy-free)

2 tablespoons (30ml) distilled white vinegar or rice vinegar

1/2 teaspoon toasted sesame oil

1 teaspoon sriracha sauce

1/4 teaspoon cayenne

1 cup (240ml) fresh orange juice (see note)

1 teaspoon orange zest (see note)

3 tablespoons (45ml) maple syrup

1 tablespoon sugar or other sweetener

1 tablespoon cornstarch

1/4 cup (60ml) water

1. Heat the safflower oil in a medium skillet over medium-low heat. Add the garlic and cook for 3 minutes. Add the ginger and continue cooking until the garlic is fragrant, stirring occasionally, 2 to 3 minutes.

2. Add the soy sauce, vinegar, sesame oil, sriracha, cayenne, orange juice, orange zest, maple syrup, and sugar, stirring to combine. Increase the heat to medium and bring the mixture to a boil, about 6 minutes.

3. Taste and adjust the seasonings. Whisk together the cornstarch and water and add the mixture to the sauce. Simmer for another 3 to 4 minutes to thicken. Store the sauce in the refrigerator for up to 1 week. Freeze it for up to 2 months.

Note: The sauce can become overly orangey depending on the oranges used and your preference. Start with 3/4 cup (180ml) of the juice and 1/2 teaspoon of the zest, taste the sauce, and add the remaining 1/4 (60ml) juice and 1/2 teaspoon zest if desired.

Variation: For a spicier version, add 1 tablespoon sambal oelek or other Asian chile sauce when you add the soy sauce.

Per 1/2 cup: Calories 188, Total Fat 6g, Saturated Fat 1g, Sodium 434mg, Total Carbs 32g, Fiber 1g, Sugars 23g, Protein 2g

Vegetables and Chickpeas in Orange Sauce

Orange Sauce with vegetables—such as cabbage, carrots, zucchini, peppers, and hearty chickpeas—makes for a satisfying stir-fry. Like most of the stir-fries in this chapter, this one can be tweaked to use any of the Asian-inspired sauces.

Prep time: 10 minutes + Orange Sauce
Active time: 25 minutes
Inactive time: 10 minutes
soy-free option, gluten-free, nut-free
Serves 4

1/2 teaspoon organic safflower or
    other neutral oil
1 medium red bell pepper, thinly
    sliced
1/2 cup (60g) thinly sliced carrots
1 1/2 to 2 cups (150 to 200g) thinly
    sliced cabbage, broccoli, green
    beans, zucchini, or more red bell
    pepper
1 (15-ounce [425g]) can chickpeas or 1
    1/2 cups (250g) cooked chickpeas,
    drained and rinsed, or 1 1/2 cups
    Crisped Tofu (page 243)
1/4 teaspoon salt, or more to taste
1/2 teaspoon red pepper flakes, di-
    vided
Dash black pepper
1 recipe Orange Sauce (page 42)
1 cup (30g) tightly packed baby spin-
    ach or other quick-cooking greens
1 teaspoon sesame seeds, for garnish
1 tablespoon finely chopped scallions,
    for garnish

1. Heat the oil in a large skillet over medium heat. Add the bell pepper and carrots and cook for 3 minutes, stirring occasionally. Add the cabbage, chickpeas, salt, 1/4 teaspoon of the red pepper flakes, and black pepper and stir to combine. Cook for 1 minute.

2. Add the orange sauce. Cover the skillet and bring the mixture to a boil, about 6 minutes. Taste and adjust the seasonings, adding the remaining 1/4 teaspoon red pepper flakes if desired. Reduce the heat to low and continue simmering for another 5 to 10 minutes, or until the vegetables are cooked to your preference and the sauce thickens. Add the spinach and cook for 1 minute. Garnish with the sesame seeds and scallions.

Per serving: Calories 354, Total Fat 9g, Saturated Fat 1g, Sodium 552mg, Total Carbs 59g, Fiber 11g, Sugars 25g, Protein 12g

Manchurian Sauce

Manchurian sauce is an Indo-Chinese sauce that evolved from Indianizing the Chinese flavors in the sauce. All the extra garlic, ginger, and chile make this sauce incredibly flavorful. Use this over Crunchy Baked Cauliflower (page 246) to make Gobi Manchurian. To reduce the heat, use mild green chiles or remove the seeds from hot chiles and use less Asian chile sauce. If you're not a fan of ketchup or tomato, omit it. The prep is much quicker using a food processor to finely chop many of the ingredients.

Prep time: 15 minutes
Active time: 25 minutes
Inactive time: 10 minutes
gluten-free, nut-free
Makes about 1 1/2 cups (360ml)

1 tablespoon organic safflower or other neutral oil

12 cloves garlic, finely chopped

1 (2 1/2-inch [6cm]) knob fresh ginger, peeled and finely chopped

2 small green or red chiles, seeded (for less heat) or unseeded (for more heat) and finely chopped

1/2 cup (60g) finely chopped red or white onion

1/2 cup (80g) finely chopped green bell pepper

2 tablespoons (20g) finely chopped celery (optional)

1 1/2 to 2 tablespoons Asian chile sauce or sambal oelek, or to taste

1/4 cup (60ml) soy sauce

1 to 1 1/2 tablespoons ketchup or tomato paste

2 teaspoons distilled white vinegar or apple cider vinegar

1/4 teaspoon ground white pepper or black pepper (or a combination)

2 to 3 teaspoons sugar or other sweetener

1 1/2 teaspoons cornstarch

3/4 cup (180ml) water

1. Heat the oil in a large skillet over medium heat. Add the garlic, ginger, and chiles and stir to combine. Cook until the garlic is golden on some of its edges, 2 to 3 minutes. Add the onion, bell pepper, and celery (if using) and cook until they are golden, about 8 to 9 minutes. Add the Asian chile sauce, soy sauce, ketchup, vinegar, pepper, and sugar. Bring the mixture to a simmer.

2. Whisk together the cornstarch and water and add the mixture to the skillet, stirring to combine. Cook until the sauce comes to a boil, about 4 minutes. Continue simmering for another few minutes to let the flavors develop. Taste and adjust the seasonings. The sauce will be very flavorful. You can adjust the consistency later depending on how you plan to use it. Add more water to keep it saucy. Refrigerate the sauce for up to 4 days or freeze it in airtight jars for up to 1 month.

Per 1/2 cup: Calories 141, Total Fat 5g, Saturated Fat 1g, Sodium 982mg, Total Carbs 22g, Fiber 2g, Sugars 9g, Protein 4g

Manchurian Chickpeas and Broccoli

Manchurian Sauce works amazingly with vegetables and chickpeas or lentils in a stir-fry. Even when making the Manchurian Sauce at the same time, the whole dish is ready in thirty minutes. You can add the ingredients directly to the simmering Manchurian Sauce and cook everything together to shorten the cooking time and make this a one-pot meal.

Prep time: 10 minutes + Manchurian Sauce
Active time: 15 minutes
Inactive: 10 minutes
gluten-free, nut-free
Serves 4

1 (15-ounce [425g]) can chickpeas or 1 1/2 cups (250g) cooked chickpeas, drained and rinsed
1 recipe Manchurian Sauce (page 44)
2 cups (200g) coarsely chopped broccoli or other vegetables, or more to taste
1 cup (240ml) water or vegetable broth
1/2 to 1 teaspoon cornstarch
1/4 teaspoon salt
Dash black pepper
Finely chopped scallions, for garnish

Heat a medium saucepan over medium heat. Add the chickpeas, Manchurian Sauce, broccoli, water, cornstarch, salt, and pepper. Partially cover the saucepan and bring the mixture to a boil, 5 minutes. Reduce the heat to medium-low and continue simmering for another 8 to 12 minutes, or until the broccoli is cooked to your preference and the sauce thickens. Taste and adjust the seasonings. Garnish with the scallions.

Variation: Use 1 1/2 to 2 cups (300 to 400g) cooked lentils or 1 recipe Crisped Tofu (page 243) instead of chickpeas.

Per serving: Calories 233, Total Fat 5g, Saturated Fat 0g, Sodium 950mg, Total Carbs 38g, Fiber 9g, Sugars 10g, Protein 11g

Manchurian Sauce Noodles

Indo-Chinese Manchurian sauce works amazingly with noodles as a stir-fry or with rice as fried rice. These noodles come together quickly if you have premade sauce. Adjust the spiciness of the sauce to your preference before using.

Prep time: 10 minutes + Manchurian Sauce
Active time: 20 minutes
Inactive time: 10 minutes
gluten-free, nut-free
Serves 4

8 ounces (227g) brown rice noodles or angel hair pasta

2 teaspoons organic safflower or other neutral oil

10 ounces (284g) firm or extra-firm tofu, drained, pressed (page 243), and cut into 1/2-inch (1cm) cubes

2 to 2 1/2 cups (200 to 250g) coarsely chopped bell peppers (any color), carrots, broccolini, zucchini, or celery

1/4 teaspoon salt

1 recipe Manchurian Sauce (page 44)

1/4 teaspoon black pepper

Finely chopped scallions, for garnish

1. Cook the noodles or pasta according to instructions on the package and set aside.

2. Heat the oil in a large skillet over medium heat. Add the tofu and cook for 7 to 8 minutes, or until some of its edges are golden, stirring occasionally.

3. Add the bell peppers and salt, stir, cover the skillet, and cook for 3 minutes. Add the Manchurian sauce and bring the mixture to a boil. Add the noodles and pepper, tossing to coat the noodles in the sauce. Cover the skillet and let the noodles and vegetables steam for 2 minutes. Take the skillet off the heat. Taste and adjust the seasonings. Garnish with the scallions and serve.

Variation: Kung Pao Sauce (page 35) is a good sauce for these noodles. Alternatively, use a half batch of Hoisin Sauce (page 40) for quick hoisin noodles to serve as a meal or as a side with other stir-fries.

Per serving: Calories 425, Total Fat 11g, Saturated Fat 2g, Sodium 911mg, Total Carbs 65g, Fiber 7g, Sugars 10g, Protein 16g

Black Pepper Tofu

This simple stir-fry is another favorite quick weeknight meal. It has plenty—I repeat, plenty—of freshly ground or crushed black pepper. The fresh black pepper is a must and so is this stir-fry. Start with 1 teaspoon black pepper if you are sensitive to the peppery heat. Serve it over cooked rice or other grains.

Prep time: 10 minutes + tofu pressing time
Active time: 15 minutes
Inactive time: 15 minutes
gluten-free, nut-free
Serves 4

21 ounces (596g) firm tofu, drained

3 teaspoons organic safflower or other neutral oil, divided

1/3 cup (80ml) soy sauce or tamari

2 teaspoons maple syrup

2 teaspoons rice vinegar

8 to 10 cloves garlic, finely chopped

1 (1-inch [3cm]) knob fresh ginger, peeled and finely chopped

3 dried red Thai chiles or chiles de árbol, chopped or broken in half (use unbroken California red chiles for a milder version)

2 cups (200g) finely chopped celery

1/2 cup (75g) finely chopped green bell pepper or onion

1/4 cup (60g) sliced mushrooms (optional)

1/4 teaspoon white pepper

1 1/2 teaspoons coarsely ground black peppercorns, or more to taste

1/4 teaspoon salt

1/2 cup (120ml) water

1. Wrap the tofu in paper towels then a kitchen towel. Place some heavy books or a heavy container on top of the wrapped tofu. Let it sit for 15 minutes (alternatively, use a tofu press to press the tofu for 15 minutes). Slice the tofu into 1/2-inch (1cm) cubes.

2. Heat 2 teaspoons of the oil in a large skillet over medium heat. Add the tofu and cook for 9 to 10 minutes, or until some sides are golden, stirring occasionally. Transfer the tofu from the skillet to a shallow bowl. Let the tofu cool slightly, then add the soy sauce, maple syrup, and vinegar and mix well. Let the tofu marinate for 10 minutes.

3. Meanwhile, heat the remaining 1 teaspoon oil in a large skillet over medium heat. Add the garlic, ginger, and Thai chiles and cook until the garlic is fragrant, 2 to 3 minutes. Add the celery, bell pepper, and mushrooms (if using). Cover the skillet and cook for 4 to 5 minutes, or until the celery is al dente, stirring once halfway through the cooking time.

4. Add the tofu along with the marinade, white pepper, black pepper, salt, and water and stir to combine. Cover the skillet and cook for 4 minutes to bring the sauce to a boil. Reduce the heat to medium-low and simmer until the sauce reaches the desired consistency. Taste and adjust the seasonings.

Per serving: Calories 315, Total Fat 18g, Saturated Fat 3g, Sodium 1000mg, Total Carbs 14g, Fiber 2g, Sugars 3g, Protein 26g

3

Masala & Saag

This chapter features masala sauces and saag. Masala can mean many things in Indian cuisine: a dry spice mix, a wet spice mix, a sauce, or just a spiced dish. Saag is a dish made with greens. And *curry* in Indian terms is used as an English translation for a dish dressed with sauce or a dish not dressed with sauce—really, any dish. However, there is no one set of spices in a curry. The spices and flavors vary by region, family recipe, and so on.

This chapter visits some of my favorite simple meals with sauces that have incredible depth of flavor, including a few Ethiopian-inspired dishes. Many of the spices used are common between Indian and Ethiopian cuisines.

Start this chapter with Tikka Masala Chickpeas (page 59). Then try the blog favorite, Mushroom Matar Masala (page 58), and move on to Lentil Balls in Masala Sauce (page 56) and Cauliflower and Chickpeas in Berbere Sauce (page 70).

Chickpea and Sweet Potato Curry (page 67)

Creamy White Masala Sauce

This sauce is like a white cream sauce you'd use for pasta or pizza but with Indian spices. It evolved from the base sauce used in dishes like methi malai mutter, which is a cream-sauce dish with greens and peas in North Indian cuisine. Use this masala sauce to make Indian-spiced spinach dip or as a white sauce on a pizza. Add it to vegetables and tofu and serve over rice or use it with lentil balls (page 31). You can also use this sauce as a dressing over my Lentil-Walnut Burgers (page 97) or other burgers.

Prep time: 20 minutes
Active time: 25 minutes
soy-free, gluten-free, nut-free option
Makes about 1 1/2 cups (360ml)

- 2 teaspoons organic safflower or other neutral oil
- 1 cup (120g) finely chopped white onion
- 1 serrano or Thai chile, seeded (if desired) and coarsely chopped
- 5 cloves garlic, finely chopped
- 1 (1/2-inch [1cm]) knob fresh ginger, peeled and finely chopped
- 1/3 to 1/2 cup (40 to 60g) raw cashews, soaked for 15 minutes
- 1 1/4 cups (300ml) nondairy milk
- 1/2 teaspoon ground cumin
- 1/2 teaspoon ground cinnamon
- 1/2 teaspoon ground cardamom
- 1 1/4 to 1 1/2 tablespoons dried fenugreek leaves or 1/2 cup (20g) chopped fresh fenugreek leaves
- 1/2 to 1 teaspoon salt
- 1/2 to 1 teaspoon sugar
- 1 teaspoon Kashmiri Garam Masala (page 245) or 1/4 teaspoon black pepper, 1/2 teaspoon ground coriander, 1/8 teaspoon ground nutmeg, and 1/8 teaspoon ground cloves

1. Heat the oil in a large skillet over medium heat. Add the onion, serrano, garlic, and ginger and cook until the onion is golden, 6 to 8 minutes, stirring occasionally.

2. Meanwhile, in a blender, combine the cashews and milk. Blend until smooth, 2 to 4 minutes, and set aside.

3. Add the cumin, cinnamon, cardamom, and fenugreek to the onion mixture and stir to combine. Cook for 30 seconds. Add the cashew cream, salt, sugar, and Kashmiri garam masala. Stir and cook over low heat until the cream just comes to a boil, 5 to 8 minutes depending the amount of cashews. Taste and adjust the seasonings. Add some water or additional milk for a saucier consistency and simmer for 1 minute or so. This can be adjusted later depending on how the sauce is used. Store the sauce in the refrigerator for up to 4 days or freeze it for up to 1 month. Reheat the sauce with 1/2 cup (120ml) or more water or milk.

Variations: Use 1/2 cup (60g) cashews for a thicker sauce and 1/3 cup (40g) if a thinner consistency is desired. For a perfectly smooth texture with no bits of onion, blend the cooked onion mixture with the cashews and milk. Transfer the cashew cream to the skillet and continue with Step 3. For a nut-free variation, use full-fat coconut milk instead of the nondairy milk and omit the cashews. Mix in 1 to 2 tablespoons unbleached all-purpose flour or rice flour to thicken the sauce if needed.

Per 1/2 cup: Calories 198, Total Fat 14g, Saturated Fat 2g, Sodium 668mg, Total Carbs 16g, Fiber 2g, Sugars 5g, Protein 5g

Tofu and Vegetables
with White Masala Sauce

The versatile Creamy White Masala Sauce works well with almost everything. Add some spinach or greens to make a spinach dip. Add vegetables and tofu for this curry. The sauce itself takes just ten minutes to put together. Cook it in parallel with the rest of the dish and you have the meal on the table in thirty minutes. To make this without tofu, add more vegetables of your choice and cook them until al dente, then proceed to add the sauce and simmer. Serve this dish over rice, quinoa, or other grains.

Prep time: 10 minutes + Creamy White
    Masala Sauce
Active time: 20 minutes
soy-free option, gluten-free, nut-free option
Serves 4

1 tablespoon organic safflower or
    other neutral oil
14 to 18 ounces (400 to 511g) firm tofu,
    drained, pressed (page 243), and
    cubed
2 medium zucchini, thinly sliced
1 medium red bell pepper, sliced
    paper thin
1 recipe Creamy White Masala Sauce
    (page 52)
1 to 2 cups (30 to 60g) baby spinach or
    other baby greens (optional)
1/2 cup (120ml) nondairy milk, if
    needed

1. Heat the oil in a large skillet over medium heat. Add the tofu and cook for 7 to 9 minutes, or until golden. Add the zucchini and bell pepper to the skillet and cook for 1 minute.

2. Add the prepared creamy white masala sauce and stir to combine. Add the spinach (if using) and bring the mixture to a boil, about 5 minutes. Taste and adjust the seasonings. Add the milk for a saucier dish if needed and bring the mixture to a boil. Serve hot.

Per serving: Calories 313, Total Fat 21g, Saturated Fat 4g, Sodium 684mg, Total Carbs 20g, Fiber 5g, Sugars 9g, Protein 18g

Makhani Sauce

This is the butter sauce, or makhani sauce, which is the general basic sauce used in most Indian restaurants—but this one is lighter and dairy-free. It was termed "liquid gold" by my recipe testers of *Vegan Richa's Indian Kitchen* and this book. For Butter and Tikka Sauce variations, see the box below.

Prep time: 10 minutes
Active time: 25 minutes
Inactive time: 10 minutes
soy-free, gluten-free, nut-free option
Makes 1 1/2 to 2 cups (360 to 480ml)

2 teaspoons organic safflower or other neutral oil
1/2 teaspoon cumin seeds
1/2 teaspoon coriander seeds
1 dried bay leaf (optional)
8 to 10 cloves garlic, coarsely chopped
1 cup (120g) finely chopped red onion
1 (1-inch [3cm]) knob fresh ginger, peeled and finely chopped
1/2 teaspoon ground turmeric
1/4 to 1/2 teaspoon cayenne
1 teaspoon Garam Masala (page 244)
1 1/2 cups (240g) fresh or canned finely chopped tomatoes
1/4 cup (30g) raw cashews or 1/4 cup (60g) silken tofu, or coconut cream, to make it nut-free
1/2 to 1 teaspoon salt
1/2 cup (120ml) water or plain unsweetened almond milk (or full-fat coconut milk to make nut-free), divided
1 1/2 teaspoons dried fenugreek leaves
1/2 teaspoon sugar

1. Heat the oil in a large skillet over medium heat. Add the cumin seeds, coriander seeds, and bay leaf (if using). Cook for 1 minute. Add the garlic and cook until it is slightly golden on some edges, about 2 minutes. Add the onion and ginger and cook until golden, 7 minutes, stirring occasionally. Add the turmeric, cayenne, and garam masala and stir for a few seconds.

2. Add the tomatoes, cashews, salt, and 1/4 cup (60ml) of the water and cook until the tomatoes are saucy, 5 to 6 minutes. Stir occasionally to avoid sticking. Cool slightly, remove and discard the bay leaf, and transfer the sauce to a blender.

3. Blend the sauce with the remaining 1/4 cup (60ml) water until smooth. Transfer the sauce to a storage bowl or the skillet if you will be using the sauce immediately. Add the fenugreek leaves and sugar and stir to combine. Taste and adjust the seasonings. The sauce can be refrigerated for up to 3 days and frozen for up to 2 months in an airtight container.

Per 1 1/2 cup: Calories 509, Total Fat 26g, Saturated Fat 4g, Sodium 1805mg, Total Carbs 61g, Fiber 12g, Sugars 21g, Protein 14g

Tikka Masala Sauce

Blend the Makhani Sauce mixture with 1 tablespoon tomato paste and 1/3 to 1/2 cup (75 to 120ml) plain unsweetened nondairy yogurt. Add the fenugreek leaves and sugar and stir. Taste and adjust the seasonings and use the sauce immediately or store.

Butter Masala Sauce

Bring the Makhani Sauce to a boil. Add your choice of vegetables, tofu, or Butler Soy Curls and an additional 1/2 to 1 cup (120 to 240ml) nondairy milk. Simmer until the sauce has thickened. Add 1 teaspoon minced ginger and 2 teaspoons minced green chile. You can also add Crisped Tofu (page 243) to make tofu makhani or tofu butter masala, Soy Curls or seitan for a chicken-free butter masala. In addition, you can use this with lentil balls (page 31) or in a pulao (page 55).

Quinoa Pulao with Masala Sauce

Pulao and fried rice are quick one-pot meals. The difference is that the grains in pulao are often cooked with the vegetables and spices in one pot, while fried rice uses precooked grains. Use quinoa or white basmati rice to make my version of pulao. Rice will take about five minutes longer to cook than quinoa and, depending on the sauce, you might need additional water. Serve this pulao with condiments like vegan yogurt raita, some Indian pickle, mango chutney, or a drizzle of cashew cream.

Prep time: 10 minutes + Creamy White Masala Sauce
Active time: 15 minutes
Inactive time: 15 minutes
soy-free option, gluten-free
Serves 3 or 4

1 recipe Creamy White Masala Sauce (page 52), Spinach Curry Sauce (page 62), or Makhani Sauce (page 54)
1 teaspoon organic safflower or other neutral oil
1/2 cup (60g) finely chopped red onion
1/4 teaspoon Garam Masala (page 244) or Curry Powder (page 245)
2 cups (200g) finely chopped green beans, cauliflower, bell peppers (any color), carrots, or zucchini
1/2 teaspoon salt, divided, or more to taste
1 (15-ounce [425g]) can chickpeas or lentils, drained and rinsed, or 1 1/2 cups (250g) cooked cubed tofu or Chickpea Flour Tofu (page 238)
1 cup (170g) quinoa, well rinsed (see note)
Sugar, to taste (optional)
Fresh lemon juice, to taste (optional)
1/2 cup (120ml) water, if needed
Toasted nuts or seeds, for garnish
Red pepper flakes, for garnish
Finely chopped fresh cilantro, for garnish

1. Pour the sauce into a large measuring cup. Add enough water to make 3 cups (720ml) of liquid and set aside.

2. Heat the oil in a large saucepan over medium heat. Add the onion and cook, stirring occasionally, until it is translucent, 4 to 5 minutes. Add the garam masala and stir to combine. Add the green beans and 1/4 teaspoon of the salt. Cover the saucepan and cook for 3 minutes. Add the chickpeas and cook for 1 minute.

3. Add the quinoa, the remaining 1/4 teaspoon salt, and sauce and stir to combine. Partially cover the saucepan and cook for 15 minutes. Reduce the heat to low. Stir, taste, and adjust the seasonings. Depending on the sauce used, you might need to add the sugar or lemon juice. For a soupier dish (or if the quinoa starts to stick), add the water. Cover the saucepan and cook until the quinoa is well done. Garnish with the toasted nuts, red pepper flakes, and cilantro.

Note: To make this with precooked quinoa, millet, or other grains, choose either the Makhani Sauce or the Creamy White Masala Sauce. Heat the oil in a large saucepan over medium heat. Add the onion and cook, stirring occasionally, until it is translucent, 4 to 5 minutes. Add the garam masala and stir to combine. Add the green beans and 1/4 teaspoon of the salt. Cover the saucepan and cook for 3 minutes. Add the chickpeas and cook for 1 minute. Add the quinoa and sauce and stir to combine. Cover and cook for 3 minutes. Fluff the quinoa, taste it, and adjust the seasonings. Garnish and serve.

Per serving (with sauce): Calories 521, Total Fat 17g, Saturated Fat 2g, Sodium 848mg, Total Carbs 75g, Fiber 16g, Sugars 15g, Protein 20g

Lentil Balls in Masala Sauce

These lentil balls work fabulously in any kind of sauce. For a non-Indian lentil ball, omit the garam masala and add 1 teaspoon or more Quick Italian Herb Blend (page 163). I usually make the sauce while the lentil mixture is chilling, so I have the balls ready when the sauce is simmering and I toss them in the sauce during the last two minutes of cooking. Depending on how you like the lentil balls (crunchy or soaked in sauce), you can serve them dressed in sauce or simmered in the sauce for 1 to 2 minutes to soak up some sauce.

Prep time: 10 minutes + sauce
Active time: 20 minutes
Inactive time: 15 minutes
soy-free, gluten-free option, nut-free option
Serves 4

1/2 cup (60g) **chopped red onion**

3 cloves **garlic**

1 (1/4-inch [0.6cm]) knob **fresh ginger, peeled**

1/3 cup (40g) **raw walnuts**

2 tablespoons (6g) **cilantro leaves (optional)**

3/4 teaspoon **salt (if using unsalted lentils)**

3/4 teaspoon **ground cumin**

3/4 teaspoon **ground coriander**

1/2 teaspoon **garlic powder**

1/4 to 1/2 teaspoon **cayenne (or 1/2 teaspoon paprika for a milder version)**

1/2 teaspoon **garam masala, curry powder, or chili powder blend**

3/4 cup (150g) **cooked brown or white rice, preferably chilled**

1 1/2 cups (300g) **cooked brown lentils or 1 (15-ounce [425g]) can lentils, drained and rinsed, divided**

1 teaspoon **ketchup or lime juice**

1 teaspoon **organic safflower oil or other neutral oil**

1 **Flax Egg (page 242)**

3 tablespoons (15g) **dry breadcrumbs or all-purpose flour (or chickpea flour to make gluten-free)**

1 recipe **Makhani Sauce or Tikka Masala Sauce (page 54) or Creamy White Masala Sauce (page 52)**

1. In a food processor, process the onion, garlic, ginger, walnuts, and cilantro (if using) until the ingredients are finely chopped. (Alternatively, cook the onion and garlic in 1/2 teaspoon oil in a small skillet over medium heat until they are golden, then add them to the food processor.) Add the salt (if using unsalted lentils), cumin, coriander, garlic powder, cayenne, garam masala, rice, and 3/4 cup (150g) of the lentils and pulse a few times until the ingredients are well combined and most of the lentils are mashed. Transfer the mixture to a large bowl. Add the remaining 3/4 cup (150g) lentils, ketchup, oil, and flax egg, mashing and mixing the ingredients to combine. Taste and adjust the seasonings. Add the breadcrumbs and stir to combine. Let the mixture chill in the refrigerator for 10 to 15 minutes.

2. After the mixture has chilled, check its consistency. If the chilled mixture is too wet, add more flour or breadcrumbs. The amount needed depends on the moisture in the vegetables and lentils. Add another flax egg if the mixture makes crumbly balls. Roll the mixture into tight, 1- to 1 1/2-inch (3- to 4cm) balls. (You should end up with at least 16 balls.)

3. Heat a large skillet over medium-high heat. Add a drizzle of oil and make sure it covers the entire bottom of the skillet. Add the lentil balls (making sure not to overcrowd the skillet) and cook for 7 to 8 minutes. Move the balls every 2 minutes to brown them on most sides. (Alternatively, to bake the lentil balls, place the balls on a large baking sheet lined with parchment paper. Spray oil on the balls and bake at 375°F [190°C] for 20 to 22 minutes.)

4. In a small saucepan, bring the sauce to a simmer over medium heat. (Add a small amount of water if using refrigerated and thickened sauce.) Add the lentil balls and simmer for 1 to 2 minutes. Serve immediately.

Note: To make the lentil balls nut-free, use 1/4 cup more cooked lentils + 2 tablespoons oats to replace the walnuts.

Per serving (with sauce): Calories 357, Total Fat 15g, Saturated Fat 2g, Sodium 898mg, Total Carbs 46g, Fiber 10g, Sugars 7g, Protein 14g

Mushroom Matar Masala

Making Indian sauces can be a multiple-step process. Thankfully, this masala sauce is easy to make: roughly chop the vegetables, blend everything together, cook the sauce, and you're ready to make Mushroom Matar Masala. To make this recipe your own, see the variation suggestions below.

Prep time: 10 minutes
Active time: 25 minutes
soy-free, gluten-free, nut-free option
Serves 4

3/4 cup (90g) coarsely chopped onion
5 cloves garlic
1 (1-inch [3cm]) knob fresh ginger, peeled
1 small green chile, seeded if desired
1 teaspoon organic safflower or other neutral oil
2 large tomatoes, coarsely chopped
1/4 cup (30g) raw cashews, soaked for 15 minutes
1/2 to 1 teaspoon Garam Masala (page 244)
1/2 teaspoon paprika
1 teaspoon dried fenugreek leaves or 1/4 teaspoon ground fenugreek seed
8 ounces (227g) sliced white mushrooms
3/4 cup (120g) fresh or thawed frozen green peas, or more to taste
3/4 cup (125g) cooked chickpeas, drained and rinsed
1/2 cup (120ml) water, plus more as needed
1/2 teaspoon salt, or more to taste
1/4 teaspoon raw sugar, or more to taste
1 cup (30g) coarsely chopped spinach (optional)
1/4 teaspoon cayenne, for garnish
2 tablespoons (6g) finely chopped cilantro, for garnish
Cooked rice or flatbread, for serving

1. In a blender, puree the onion, garlic, ginger, and chile with a few tablespoons water. Heat the oil in a large skillet over medium heat. Add the onion puree. Cook, stirring occasionally, for 5 to 7 minutes, or until the raw-onion smell has dissipated.

2. Meanwhile, blend the tomatoes and cashews in the same blender until smooth. Add the tomato puree, garam masala, paprika, and fenugreek to the skillet. Cook for 7 to 8 minutes, stirring occasionally.

3. Add the mushrooms, peas, chickpeas, water, salt, and sugar. Cover the skillet and cook for 10 minutes, or until the mushrooms are cooked to your preference. Add the spinach, if using. Taste and adjust the seasonings. Garnish with the cayenne and cilantro and serve over rice or with flatbread.

Variation: If you're craving variety, add other vegetables, baked tofu, Butler Soy Curls, chickpeas, or lentils. Make the sauce creamier with more cashews or tangier with more tomatoes.

Note: To make the sauce without nuts, use 1/3 cup (80g) silken tofu or plain unsweetened nondairy yogurt or coconut cream (the thick coconut milk from a can of full-fat coconut milk).

Per serving: Calories 185, Total Fat 6g, Saturated Fat 2g, Sodium 334mg, Total Carbs 27g, Fiber 6g, Sugars 9g, Protein 9g

Tikka Masala Chickpeas

Chickpeas in Tikka Masala Sauce is a current favorite in my house. Tikka masala is always associated with grilled meats or paneer. Tofu, tempeh, seitan, or Butler Soy Curls make for the most-used substitutes for animal products, but there are lots more you can add to this sauce. Add chickpeas, lentils, or some roasted vegetables for a great dinner. Try this recipe below with chickpeas and you might never go back to tofu. Serve this dish over cooked rice or with flatbread.

Prep time: 10 minutes + Tikka Masala Sauce
Active time: 20 minutes
Inactive time: 10 minutes
soy-free, gluten-free, nut-free option
Serves 4

1 recipe Tikka Masala Sauce (page 54)
2 (15-ounce [425g]) cans chickpeas or 3 cups (500g) cooked chickpeas, drained and rinsed
1 cup (240ml) water or plain unsweetened nondairy milk
Salt, to taste
1 cup (30g) tightly packed baby spinach (optional)
Dash cayenne
Dash Garam Masala (page 244)
1/4 cup (10g) chopped fresh cilantro

Combine the tikka masala sauce, chickpeas, and water in a medium saucepan over medium heat. Cover the saucepan and bring the mixture to a boil, about 5 minutes. Add the salt. Taste and adjust the seasonings. Continue to cook for another 10 minutes so the sauce thickens and the chickpeas soften. Add the spinach (if using) during the last 2 minutes of cooking. Garnish with the cayenne, garam masala, and cilantro.

Variation: Use 3 cups (600g) cooked lentils instead of the chickpeas. Use 1 1/2 cups (250g) cooked chickpeas and 1 1/2 cups (100g) finely chopped vegetables, such as cauliflower, bell peppers, sweet potatoes, or zucchini.

Per serving: Calories 340, Total Fat 10g, Saturated Fat 1g, Sodium 803mg, Total Carbs 50g, Fiber 13g, Sugars 11g, Protein 15g

Bombay Potatoes and Peas

Bombay potatoes is a spiced potato dish made with whole spices. It is a quick potato side with many variations. It can include curry leaves, different spices, peanuts, and so on. This version uses mustard seeds, cumin seeds, and peas to add some color and protein. Add some other vegetables or some cooked chickpeas to make it a meal. This recipe also works well with sweet potatoes. Serve it hot over rice or use it as a filling for flatbread or tacos.

Prep time: 10 minutes
Active time: 35 minutes
Inactive time: 20 minutes
soy-free, gluten-free, nut-free
Serves 4

2 teaspoons organic safflower or other neutral oil
1/2 teaspoon cumin seeds
1 teaspoon mustard seeds
1 small red onion, finely chopped
1 large tomato, coarsely chopped
7 cloves garlic
1 (1-inch [3cm]) knob fresh ginger, peeled and coarsely chopped
1/2 teaspoon ground turmeric
1/4 to 1/2 teaspoon cayenne
1 teaspoon ground coriander
1/2 teaspoon ground cumin
1/2 teaspoon Garam Masala (page 244), or more to taste
3 medium Yukon gold potatoes, cut into 1/2-inch [1cm] pieces
1 teaspoon salt, or more to taste
1 cup (240ml) water, or more as needed
1 cup (160g) fresh or thawed frozen peas
1/4 cup (10g) finely chopped cilantro
Fresh lemon juice, to taste (optional)

1. Heat the oil in a large skillet over medium heat. Add the cumin and mustard seeds. Cook until the cumin seeds change color, 1 to 2 minutes. Add the onion and cook until it is translucent, 5 to 6 minutes.

2. Meanwhile, in a blender, blend the tomato, garlic, and ginger into a coarse puree. Add the tomato mixture, turmeric, cayenne, coriander, ground cumin, and garam masala to the skillet. Cook, stirring occasionally, until the puree thickens and the garlic is fragrant, 5 to 6 minutes.

3. Add the potatoes, salt, and water. Cover the skillet and cook for 10 to 11 minutes. Add the peas. Taste and adjust the seasonings. Reduce the heat to medium low. Simmer for another 10 to 12 minutes, or until the potatoes are cooked to your preference. Add additional water if the potatoes start to stick or if you prefer more curry. Add the cilantro and lemon juice (if using).

Variations: To make this recipe with boiled potatoes, add boiled cubed potatoes, salt, 1/4 cup (60ml) water, and peas after the puree has thickened and the garlic has become fragrant. Cover the skillet and cook for 5 to 8 minutes. Add the cilantro and lemon juice (if using) and serve. Add 1/2 to 1 teaspoon amchur (dried mango powder). Use 2 to 3 tomatoes for more sauce. Add some roughly chopped greens of your choice with the peas.

Per serving: Calories 157, Total Fat 3g, Saturated Fat 0g, Sodium 648mg, Total Carbs 29g, Fiber 5g, Sugars 5g, Protein 6g

Spinach Curry Sauce

This is the simple palak tofu sauce from the blog (it's also in *Vegan Richa's Indian Kitchen*). Try it in the Chickpeas and Potatoes in Spinach Curry Sauce (page 63) or the Quinoa Pulao with Masala Sauce (page 55), substituting the masala sauce with this one. Additionally, if you want to create your own special dish, add Crisped Tofu (page 243), roasted vegetables, chickpeas, or whatever you're craving to this sauce.

Prep time: 15 minutes
Active time: 15 minutes
soy-free, gluten-free, nut-free option
Makes 2 cups (480ml)

4 cups (120g) tightly packed fresh spinach, coarsely chopped, or 3 cups (570g) frozen spinach, thawed and squeezed

1/2 cup (120ml) water

1 cup (240ml) plain unsweetened almond milk (or full-fat coconut milk to make nut-free)

1/3 cup (40g) raw cashews, soaked for 15 minutes, or 1/3 cup (50g) ground raw cashews (or omit to make nut-free)

6 cloves garlic

1 (1 1/2-inch [4cm]) knob fresh ginger, peeled and coarsely chopped

1 small serrano or other hot green chile (seeded for a milder version if desired)

2 large tomatoes, coarsely chopped

3/4 teaspoon salt, or to taste

1 1/2 teaspoons raw sugar or maple syrup

1 teaspoon Garam Masala (page 244) or Curry Powder (page 245)

1/4 to 1/2 teaspoon ground cinnamon

1/4 to 1/2 teaspoon cayenne

1. Add the spinach, water, milk, cashews, garlic, ginger, serrano, tomatoes, salt, sugar, garam masala, cinnamon, and cayenne to a blender. Blend into a smooth puree. Alternatively, for a chunkier sauce, blend half the spinach with the rest of the ingredients to a smooth puree. Transfer to a bowl. Pulse the other half of the spinach until coarsely blended and mix the two purees together in the bowl.

2. To store the spinach curry sauce or use it as a dressing, bring the sauce to a boil in a small saucepan over medium-high heat. Simmer for a few minutes, until the raw garlic smell and taste are cooked out. Refrigerate the sauce up to 3 days or freeze it up to 1 month. Note that the color of the sauce might change after freezing.

Variation: Use more cashews to make a thicker sauce. For a flavor variation, add 1/4 teaspoon onion powder and 1/8 teaspoon ground cloves to the blender before pureeing the spinach.

Per 1/2 cup: Calories 100, Total Fat 5g, Saturated Fat 1g, Sodium 544mg, Total Carbs 11g, Fiber 2g, Sugars 2g, Protein 4g

Chickpeas and Potatoes in Spinach Curry Sauce

This is a variation of the very popular palak tofu (or saag tofu) from the blog. I use chickpeas and carrots or potatoes in this version. Feel free to use 14 ounces (400g) Crisped Tofu (page 243) or 2 to 3 cups (180 to 270g) roasted vegetables seasoned with Garam Masala instead. Serve this curry over rice or with flatbread.

Prep time: 10 minutes + Spinach Curry Sauce
Active time: 25 minutes
Inactive time: 15 minutes
soy-free, gluten-free
Serves 4

1/4 cup (30g) raw cashews
2 1/2 cups (415g) cooked chickpeas, drained and rinsed
1 cup (120g) thinly sliced carrots or 1/2-inch (1cm) dice potatoes
1/2 teaspoon smoked or sweet paprika
1 recipe Spinach Curry Sauce (page 62)
1/2 cup (120ml) water, or as needed
Red pepper flakes, for garnish
Garam Masala (page 244), for garnish
2 tablespoons (30ml) cashew cream, for garnish (optional)

1. Heat a large skillet over medium heat. Add the cashews and toast them, stirring occasionally, until golden, 2 to 3 minutes. Add the chickpeas, carrots, and paprika and cook for 1 minute. Add the spinach curry sauce. Cover the skillet and bring the curry to a boil, 6 to 7 minutes. Taste and adjust the seasonings. Add the water to thin the sauce to your preference.

2. Reduce the heat to medium-low and simmer the curry for 10 to 15 minutes. Garnish with the red pepper flakes, garam masala, and cashew cream (if using).

Per serving: Calories 338, Total Fat 13g, Saturated Fat 2g, Sodium 576mg, Total Carbs 45g, Fiber 12g, Sugars 10g, Protein 16g

Curried Vermicelli with Spinach

These curried noodles are my fusion version of Singapore noodles. I almost always prefer garam masala in these rather than curry powder. Vermicelli or brown rice mai fun noodles and plenty of vegetables make this a great weekday meal or side. Note that these noodles are meant to be on the dryer side. If you prefer more moisture in your noodles, add more liquid and cook the noodles for a minute less.

Prep time: 15 minutes
Active time: 20 minutes
gluten-free, nut-free option
Serves 4

8 ounces (227g) vermicelli or brown rice mai fun noodles

1 teaspoon organic safflower or other neutral oil

7 to 8 ounces (200 to 227g) extra-firm tofu, drained, pressed (page 243) and cut into 1/2-inch (1cm) cubes

3 cloves garlic, minced

1/4 cup (50g) thinly sliced onion

1 green bell pepper, thinly sliced

1 red bell pepper, thinly sliced

1 to 2 cups (75 to 150g) snow peas, thinly sliced carrots, thinly sliced mushrooms, or a combination

1 tablespoon mild curry powder, divided (see note)

1/4 teaspoon salt, or more to taste

2 tablespoons (30ml) soy sauce

1/2 teaspoon toasted sesame oil

1 tablespoon maple syrup

2 cups (60g) loosely packed baby spinach, or more to taste

1/2 cup (50g) fresh bean sprouts (optional)

Ground black pepper, to taste

1 tablespoon fresh lemon juice, divided

Red pepper flakes, to taste

2 tablespoons (20g) finely chopped roasted unsalted peanuts

2 tablespoons (6g) finely chopped fresh cilantro

1. Bring a medium saucepan of water to a boil over high heat. Add the vermicelli and cook for 2 to 4 minutes. Drain the vermicelli and set aside.

2. Heat the safflower oil in a large skillet over medium-high heat. Add the tofu and cook for 2 to 3 minutes, or until it is golden on some edges. Add the garlic and onion and cook, stirring occasionally, for 1 to 2 minutes. Add the green bell pepper, red bell pepper, and snow peas and toss well.

3. Add 1 to 2 teaspoons of the curry powder and the salt and stir to combine. Cook for 2 minutes. Add the soy sauce, sesame oil, and maple syrup and stir to combine. Add the noodles and the remaining 1 to 2 teaspoons curry powder. Toss well using tongs or two spatulas. Cook the noodles for 3 minutes or until they start to slightly scorch on the bottom. (Cook only 1 minute if using noodles other than vermicelli.)

4. Add the spinach, bean sprouts (if using), black pepper, and 1/2 tablespoon of the lemon juice. Toss well, taste, adjust the seasonings, and add the red pepper flakes. Garnish with the peanuts, cilantro, and the remaining 1/2 tablespoon lemon juice.

Note: If you do not have mild curry powder, you can substitute it with 1 1/2 teaspoons Garam Masala (page 244), 1 teaspoon ground coriander, and 1/2 teaspoon turmeric that have been well combined in a bowl.

Per serving: Calories 364, Total Fat 8g, Saturated Fat 1g, Sodium 418mg, Total Carbs 61g, Fiber 6g, Sugars 8g, Protein 14g

Chickpea and Sweet Potato Curry

This one-pot curry hits all my vegan meal requirements: chickpeas, sweet potatoes, spinach, curry. If you like, you can use other cooked beans, such as black-eyed peas, kidney beans, or white beans. Serve this dish with cooked rice or flatbread.

Prep time: 10 minutes
Active time: 30 minutes
soy-free, gluten-free, nut-free
Serves 4

1 teaspoon organic safflower or other neutral oil

1/2 to 3/4 teaspoon cumin seeds

3/4 cup (90g) finely chopped red or white onion

3 cloves garlic, finely chopped

1 (1/2-inch [1cm]) knob fresh ginger, peeled and finely chopped

1 teaspoon ground coriander

1/2 to 1 teaspoon Garam Masala (page 244), Curry Powder (page 245), Dry Berbere Spice Blend (page 68), Baharat Spice Blend (page 100), or store-bought versions

1/2 teaspoon ground turmeric

1/4 teaspoon ground cinnamon

1/4 teaspoon ground black pepper

1/4 to 1/2 teaspoon cayenne

2 medium tomatoes, chopped

1 (15-ounce [425g]) can chickpeas or 1 1/2 cups (250g) cooked chickpeas, drained and rinsed

1 1/2 cups (190g) coarsely chopped sweet potato

2 cups (480ml) water (see variation)

3/4 teaspoon salt, or more to taste

1 1/2 to 2 cups (45 to 60g) coarsely chopped baby spinach or 1 cup (190g) frozen spinach, thawed

1 teaspoon fresh lemon juice

Paprika, for garnish

Finely chopped fresh cilantro, for garnish

1. Heat the oil in a large skillet over medium heat. Add the cumin seeds and cook until they change color and get fragrant. Add the onion, garlic, and ginger and cook until the onion is translucent. Add the coriander, garam masala, turmeric, cinnamon, pepper, and cayenne and stir to combine. Cook for 30 seconds. Add the tomatoes and a splash of water, stir, cover the skillet, and cook until the tomatoes get saucy, 4 to 5 minutes. Mash the larger pieces of tomato with the back of a wooden spoon.

2. Add the chickpeas, sweet potato, water, and salt. Stir, cover the skillet, and cook for 15 to 20 minutes, or until the sweet potato is just done. Add the spinach and lemon juice, stirring to combine. Reduce the heat to medium-low and continue to simmer for 5 minutes, or until the mixture reaches the desired consistency. Taste and adjust the seasonings. Garnish with the paprika and cilantro and serve.

Variation: For a creamier curry, substitute the 2 cups (480ml) water with 1 cup (240ml) full-fat coconut milk mixed with 1 cup (240ml) water.

Per serving: Calories 193, Total Fat 3g, Saturated Fat 0g, Sodium 522mg, Total Carbs 35g, Fiber 8g, Sugars 7g, Protein 8g

Oil-Free or Pressure-Cooked Curry

Oil-free version: Heat a large skillet over medium heat. Add the cumin seeds and dry roast them until they are fragrant. Add the onion, garlic, ginger, and a splash of water and cook until the onion is translucent. Add more water if needed. Continue with the rest of the directions.

Pressure cooker or Instant Pot version: Follow step 1 over medium heat or in a separate pan. Add the cooked chickpeas, sweet potato, 1 1/2 cups (360ml) water, and salt. Close the pressure cooker's lid, set the timer to 8 to 10 minutes at high pressure. (Bring the stove top cooker to high pressure over medium heat. Cook for 6 to 8 minutes.) Let the pressure release naturally. Add the spinach immediately and mix in while the curry is still hot, or cook the curry with the spinach for a few minutes over medium heat.

Berbere Paste

This flavorful paste can be used to make Ethiopian wots with lentils or split peas. The flavor gets stronger as it sits. Use whichever spices you have to make this paste, as there are enough spices to balance. The heat in the paste can be adjusted by reducing the cayenne and paprika. This is probably not an everyday sauce recipe, but homemade berbere is great to have around. You can adjust the oil to your preference. Use this paste to make Jackfruit–Split Pea Wot (page 73), Berbere Tofu Bowl with Couscous (page 75), or a batch of Cauliflower and Chickpeas in Berbere Sauce (page 70).

Prep time: 15 minutes
Active time: 25 minutes
Inactive time: 10 minutes
soy-free, gluten-free, nut-free
Makes about 3/4 cup (314g)

- 2 tablespoons (30ml) **organic safflower or other neutral oil**
- 1 teaspoon **coriander seeds**
- 1/2 teaspoon **nigella seeds**
- 1/4 teaspoon **fenugreek seeds**
- 1/2 cup (60g) **finely chopped onion**
- 10 cloves **garlic, finely chopped**
- 1 (1-inch [3cm]) knob **fresh ginger, peeled and finely chopped**
- 1/2 teaspoon **ground cinnamon**
- 1/2 teaspoon **ground cardamom**
- 1/8 teaspoon **ground cloves**
- 1/4 teaspoon **ground allspice**
- 2 tablespoons (16g) **New Mexico chili powder**
- 1/2 teaspoon **paprika**
- 1/2 to 1 teaspoon **cayenne**
- 1/4 teaspoon **black pepper**
- 1/2 teaspoon **salt**
- 4 **fresh basil leaves**
- 1/2 cup (120ml) **water, or more as needed**

1. Heat the oil in a medium skillet over medium-low heat. Add the coriander seeds, nigella seeds, and fenugreek seeds and cook for 5 minutes.

2. Add the onion, garlic, and ginger and cook for 15 minutes, stirring occasionally. Add the cinnamon, cardamom, cloves, allspice, chili powder, paprika, cayenne, pepper, and salt and stir to combine. Cook for another 5 minutes.

3. Transfer the mixture to a blender. Add the basil leaves and blend with the water to a smooth paste. Add more salt or cayenne if needed. The paste ages well and the flavors (and heat) will get stronger as it sits. Refrigerate in an airtight jar or freeze in 2-tablespoon (30g) portions. The paste will keep refrigerated for up to 5 days and frozen for up to 1 month.

Per 2 tablespoons: Calories 382, Total Fat 16g, Saturated Fat 2g, Sodium 1670mg, Total Carbs 58g, Fiber 21g, Sugars 6g, Protein 16g

Spiced Oil

In traditional Ethiopian cuisine, clarified butter is slow-cooked with whole spices to make a flavorful spiced butter. A small amount of this spiced butter adds a deep flavor to food. This oil-based version is a simplified way to add the signature flavor profile to Ethiopian dishes.

Prep time: 5 minutes
Active time: 5 minutes
soy-free, gluten-free, nut-free
Makes 1 tablespoon (15ml)

1 tablespoon organic safflower or
   other neutral oil
1/2 teaspoon coriander seeds
1/4 teaspoon nigella seeds
1/4 teaspoon fenugreek seeds
1 whole clove, ground
Pinch cayenne (optional)

Heat the oil in a small skillet over low heat. Add the coriander seeds, nigella seeds, and fenugreek seeds and cook for 8 to 10 minutes. Add the clove and cayenne (if using) and stir to combine. Take the skillet off the heat and cool completely. Use the oil immediately or store it, refrigerated, for up to 1 week. Note that you can remove and discard the seeds prior to storing the oil or you can store the oil with the spices in it and use a spoon to measure out just the oil.

Per 1 tablespoon: Calories 132, Total Fat 14.3g, Saturated Fat 2g, Sodium 2mg, Total Carbs 1.8g, Fiber 1g, Sugars 0g, Protein 0.6g

Dry Berbere Spice Blend

This quick berbere-like spice blend uses the more commonly available substitutions for some ingredients that traditionally used in berbere.

1 teaspoon ground coriander
2 1/2 teaspoons paprika (a combination of sweet and smoky)
1/2 teaspoon New Mexico chile powder or more sweet paprika
1/2 teaspoon ground cumin
1/4 teaspoon fenugreek seed powder or ground mustard
1/2 teaspoon ground black pepper (reduce for less heat)
1/4 teaspoon ground cardamom
Generous pinch each: ground cloves, ground ginger, allspice, cinnamon, and cayenne

Combine the spices in a bowl and mix well. Store in airtight container for up to 3 months.

Makes about 2 tablespoons

Cauliflower and Chickpeas in Berbere Sauce

Berbere paste makes an amazing sauce in which you can cook vegetables, chickpeas, tofu, and other ingredients. This recipe boasts a sauce with onion and my homemade berbere paste. Serve this dish with flatbread or injera or over rice.

Prep time: 10 minutes + Berbere Paste
Active time: 15 minutes
Inactive time: 15 minutes
soy-free, gluten-free, nut-free
Serves 4

1 teaspoon organic safflower or other neutral oil
1 1/2 cups (180g) chopped onion
1/8 teaspoon sugar
1/8 teaspoon ground cardamom
1/8 teaspoon ground cinnamon
4 to 6 tablespoons (80 to 100g) Berbere Paste (page 68)
1 (15-ounce [425g]) can chickpeas or 1 1/2 cups (250g) cooked chickpeas, drained and rinsed
1 1/2 cups (160g) chopped cauliflower
1 cup (150g) chopped zucchini, carrots, bell peppers, or corn
1 cup (160g) chopped tomatoes
1/2 teaspoon salt, or to taste
1/2 cup (120ml) water, plus more as needed
1 teaspoon Spiced Oil (page 69) or extra-virgin olive oil, for garnish

1. Heat the oil in a large skillet over medium heat. Add the onion, sugar, and a pinch salt. Cook until the onion is golden, stirring occasionally, 9 to 11 minutes. You want some of the onion to start to caramelize. Add the cardamom and cinnamon, stirring to combine. Add the berbere and stir. Cook for 1 minute to roast the paste. Add the chickpeas, cauliflower, zucchini, tomatoes, salt, and water and stir to combine.

2. Cover the skillet and cook for 10 to 15 minutes, or until the cauliflower has cooked through, stirring occasionally. Taste and adjust the seasonings. Add more water if needed. Garnish with the spiced oil.

Note: To make this with store-bought dry berbere spice blend, add 4 cloves finely chopped garlic and 1 tablespoon minced ginger with the onion at Step 1. Add 2 tablespoons or more of the spice blend to the caramelizing onions, and proceed with the recipe.

Per serving: Calories 211, Total Fat 5g, Saturated Fat 1g, Sodium 541mg, Total Carbs 36g, Fiber 10g, Sugars 9g, Protein 10g

Jackfruit-Split Pea Wot

This Ethiopian wot fusion has jackfruit and split peas with some homemade berbere paste. The texture from jackfruit and earthy split peas work really well together. Like any well-spiced meal, the dish gets tastier as it sits, making it a perfect make-ahead meal. To make this without jackfruit, use another 1/2 cup (100g) split peas, add another 1/2 cup (120ml) water, and add more salt to taste. Serve this delicious wot over injera, flatbread, or rice or make wraps with lettuce leaves.

Prep time: 10 minutes + Berbere Paste
Active time: 20 minutes
Inactive time: 40 minutes
soy-free, gluten-free, nut-free
Serves 4

1/2 cup (100g) split peas or split chickpeas, picked over, rinsed, and drained

1 (20-ounce [567g]) can young green jackfruit

2 teaspoons organic safflower or other neutral oil

1/4 teaspoon coriander seeds

1 large onion, finely chopped

8 cloves garlic, minced

1 (1 1/2-inch [4cm]) knob fresh ginger, peeled and minced

4 to 6 tablespoons (80 to 100g) Berbere Paste (page 68) or 2 to 3 teaspoons Baharat Spice Blend (page 100)

1 cup (160g) coarsely chopped tomatoes

2 1/2 cups (600ml) water

1 teaspoon salt

1 teaspoon extra-virgin olive oil, for garnish (see variation)

Fresh lemon juice, for garnish

1. Soak the rinsed split peas in hot water for at least 30 minutes. Meanwhile, drain and rinse the jackfruit. Squeeze excess water from the jackfruit by pressing the pieces between your palms. Shred the jackfruit using a fork or food processor and set aside.

2. Heat the safflower oil in a large skillet or saucepan over medium heat. Add the coriander seeds and cook for a few seconds, until they change color. Add the onion, garlic, ginger, and a pinch salt. Cook for 10 to 12 minutes, until the vegetables are golden, stirring occasionally. Add the berbere, stirring to combine. Cook for 1 minute. Add the tomatoes and stir to combine.

3. Drain the split peas and add them to the saucepan. Add the jackfruit and water. Cover the skillet and cook for 20 minutes. Add the salt. Continue to cook, partially covered, for 20 to 25 minutes, or until the split peas are cooked. Taste and adjust the seasonings. Garnish the wot with the olive oil and lemon juice.

Note: Split chickpeas are also called chana dal. Look for either term when purchasing ingredients for your Indian-inspired meals.

Variation: If you're craving a bit more spice, you can substitute an equal amount of Spiced Oil (page 69) for the olive oil.

Per serving: Calories 218, Total fat 4g, Saturated Fat 1g, Sodium 612mg, Total Carbs 40g, Fiber 9g, Sugars 15g, Protein 8g

Pressure-Cooked Wot

To make this recipe using a pressure cooker or Instant Pot: Follow steps 1 and 2 on sauté mode in the Instant Pot. Add the split peas, jackfruit, salt, and 1 1/2 cups (360ml) water. Cook on manual for 7 to 10 minutes. Let the pressure release naturally. Taste and adjust the seasonings. Continue with the recipe directions and serve.

Berbere Tofu Bowl with Couscous

I love bowls of food with many textures. This bowl has chewy tofu marinated in a flavorful, smooth berbere sauce, and the breadcrumbs provide crispiness. Chopped juicy vegetables and a splash of fresh lemon juice brighten up the bowl. To make this gluten-free, use gluten-free breadcrumbs and Turmeric Cauliflower Rice (page 131) instead of couscous.

Prep time: 15 minutes + marinating time
Active time: 25 minutes
Inactive time: 10 minutes
gluten-free option, nut-free
Serves 4

Tofu

1/2 cup (150g) **Berbere Paste (page 68)**, or to taste
1/4 teaspoon **ground cinnamon**
1/2 teaspoon **ground allspice**
1 teaspoon **fresh lime juice**
1/4 teaspoon **salt**
1/4 teaspoon **black pepper**
1 teaspoon **cornstarch**
21 ounces (596g) **firm tofu**, drained, pressed (page 243), and cut into 1/4-inch (0.6cm) thick slices

Breading

1 cup (80g) **dry breadcrumbs (or gluten-free crumbs)**
1/4 teaspoon **salt**
1/4 to 1/2 teaspoon **cayenne**
1 tablespoon **nutritional yeast**

Couscous

1 1/2 cups (360ml) **water**
1/2 teaspoon **ground turmeric**
1/2 teaspoon **garlic powder**
1/2 teaspoon **Garam Masala (page 244) or Curry Powder (page 245)**
1/2 teaspoon **salt**
1 cup (170g) **couscous**
1/2 teaspoon **fresh lemon juice**, plus more for garnish
1/2 cup (80g) **fresh or thawed frozen green peas**
1 cup (160g) **chopped cucumber or tomatoes**

1. Tofu: In a large bowl, combine the berbere paste, cinnamon, allspice, lime juice, salt, pepper, and cornstarch. Dip each tofu slice into the marinade to coat well. Alternatively, brush all sides of the tofu with the marinade and place the slices in an airtight container. Save any remaining marinade to use as berbere paste in other recipes. Cover the container and let the tofu marinate for 1 hour or up to overnight.

Breading: In a shallow bowl, combine the breadcrumbs, salt, cayenne, and nutritional yeast. Place each tofu slice in the breadcrumb mixture to coat well. Flip the tofu to coat all sides. Cook the tofu slices on a grill pan over medium-high heat for 7 to 9 minutes. Alternatively, bake the tofu on a large baking sheet at 400°F (200°C) for 20 to 25 minutes.

2. Couscous: Combine the water, turmeric, garlic powder, garam masala, and salt in a medium saucepan over medium heat. When the water comes to a rolling boil, add the couscous, lemon juice, and peas and stir to combine. Cover the saucepan and cook for 1 minute. Take the saucepan off the heat and let it sit for 10 minutes. Fluff the couscous. Add a generous helping of couscous to each serving bowl. Top with the cucumber and a drizzle of lemon juice. For additional dressing, use the Tahini Garlic Sauce on page 123.

Variation: Use other sauces, like the Tikka Masala Sauce (page 54) or Barbecue Sauce (page 241), instead of berbere paste.

Per serving: Calories 464, Total Fat 12g, Saturated Fat 2g, Sodium 824mg, Total Carbs 50g, Fiber 10g, Sugars 5g, Protein 29g

4

Buffalo & Firecracker

If you love food that is hot and tangy, this is the chapter for you. These recipes feature Buffalo hot sauce, made famous in the city of Buffalo, New York, and a sweet and tangy hot sauce called Firecracker Sauce. Along with heat, these sauces add amazing flavors to a meal. Both of these sauces can be made mild, medium-hot, or incredibly hot. You will want to adjust the heat to suit your own palate.

Start with the popular Buffalo Chickpea Pizza with White Garlic Sauce (page 88), then definitely try the Firecracker Jackfruit Sandwiches (page 83). If the final dish is too hot to handle, add more vegetables or other cooling ingredients to the dish (or simply scrape off some of that sauce).

Buffalo Sauce (page 84)

Firecracker Sauce

This sauce can get hot! It is called Firecracker, after all—be careful when you sample its flavor. You want it to be a little hotter than you'd normally prefer, as it gets paired with things like legumes, avocado, and creamy condiments and dressings to tone things down. This sweet hot sauce pairs well with chickpeas in a salad (page 80), with jackfruit (page 83), with Crunchy Baked Cauliflower (page 79), or with other vegetables.

Prep time: 5 minutes
Active time: 10 minutes
soy-free, gluten-free, nut-free
Makes about 1 cup (240ml)

- 3 tablespoons (45ml) sriracha sauce
- 1/4 cup (60ml) distilled white vinegar
- 2 to 3 tablespoons (30 to 45ml) hot sauce or 1 tablespoon vinegar plus 1 tablespoon sriracha sauce
- 2 1/2 teaspoons garlic powder
- 1/2 to 1 teaspoon cayenne (see note)
- 1/2 teaspoon salt, or more to taste
- 1 teaspoon organic safflower or other neutral oil (optional)
- 3 to 5 tablespoons (36 to 60g) raw sugar
- 3/4 cup (180ml) water
- 2 teaspoons cornstarch
- 2 tablespoons (6g) chopped scallions (optional)

Add the sriracha, vinegar, hot sauce, garlic powder, cayenne, salt, oil (if using), sugar, water, and cornstarch to a small saucepan over medium heat and whisk to combine. Bring the sauce to a boil, about 4 minutes. Continue to cook for another 2 to 4 minutes to thicken the sauce slightly. Add the scallions (if using). Refrigerate in a clean, airtight jar for up to 1 week with scallions and up to 1 month without scallions.

Note: For less heat, substitute the cayenne with one part paprika and one part cayenne. If you are unsure how much spiciness you can tolerate, start with the lesser amount of cayenne or do not use any cayenne at all, as there is already heat from the hot sauces.

Per 1/2 cup: Calories 128, Total Fat 3g, Saturated Fat 0.4g, Sodium 1595mg, Total Carbs 31g, Fiber 1.4g, Sugars 24g, Protein 1.5g

Firecracker Cauliflower Bites

This spicy recipe is one of the ways I learned to like broccoli. Once you master the Crunchy Baked Cauliflower (or broccoli, prepared in the same manner), this comes together easily. Serve this cauliflower as finger food or a salad topping. These bites are also delicious with Buffalo Sauce (page 84).

Prep time: 15 minutes

soy-free , gluten-free option, nut-free option

Serves 4

1 recipe **Crunchy Baked Cauliflower (page 246)**

1 recipe **Firecracker Sauce (page 78)**

Celery ribs or cucumber sticks, for serving

1 recipe **Celery Ranch Sauce (page 87) or other creamy sauce, for serving (optional)**

Place the cauliflower in a large serving bowl. Drizzle the firecracker sauce all over the cauliflower (use less sauce for milder cauliflower bites). Alternatively, you can serve the sauce on the side to dip and eat. Serve the cauliflower bites with the celery ribs and celery ranch sauce (if using).

Per serving (with Firecracker Sauce and Celery Ranch Sauce): Calories 463, Total Fat 14g, Saturated Fat 2g, Sodium 1437mg, Total Carbs 80g, Fiber 6g, Sugars 19g, Protein 13g

Firecracker Chickpea Salad with Peanut Dressing

This bowl has many flavors and textures. Crunchy vegetables, hot Firecracker Sauce, and sweet and nutty peanut sauce all come together in a fabulous fusion bowl.

Prep time: 15 minutes + Firecracker Sauce
Active time: 20 minutes
soy-free option, gluten-free, nut-free option
Serves 4

Salad

3 cups (225g) thinly sliced romaine lettuce

1 1/2 cups (180g) shredded or thinly sliced carrots

2 large red bell peppers, thinly sliced

1 medium zucchini or cucumber, thinly sliced

1/4 cup (10g) chopped scallions or fresh cilantro, for garnish

4 tablespoons (38g) roasted peanuts, for garnish (optional)

Chickpeas

2 1/2 cups (415g) cooked chickpeas, drained and rinsed (see variation)

1/2 to 1 recipe Firecracker Sauce (page 78)

Peanut Dressing

1 (1 1/2-inch [4cm]) knob fresh ginger, peeled and chopped

2 cloves garlic

1/2 cup (130g) smooth peanut butter or almond butter (or sunflower seed butter or soy nut butter to make nut-free)

1 tablespoon soy sauce

2 teaspoons fresh lemon juice

1/2 to 1 teaspoon sriracha sauce, to taste

1 tablespoon maple syrup

4 to 6 tablespoons (60 to 90ml) water

1. **Salad:** Combine the lettuce, carrots, bell peppers, and zucchini in a large serving bowl. Toss the salad to evenly distribute the vegetables throughout the lettuce.

2. **Chickpeas:** In a medium skillet over medium heat, combine the chickpeas and firecracker sauce. Cook until the sauce thickens, stirring occasionally, 4 to 5 minutes. Taste carefully and adjust the seasonings. (If the chickpeas are too spicy for your taste, add more chickpeas and some maple syrup to lessen the heat.) Simmer for about 1 minute. Take the skillet off the heat, let the chickpeas cool slightly, and add them to the serving bowl.

3. **Peanut Dressing:** In a blender, process the ginger, garlic, peanut butter, soy sauce, lemon juice, sriracha, maple syrup, and enough water to create the desired consistency. Taste and adjust the seasonings, adding more maple syrup, lemon juice, or salt, if desired. Drizzle the sauce over the salad. Sprinkle the scallions and peanuts (if using) on top of the salad and serve.

Variation: Instead of chickpeas, use Crisped Tofu (page 243) or Crunchy Baked Cauliflower (page 246) with the Firecracker Sauce. Use the Firecracker Sauce as dressing too. Ranch Dressing (page 87) also goes well with this salad.

Note: To make it gluten-free, substitute tamari or coconut aminos for the soy sauce.

Per serving (with 1/2 recipe Firecracker Sauce): Calories 537, Total Fat 25g, Saturated Fat 5g, Sodium 631mg, Total Carbs 63g, Fiber 15g, Sugars 27g, Protein 22g

Firecracker Jackfruit Sandwiches

These handy sandwiches use jackfruit with Firecracker Sauce (page 78) to make amazing sliders, which are perfect for game-day finger food or an everyday light lunch. Spicy, sweet, and garlicky, the Firecracker Sauce can get really hot for some, so adjust the cayenne and sriracha to your preference. The heat from the sauce pairs well with a cooling topping, such as the Ranch Dressing, but it's also good with Peanut Butter Sauce (page 2).

Prep time: 15 minutes
Active time: 20 minutes
Inactive time: 35 minutes
soy-free , gluten-free option , nut-free option
Makes 6 to 7 slider sandwiches

2 (20-ounce [567g]) cans young green jackfruit (see note)
2 recipes Firecracker Sauce (page 78), divided
1 cup (240ml) water
2 teaspoons nutritional yeast
Slider buns or tortillas (gluten-free if necessary)
1/4 cup (60ml) Ranch Dressing (page 87) or Nut-Free Ranch Dressing (page 86), for serving
Sliced avocado or mango, for serving
Lettuce leaves, for serving (optional)

1. Drain the jackfruit and rinse it well in a bowl of water. Drain the jackfruit and squeeze out the excess liquid. Shred the jackfruit using a fork or a food processor.

2. Add the jackfruit, 1 recipe of the Firecracker Sauce, water, and nutritional yeast to a large skillet over medium-low heat. Partially cover the skillet and cook the jackfruit mixture for 25 to 30 minutes, or until the sauce sticks to the jackfruit and the liquid evaporates.

3. Lay the bottom slider buns on a serving tray or individual plates. Layer the ranch, avocado, lettuce (if using), and jackfruit on the buns. Drizzle the remaining 1 recipe Firecracker Sauce over the jackfruit, place the top buns on the sandwiches, and serve.

Note: Don't have jackfruit? Use shredded sweet potatoes, butternut squash, or hearts of palm instead. Add some barbecue chickpeas from the Buddha Bowl with Nacho-Spiced Sweet Potatoes (page 136) or some Jamaican jerk black beans from the Barbecue Pizza with Jerk Beans and Vegetables (page 160) for a heartier meal.

Per serving (does not include buns, avocado, or lettuce): Calories 281, Total Fat 5g, Saturated Fat 1g, Sodium 1170mg, Total Carbs 60g, Fiber 5g, Sugars 46g, Protein 7g

Buffalo Sauce

I use this Buffalo sauce with my Buffalo Chickpea Pizza with White Garlic Sauce (page 88), often with the extra vinegar and cayenne. The extra zing works well when paired with cooling Ranch Dressing (page 87) or other creamy sauces. The heat and tang end up balancing the other flavors perfectly. Use this spicy sauce with Buffalo Lentil Tacos (page 90), Buffalo Chickpea Tacos (page 91), and, of course, over Crunchy Baked Cauliflower (page 246).

Prep time: 2 minutes
Active time: 5 minutes
soy-free, gluten-free, nut-free
Makes 2/3 cup (160ml) sauce

1/3 cup (80ml) hot sauce
3 tablespoons (45ml) sriracha sauce
2 tablespoons (30ml) extra-virgin olive oil or melted nondairy butter
1 teaspoon distilled white vinegar (optional)
1/2 teaspoon cayenne (optional)

In a small bowl, whisk together the hot sauce, sriracha, oil, vinegar (if using), and cayenne (if using). Taste and adjust the seasonings. Store this sauce in an airtight container in the refrigerator for 4 to 6 weeks.

Per 2/3 cup: Calories 262, Total Fat 23g, Saturated Fat 6g, Sodium 3242mg, Total Carbs 12g, Fiber 2g, Sugars 10g, Protein 2g

White Garlic Sauce

This sauce is very versatile. It makes a great base for mac and cheese, Vegetable Lasagna (page 162), Alfredo Spinach Pizza (page 156), and Buffalo Chickpea Pizza with White Garlic Sauce (page 88). Heat the sauce to thicken it and use dollops of it instead of mozzarella in any recipe calling for that familiar white cheese. (For a nut-free version of this sauce, see page 86.)

Prep time: 15 minutes + soaking time
Active time: 5 minutes
soy-free, gluten-free
Makes 1 1/4 cups (300ml)

- 1/2 cup (60g) raw cashews, soaked for 15 minutes, or 1/2 cup (80g) ground raw cashews
- 3/4 cup (180ml) plain unsweetened nondairy milk
- 1 tablespoon cornstarch or arrowroot starch
- 1/2 teaspoon salt, or more to taste
- 1 tablespoon extra-virgin olive oil
- 1/8 teaspoon black pepper
- 1 teaspoon garlic powder or 4 cloves roasted garlic
- 1/4 teaspoon onion powder
- 1/4 teaspoon ground mustard (optional)
- 1/2 to 1 teaspoon Quick Italian Herb Blend (page 169)
- 1 to 2 tablespoons nutritional yeast
- 1 teaspoon apple cider vinegar or distilled white vinegar

Process the cashews, milk, cornstarch, salt, oil, pepper, garlic powder, onion powder, ground mustard (if using), quick Italian herb blend, nutritional yeast, and vinegar in a blender until smooth and creamy. Taste and adjust the seasonings. Store in an airtight container in the refrigerator for up to 4 days.

Per 1 1/4 cups: Calories 611, Total Fat 45g, Saturated Fat 7g, Sodium 1320mg, Total Carbs 37g, Fiber 7g, Sugars 4g, Protein 22g

Nut-Free White Garlic Sauce

This sauce has a similar texture and flavor to the cashew-based White Garlic Sauce on page 85, but it has the benefit of being nut-free. Hemp seeds and chickpea flour make up the volume and texture. Use this nut-free option wherever you need White Garlic Sauce. This sauce can also be made with pepitas instead of hemp seeds, but be aware that you'll need to blend them longer so the mixture is smooth.

Prep time: 5 minutes
Active time: 20 minutes
soy-free, gluten-free, nut-free
Makes about 1 1/4 cups (300ml)

1 1/2 tablespoons hemp seeds

1/3 cup (80ml) hot water

3 tablespoons (18g) chickpea flour

1 cup (240ml) water

2 teaspoons cornstarch or arrowroot starch

1/2 teaspoon salt, or more to taste

1 tablespoon extra-virgin olive oil

1/8 teaspoon black pepper

4 cloves roasted garlic, 3/4 teaspoon garlic powder, or 4 cloves garlic, finely chopped and sautéed in 1/2 teaspoon oil until fragrant

1/4 teaspoon onion powder

1/4 teaspoon ground mustard

1/2 to 1 teaspoon Quick Italian Herb Blend (page 163) or equal quantities dried thyme, oregano, and basil

1 to 2 tablespoons nutritional yeast

1 teaspoon apple cider vinegar or distilled white vinegar

1. Soak the hemp seeds in the hot water and set aside for 10 minutes. While the hemp seeds are soaking, whisk together the chickpea flour and water in a medium saucepan over medium heat. (The flour lumps will dissolve as the liquid heats up.) Cook, stirring frequently, until the mixture resembles a roux, 6 to 7 minutes. Taste the mixture carefully to see if the raw flour flavor has been cooked out.

2. Transfer the hemp seeds and soaking water to a small blender (see note). Add the cornstarch, salt, oil, pepper, roasted garlic, onion powder, ground mustard, quick Italian herb blend, nutritional yeast, and vinegar to the blender. Blend for 2 to 3 minutes in 1-minute intervals.

3. Transfer the hemp seed mixture to the roux. Cook for 2 minutes, stirring frequently, until the mixture thickens slightly. Carefully taste and adjust the seasonings. Take the saucepan off the heat. Use the sauce immediately or store it, refrigerated, for up to 4 days. To use, reheat the sauce with a bit of water to thin out the consistency if needed.

Note: If you do not have a small blender, use a food processor or mortar and pestle to grind the dry hemp seeds into powder and soak the powder in the water. Mix with the rest of the ingredients in the saucepan.

Per 1 1/4 cups: Calories 368, Total Fat 22g, Saturated Fat 3g, Sodium 1200mg, Total Carbs 26g, Fiber 7g, Sugars 2g, Protein 18g

Nut-Free Ranch Dressing

To turn this sauce into nut-free ranch dressing, add 1/4 teaspoon onion powder, 1/4 teaspoon dried parsley, 1/4 teaspoon dried thyme, and 1/4 teaspoon dried dill when you take the saucepan off the stove.

Ranch Dressing

This ranch dressing is easy to make and tastes amazing. Use it wherever you use Buffalo Sauce (page 84), like the Buffalo Chickpea Pizza with White Garlic Sauce (page 88) or the Buffalo Chickpea Tacos (page 91). You can also use this recipe to dress a salad or the Buddha Bowl with Nacho-Spiced Sweet Potatoes (page 136). And, of course, this goes great with any of the burgers in chapter 5.

Prep time: 15 minutes soaking time + 5 minutes
Active time: 5 minutes
soy-free, gluten-free
Makes about 1 cup (240ml)

- 1/2 cup (60g) raw cashews, soaked for 15 minutes and drained, or ground raw cashews
- 2/3 cup (160ml) plain unsweetened nondairy milk or 1/2 cup (120ml) water
- 1/2 teaspoon salt
- 2 teaspoons extra-virgin olive oil
- 1/4 teaspoon black pepper
- 1 teaspoon garlic powder or 4 cloves roasted garlic
- 3/4 teaspoon onion powder
- 1 to 2 tablespoons nutritional yeast
- 2 teaspoons apple cider vinegar or distilled white vinegar
- 1/2 teaspoon dried parsley
- 1/2 teaspoon dried thyme
- 1/4 teaspoon dried dill
- 2 teaspoons finely chopped fresh chives or 1 teaspoon dried chives (optional)

In a blender, combine the cashews, milk, salt, oil, pepper, garlic powder, onion powder, nutritional yeast, vinegar, parsley, thyme, and dill. Blend until smooth and creamy. Taste and adjust the seasonings. Add the chives (if using) and stir gently to combine.

Variation: Use 1 1/2 to 2 teaspoons premade nondairy ranch seasoning instead of parsley, thyme, and dill.

Per 1 cup: Calories 676, Total Fat 56g, Saturated Fat 9g, Sodium 1194mg, Total Carbs 30g, Fiber 7g, Sugars 4g, Protein 21g

More Ranch Variations

Quick Ranch Seasoning: In a small airtight container, combine 2 teaspoons garlic powder, 2 teaspoons onion powder, 2 teaspoons dried onion flakes, 1 1/2 tablespoons (5g) dried parsley, 1 1/2 teaspoons dried dill, 1 teaspoon dried thyme, 1 teaspoon black pepper, and 1 teaspoon dried chives (or more to taste). Store for up to 3 months.

Celery Ranch Sauce: Add 1/2 teaspoon celery seeds to the ranch dressing.

Chipotle Ranch Sauce: Add 1/2 teaspoon smoked paprika and 1/2 teaspoon chipotle chili powder to the ranch dressing. Mix in a good pinch sugar to balance the heat if you like.

Buffalo Chickpea Pizza with White Garlic Sauce

This is a very popular pizza on the blog. It seems like there are many components, but they come together quickly. I usually make this pizza from start to finish in thirty minutes and then rest while it bakes. Make the dough, toss the chickpeas in sauce, make the garlic sauce and ranch, assemble the pizza, and bake—pretty simple! For an even quicker option, add some Quick Ranch Seasoning (page 87) to the remaining white sauce instead of making a ranch sauce separately.

Prep time: 25 minutes
Active time: 30 minutes
Inactive time: 15 minutes
gluten-free option, soy-free, nut-free option
Serves 4 to 6

Buffalo Chickpeas

2 to 2 1/2 cups (330 to 415g) cooked chickpeas, drained and rinsed
1/3 cup (80ml) hot sauce
3 tablespoons (45ml) sriracha sauce
2 tablespoons (30ml) extra-virgin olive oil or melted nondairy butter
1 teaspoon distilled white vinegar (optional)
1/2 teaspoon cayenne (optional)

Pizza

1 recipe Easy Pizza Dough (page 230) or store-bought pizza dough
1 recipe White Garlic Sauce (page 85)
2 cups (60g) baby spinach
1/2 recipe Celery Ranch Sauce (page 87)
Nondairy shredded mozzarella cheese (optional)

1. Buffalo Chickpeas: Add the chickpeas to a medium bowl. Add the hot sauce, sriracha, oil, vinegar (if using), and cayenne (if using). Toss the chickpeas to coat them in the sauce, mashing a few chickpeas for texture if desired.

2. Pizza: Preheat the oven to 425°F (220°C). Divide the pizza dough into 2 balls and shape them to make 2 (12-inch [30cm]) pizzas. Place the pizza crusts on two pizza stones or medium baking sheets. (The crust doubles in thickness, so keep it thin to avoid an overly bready crust; however, keep the edges thick to hold the sauces.)

3. Spread a layer of the white garlic sauce on the crusts. Add a layer of spinach. Using a spoon, distribute the chickpeas over the spinach. Drizzle some or all of the remaining Buffalo sauce on the pizza, depending on your heat preference. (You can also drizzle some of the Buffalo sauce over the baked pizzas right before serving.) Drizzle the celery ranch sauce liberally over the chickpeas and spinach. Top the pizzas with the mozzarella (if using). Let the pizzas sit near the warm oven for 5 minutes. Bake the pizzas for 17 to 19 minutes. Broil for 30 seconds to brown the tops, if needed. After removing the pizzas from the oven, let them cool for 1 minute, then slice and serve.

Variation: Use seitan or vegan chicken strips instead of chickpeas. For a gluten-free option, make the Gluten-Free Pizza Crust (page 232).

Per serving: Calories 324, Total Fat 18g, Saturated Fat 3g, Sodium 873mg, Total Carbs 30g, Fiber 8g, Sugars 6g, Protein 12g

Cover the crust with spinach leaves.

Spread the Buffalo Chickpeas on top.

Drizzle with the Celery Ranch Sauce.

Bake and enjoy.

Buffalo Lentil Tacos

Buffalo Sauce goes wonderfully with earthy lentils to make these especially easy tacos. If you like, use other vegetables (such as raw celery, sliced radishes, or roasted cauliflower or broccoli) instead of the asparagus, and top the tacos with crunchy lettuce. Serve the Buffalo lentils over baked sweet potatoes or baked russet potatoes to make a grain-free meal.

Prep time: 15 minutes + Lentils + Buffalo Sauce
Active time: 25 minutes
soy-free, gluten-free option, nut-free
Serves 4

Buffalo Lentils

2 1/2 to 3 cups (500 to 600g) cooked lentils, drained and rinsed
1 recipe Buffalo Sauce (page 84) or Firecracker Sauce (page 78)
Salt, to taste (if using unsalted lentils)

Cilantro-Avocado Cream

1 cup (40g) fresh cilantro
1/2 ripe Hass avocado, pitted and peeled
1/4 cup (60ml) full-fat coconut milk
1/4 teaspoon garlic powder or 1 clove garlic
2 teaspoons fresh lemon juice
1/4 teaspoon salt
Dash black pepper

Garlicky Asparagus

1 teaspoon organic safflower or other neutral oil
1 1/2 cups (200g) coarsely chopped asparagus
4 cloves garlic, minced

For Serving

Tortillas
Salsa or pico de gallo
Roasted vegetables or lettuce (optional)

1. Buffalo Lentils: Combine the lentils, Buffalo sauce, and salt (if using unsalted lentils) in a medium saucepan over medium heat. Bring the lentils to a boil, 6 to 8 minutes. Simmer for another few minutes, until the sauce coats and flavors the lentils. Taste and adjust the seasonings, adding more Buffalo sauce if needed.

2. Cilantro-Avocado Cream: In a blender, process the cilantro, avocado, milk, garlic powder, lemon juice, salt, and pepper until the ingredients have combined. Add water to adjust the consistency to your preference and blend again. Taste and adjust the seasonings.

3. Garlicky Asparagus: Heat the oil in a medium skillet over medium heat. Add the asparagus and garlic and cook for 4 to 5 minutes, stirring occasionally.

4. For Serving: Warm the tortillas. Load them up with the saucy lentils and asparagus. Drizzle a generous amount of the cilantro-avocado cream over each taco. Add salsa and roasted vegetables (if using) and serve.

Per serving (with Buffalo Sauce and without tortillas): Calories 295, Total Fat 10g, Saturated Fat 3g, Sodium 916mg, Total Carbs 40g, Fiber 12g, Sugars 4g, Protein 16g

Buffalo Chickpea Tacos

These tacos are a quick alternative to the Buffalo Chickpea Pizza with White Garlic Sauce (page 88). Toss the chickpeas in Buffalo Sauce, add some roasted vegetables and greens, top the tacos generously with ranch dressing, and supper is done. To make this nut-free, use Nut-Free Ranch Dressing (page 86).

Prep time: 10 minutes + Celery Ranch
　　Sauce
Active time: 20 minutes
soy-free, gluten-free option, nut-free option
Serves 4

1/3 cup (80ml) hot sauce

3 tablespoons (45ml) sriracha sauce

2 tablespoons (30ml) extra-virgin olive oil or melted nondairy butter

1 teaspoon distilled white vinegar (optional)

2 to 2 1/2 cups (330 to 415g) room-temperature cooked chickpeas, drained and rinsed, or 1 recipe Chickpea Flour Tofu (page 238)

1 recipe Celery Ranch Sauce (page 87), divided

1 1/2 cups (200g) finely chopped celery or cucumber

1 teaspoon organic safflower or other neutral oil

1 medium green bell pepper, thinly sliced

1 medium red bell pepper, thinly sliced

1/2 teaspoon salt, divided

8 to 10 tortillas or taco shells

2 cups (60g) baby spinach

1. Combine the hot sauce, sriracha, olive oil, and vinegar (if using) in a medium bowl. Add the chickpeas, tossing to coat them in the sauce, and set aside. In another medium bowl, combine half the celery ranch sauce with the celery. In a third medium bowl, thin the other half of the celery ranch sauce with water if needed.

2. Heat the safflower oil in a large skillet over medium-high heat. Add the green bell pepper, red bell pepper, and 1/4 teaspoon of the salt. Cook the bell peppers until they are golden on some sides, 4 to 5 minutes, stirring occasionally. Warm the tortillas if desired.

3. Add some of the baby spinach, roasted bell peppers, and celery to every taco. Divide the remaining 1/4 teaspoon salt between all the tacos. Add some Buffalo chickpeas and a generous drizzle of the celery ranch sauce to each taco and serve.

Per serving (without tortillas): Calories 440, Total Fat 24g, Saturated Fat 4g, Sodium 1260mg, Total Carbs 44g, Fiber 12g, Sugars 11g, Protein 16g

5

Burgers & More

Veggie burgers can sometimes be too crumbly, squishy, or bland. This chapter changes all that with my next generation of firm and flavorful burgers made with vegetables, lentils, beans, and whole grains. These burgers come together quickly, and with a bit of practice on your part, they will rival the best burgers out there.

Veggie burgers come in varied textures and flavors. Some are meaty and sturdy and compete with their nonvegan counterparts while others can hold their own unique taste. Most can be made oil-free by baking them without oil, and many can comply with whole-food diets when made with coarsely ground oats instead of breadcrumbs.

You can also serve these patties in a bowl, sandwich, or wrap or over a salad. Many of the burgers in this chapter can be made into loaves, and some of them also make excellent veggie balls to add to spaghetti, curries, and so on. They can also be made in advance and frozen. Lightly pan-fry or bake them to reheat.

Start your veggie-burger adventures with the Easiest Black Bean Burgers (page 94), the earthy Lentil-Walnut Burgers (page 97), and the umami-rich Baharat Chickpea Burgers (page 103). Also try the Lentil-Quinoa Loaf with Spicy Glaze (page 118).

Lentil-Quinoa Loaf with Spicy Glaze (page 118)

Easiest Black Bean Burgers

These crazy-easy burgers are accessible to everyone. If you have never made burger patties, these are the ones you want to make first. With a simple list of ingredients—such as beans, walnuts, oats, and spices—you can kick-start your veggie-burger adventure here.

Prep time: 15 minutes
Active time: 25 minutes
Inactive time: 15 minutes
soy-free, gluten-free option
Makes 7 to 8 patties

1/2 cup (60g) raw walnuts

1/2 cup (40g) old-fashioned oats

2 cloves garlic

1 (1/2-inch [1cm]) knob fresh ginger, peeled and coarsely chopped

1/4 cup (30g) coarsely chopped onion

1 to 2 tablespoons pickled jalapeño slices

1 (15-ounce [425g]) can black beans or 1 1/2 cups (250g) cooked black beans, drained and rinsed

1/4 cup (10g) coarsely chopped cilantro

1/2 teaspoon ground cumin

1/2 teaspoon dried oregano

1/2 teaspoon chipotle chili powder

1/2 teaspoon salt

1/4 teaspoon black pepper, or more to taste

1 tablespoon ground flax seed or chia seed

2 to 3 tablespoons (10 to 15g) dry breadcrumbs or flour (gluten-free if necessary)

1. In a food processor, combine the walnuts, oats, garlic, ginger, onion, and jalapeños and pulse a few times, until the walnuts and onions are evenly chopped, 5 to 10 seconds. Add the beans, cilantro, cumin, oregano, chili powder, salt, pepper, and flax seed and process in 5-second intervals, until most of the beans break down. Do not puree—there should still be some whole beans for texture.

2. Transfer the mixture to a bowl. Cover the bowl and chill for 15 minutes. If the mixture is too wet, add the breadcrumbs and stir to combine.

3. Divide the mixture into 7 to 8 equal portions. Shape into tightly packed patties. Heat a large skillet over medium-high heat (add oil if desired). Place the patties in the skillet and cook for 4 to 6 minutes per side, or until golden brown. Alternatively, preheat the oven to 400°F (200°C). Place the patties on a medium baking sheet lined with parchment paper. Bake the burgers for 15 minutes, flip, and bake another 10 minutes, or until the burgers are golden. Serve with your favorite burger fixings.

Per serving: Calories 128, Total Fat 6g, Saturated Fat 1g, Sodium 175mg, Total Carbs 16g, Fiber 5g, Sugars 1g, Protein 5g

Lentil-Walnut Burgers

These scrumptious and filling patties are made earthy and hearty by lentils, brown rice, and walnuts. I use cumin, coriander, and Garam Masala in these, but the herbs and spices can easily be changed to reflect Italian, Ethiopian, Mexican, or other inspired flavors. Feel free to use your own combination of flavors. These also make fantastic "meat"balls in curries or pasta sauce. I serve these with a vegan cheese slice melted on the patties, lettuce, juicy tomatoes, onions, pickled jalapeño, and a creamy dressing.

Prep time: 15 minutes
Active time: 25 minutes
Inactive time: 15 minutes
soy-free, gluten-free option
Makes 6 patties

- 1/2 cup (60g) **coarsely chopped red onion**
- 3 **cloves garlic**
- 1 (1/4-inch [0.6cm]) **knob fresh ginger, peeled and coarsely chopped**
- 1/3 cup (40g) **raw walnuts**
- 1/4 cup (10g) **tightly packed fresh cilantro**
- 3/4 **teaspoon salt, or more to taste (if using unsalted lentils)**
- 3/4 **teaspoon ground cumin**
- 3/4 **teaspoon ground coriander**
- 1/2 **teaspoon garlic powder**
- 1/2 **teaspoon cayenne (see note)**
- 1/2 **teaspoon Garam Masala (page 244), Curry Powder (page 245), or chili powder blend**
- 3 to 4 **fresh basil leaves (optional)**
- 3/4 cup (150g) **cooked brown or white rice**
- 1 1/2 cups (300g) **cooked brown lentils or 1 (15-ounce [425g]) can lentils, drained and rinsed, divided**
- 2 **teaspoons ketchup or Barbecue Sauce (page 241)**
- 2 **teaspoons organic safflower or other neutral oil, divided**
- 1 **Flax Egg (page 242)**
- 3 to 4 **tablespoons (15 to 20g) breadcrumbs or flour (gluten-free if desired), plus more as needed**

1. In a food processor, process the onion, garlic, ginger, walnuts, and cilantro until the ingredients are finely chopped. (Alternatively, finely chop the onion and garlic and cook them in 1/2 teaspoon oil over medium heat, until they are golden. Add them to the processor.)

2. Add the salt (if using unsalted lentils), cumin, coriander, garlic powder, cayenne, garam masala, basil (if using), rice, and 3/4 cup (150g) of the lentils and process in 5-second intervals, until well combined and most of the rice has broken down. Transfer the mixture to a bowl. Add the remaining 3/4 cup (150g) lentils, ketchup, 1 teaspoon of the oil, and flax egg and mix everything thoroughly. Taste and adjust the seasonings. Add the breadcrumbs and stir to combine. Let the mixture chill for 10 to 15 minutes.

3. If the chilled mixture is too wet, add more breadcrumbs. Mash the mixture slightly if it is too chunky. Divide the mixture into 5 or 6 equal portions and shape them into tightly packed patties.

4. Heat the remaining 1 teaspoon oil in a large skillet over medium-high heat. Place the patties in the skillet and cook for 4 to 6 minutes per side, or until they are golden brown. Brush oil on the patties if needed. Alternatively, preheat the oven to 400°F (200°C). Place the patties on a medium baking sheet lined with parchment paper. Bake the burgers for 15 minutes, flip, and bake another 10 minutes or until golden.

Note: For milder burgers, substitute the cayenne with an equal amount paprika plus a dash of black pepper.

Variation: Sauté 1 cup (240g) sliced mushrooms with the onion and garlic until golden, add them to the processor, and proceed with the remaining directions. Add 2 tablespoons (4g) nutritional yeast for a cheese-like flavor profile.

Per serving (burger patties only): Calories 165, Total Fat 6g, Saturated Fat 0.6g, Sodium 324mg, Total Carbs 23g, Fiber 5g, Sugars 2g, Protein 7g

Sweet Potato, Peanut, and Chickpea Burgers

These burgers were created for one of those fall days when I was craving sweet potatoes with some Asian flavors and also a burger that I could hold and eat. These patties have a unique flavor and have been a favorite on the blog. To make these peanut-free, use toasted almonds.

Prep time: 10 minutes
Active time: 15 minutes
Inactive time: 30 minutes
soy-free option, gluten-free option
Makes 6 patties

1/2 cup (40g) raw or lightly toasted unsalted peanuts

1/4 cup (20g) old-fashioned oats (gluten-free if necessary)

1 (1 1/2-inch [4cm]) knob fresh ginger, peeled and coarsely chopped

3 cloves garlic

1 (15-ounce [425g]) can chickpeas or 1 1/2 cups (250g) cooked chickpeas, drained and rinsed

2 tablespoons (6g) tightly packed fresh cilantro

1 teaspoon tamari or soy sauce (or coconut aminos to make soy-free)

2 teaspoons rice vinegar

2 teaspoons toasted sesame oil

3/4 teaspoon salt, or more to taste

1/2 to 1 teaspoon sriracha sauce or red pepper flakes, to taste

2 tablespoons (16g) ground flax seed or chia seed

1/2 cup (125g) sweet potato puree or mash

2 to 3 tablespoons (10 to 15g) oat flour, chickpea flour, or dry breadcrumbs (gluten-free if necessary)

Almond-Sriracha Sauce (page 100), for serving

1. Preheat the oven to 400°F (200°C). Process the peanuts, oats, ginger, and garlic in a food processor to make a coarse meal. Add the chickpeas and cilantro. Process until almost all the chickpeas are broken down. Transfer the mixture to a bowl. Add the tamari, vinegar, oil, salt, sriracha, flax seed, and sweet potato. Mix well to combine.

2. Add the flour to help reduce the moisture in the mixture and to make it slightly sticky. Taste and adjust the seasonings. Chill the mixture for 15 minutes. Divide the mixture into 6 portions and shape into patties. Use greased hands or press the mixture through a cookie cutter to shape the patties. Place the burgers on a medium baking sheet lined with parchment paper. Bake the burgers for 20 minutes, flip, and bake for another 10 minutes or until they are firm and golden on both sides.

3. Alternatively, to pan-fry the burgers, chill the mixture for 1 hour. Add more breadcrumbs if needed. Divide the mixture into 6 portions and shape into patties. Use greased hands or press the mixture through a cookie cutter to shape the patties. Heat 1 teaspoon oil in a large skillet over medium heat. Add the patties and cook for 4 to 6 minutes on each side. Serve the burgers with the almond-sriracha sauce or the peanut dressing from the Firecracker Chickpea Salad with Peanut Dressing (page 80) and your favorite burger fixings.

Per serving: Calories 210, Total Fat 11g, Saturated Fat 2g, Sodium 375mg, Total Carbs 23g, Fiber 6g, Sugars 4g, Protein 9g

Almond-Sriracha Sauce

This sauce is my go-to dressing with peanut-based burger patties or Thai-style salad bowls. It is similar to a peanut butter dressing and works really well to enhance the flavor profile of the Sweet Potato, Peanut, and Chickpea Burgers (page 98).

Active time: 10 minutes
soy free, gluten free, nut-free option
Makes about 1/2 cup (120ml)

3 tablespoons (48g) almond butter or other nut butter (or sunbutter to make nut-free)

2 teaspoons finely chopped fresh ginger

1/4 teaspoon garlic powder

1 to 2 teaspoons sriracha sauce

1 teaspoon apple cider vinegar

2 teaspoons maple syrup

1/2 teaspoon sesame oil

3 tablespoons (45ml) full-fat coconut milk

Pinch salt

Combine the almond butter, ginger, garlic powder, sriracha, vinegar, maple syrup, oil, milk, and salt in a small blender and blend until smooth. Taste and adjust the seasonings.

Per 1/2 cup: Calories 430, Total Fat 36g, Saturated Fat 9g, Sodium 148mg, Total Carbs 22g, Fiber 5g, Sugars 13g, Protein 11g

Baharat Spice Blend

Baharat is a very flavorful and strong spice blend. When used over neutral vegetables or chickpeas, it adds an aroma that is reminiscent of meaty kebabs. Try this blend with roasted vegetables, in burger patties, to flavor a cheese sauce, and in stews.

Makes about 1/3 cup (40g)

1 tablespoon black peppercorns

1 tablespoon coriander seeds or ground coriander

1 tablespoon cumin seeds

1 tablespoon Hungarian sweet paprika

2 to 3 teaspoons ground cinnamon

1/2 teaspoon ground cloves

1/2 to 1 teaspoon ground allspice

3/4 teaspoon ground cardamom

1/2 teaspoon ground nutmeg

In a blender or spice grinder, grind the peppercorns, coriander seeds, cumin seeds, paprika, cinnamon, cloves, allspice, cardamom, and nutmeg. Store the spice blend in an airtight container.

Per 1 tablespoon: Calories 21, Total Fat 1g, Saturated Fat 0g, Sodium 4mg, Total Carbs 4g, Fiber 2g, Sugars 0g, Protein 1g

Tips for Making Great Veggie Burgers

I generally need only a few tablespoons of breadcrumbs or flour to bind or balance out the moisture in the patties. Use gluten-free breadcrumbs, coarsely ground oats, chickpea flour, or rice flour to keep the patties gluten-free. Most of the patties can be adjusted to preference.

Keep the mixture moist. Use an egg replacer or similar binder. If the mixture feels dry, mash it well and add a Flax Egg (page 242), 2 to 3 tablespoons (30 to 45ml) aquafaba, applesauce, or sweet potato puree, until the mixture can be easily shaped without falling apart.

If the mixture is too wet, chill it at least 15 minutes or add more breadcrumbs or flour.

Keep track of the extra moisture from the vegetables. Some vegetables, like cauliflower or zucchini, will keep leaking moisture into the patties. Precook the vegetables before adding them to the burger mixture, or keep the time lag between prepping and forming the burger mixture and cooking the burgers minimal.

If the patties are mushy after pan-frying because of excess moisture inside, bake them for 10 to 15 minutes to dry them out.

Mash the burger mixture well. Larger beans or coarsely chopped vegetables will lead to the patties breaking easily. Thoroughly mash the beans and finely chop the vegetables. Pack the patties well. For pretty and well-packed patties, use large cookie cutters.

To pan-fry burgers: Heat 1 teaspoon oil in a skillet over medium heat. Place the patties in the skillet and cook for 4 to 6 minutes per side, or until they are golden brown. Brush oil on the patties if needed.

To bake burgers: Place the patties on a baking sheet lined with parchment paper. Brush oil on the patties if needed. Bake at 400°F (200°C) for 15 minutes, then flip the burgers and bake another 10 minutes, or until they are golden.

To pan-fry and then bake the burgers: Follow the previous instructions in order. This two-step method is meant mostly for larger or fatter patties, which may not cook through in the middle when pan-frying. Baking after pan-frying gives the patties a crisp exterior, cooks them well, and bakes out excess moisture.

Baharat Chickpea Burgers

Baharat spice is a flavorful spice blend that works very well in meaty dishes. *Baharat* means *spices* in Arabic. The blend is used in Middle Eastern cuisine as an all-purpose seasoning, like garam masala is used in India. Try the spice blend in stews, rub some on vegetables or tofu, or add some to burger patties. The earthy, complex flavor profile adds a deep umami flavor that you want to bite into. These patties pair well with creamy dressings like the Tahini Garlic Sauce. Serve the patties as burgers, over salads, or make veggie balls that you can serve with Makhani Sauce (page 54).

Prep time: 15 minutes
Active time: 20 minutes
Inactive time: 10 minutes
soy-free, gluten-free option, nut-free option
Makes 5 to 6 patties

2 teaspoons organic safflower or other neutral oil, divided

2 cloves garlic

1/2 cup (60g) chopped onion

3 teaspoons Baharat Spice Blend (page 100), divided

1/2 cup (40g) old-fashioned oats (gluten free if necessary)

1/4 cup (40g) almond meal or 1/4 cup (40g) raw almonds (or sunflower seeds to make nut-free)

1/3 cup (60g) coarsely chopped potato, zucchini, or carrots

1 (15-ounce [425g]) can chickpeas or 1 1/2 cups (250g) cooked chickpeas, drained and rinsed

1/2 teaspoon salt, or to taste

1/2 teaspoon garlic powder

1/4 to 1/2 teaspoon cayenne

1/2 teaspoon soy sauce or tamari (optional)

1 tablespoon ketchup

2 teaspoons extra-virgin olive oil, divided, or more if needed

1 Flax Egg (page 242)

2 to 4 tablespoons (10 to 20g) breadcrumbs or flour, if needed

Tahini Garlic Sauce (page 123)

Caramelized Onions (page 242)

Sliced tomatoes

Finely chopped fresh cilantro

1. Heat 1 teaspoon oil in a small skillet over medium heat. Add the garlic, onion, and a pinch salt. Cook for 3 minutes, stirring occasionally. Sprinkle 1 teaspoon of the baharat spice blend over the garlic and onion and stir to combine. Cook for 1 minute and take the skillet off the heat.

2. In a food processor, process the oats, almond meal, and potato until most of the oats are a coarse meal. Add the chickpeas, salt (if using unsalted chickpeas), garlic powder, cayenne, soy sauce, ketchup, olive oil, flax egg, the remaining 2 teaspoons baharat spice blend, and the onion and garlic mixture. Pulse until almost all of the chickpeas are mashed.

3. Transfer the mixture to a bowl and mash it a bit with your hands. Add the breadcrumbs and mix. Taste and adjust the seasonings. The mixture should hold together well. If the mixture is too moist, add more breadcrumbs. If it's too dry and crumbly, add another flax egg. Divide the mixture into 6 portions and shape into tightly packed patties.

4. Heat the remaining 1 teaspoon safflower oil in a large skillet over medium heat. Place the patties in the skillet and cook for 4 to 6 minutes on each side, or until golden brown.

5. Alternatively, to bake the burgers, preheat the oven to 400°F (200°C). Brush oil on the patties and place them on a medium baking sheet lined with parchment paper. Bake the burgers for 15 minutes, flip, and bake another 10 minutes, until the burgers are golden. Serve with the tahini garlic sauce, caramelized onions, tomatoes, and cilantro.

Variation: Add a handful of fresh mint or cilantro to the processor with the chickpeas.

Per serving: Calories 176, Total Fat 7g, Saturated Fat 1g, Sodium 225mg, Total Carbs 24g, Fiber 6g, Sugars 4g, Protein 7g

Chickpea Jackfruit Burgers

Brown chickpeas (also known as kala chana) are nutty and sturdy beans. They are amazing in burger patties. Combined with jackfruit, the little legumes create a patty that is filling with a great texture from the jackfruit and a unique flavor profile. These patties were a favorite of my recipe testers.

Prep time: 10 minutes + chickpea cooking time (if making from scratch)
Active time: 30 minutes
Inactive time: 10 minutes
soy-free, gluten-free option, nut-free
Makes 4 to 6 patties

10 ounces (300g) canned young jackfruit (in water or brine)
3/4 cup (120g) cooked brown chickpeas, drained and rinsed (see note)
1/2 cup (100g) coarsely chopped potato
1/4 cup (30g) coarsely chopped onion
1/4 cup (10g) tightly packed fresh cilantro
3/4 teaspoon garlic powder
1/4 teaspoon onion powder
1/4 teaspoon dried thyme
1/2 teaspoon dried sage
Dash black pepper
1/2 teaspoon salt, or more to taste
2 tablespoons (12g) nutritional yeast (optional)
1/2 teaspoon ground cumin
1/2 teaspoon chipotle chili powder or 1 small chipotle chile in adobo sauce, or more to taste
3 teaspoons extra-virgin olive oil, divided, plus more as needed
2 teaspoons ketchup or 2 teaspoons tomato paste
2 to 4 tablespoons (10 to 20g) flour or dry breadcrumbs (gluten-free if necessary)
For serving: Caramelized Onions (page 242), Tahini Garlic Sauce (page 123), sliced tomatoes, and lettuce

1. If using canned jackfruit packed in brine, drain and chop the jackfruit into small pieces. (No need to remove the tender stem.) Soak the jackfruit in water for 10 minutes. Drain the jackfruit, rinse well, and squeeze out the liquid.

2. Add the jackfruit, chickpeas, potato, onion, cilantro, garlic powder, onion powder, thyme, sage, pepper, salt, nutritional yeast (if using), cumin, chili powder, 2 teaspoons of the oil, and ketchup to a food processor. Process in 5-second intervals, until most of the chickpeas are mashed but there is still some texture.

3. Transfer the mixture to a large bowl. Taste and adjust the seasonings. Add the flour if the mixture is too moist. Divide the mixture into 4 to 6 equal portions and shape into fat, sturdy patties.

4. Heat the remaining 1 teaspoon oil in a large skillet over medium heat. Add the patties and cook for 4 to 6 minutes on each side. Brush more oil on the burgers if needed.

5. Alternatively, to bake the burgers, preheat the oven to 400°F (200°C). Place the patties on a medium baking sheet lined with parchment paper and bake for 15 minutes, flip, and bake another 10 minutes, until the burgers are golden. Serve the burgers with the caramelized onions, tahini garlic sauce, tomatoes, and lettuce.

Note: Brown chickpeas are easily available at whole-food stores, Indian markets, and online. (If you cannot find brown chickpeas, use regular white chickpeas. The patties will be softer.) To make brown chickpeas from scratch, soak 1/2 cup (80g) dried brown chickpeas in warm water for at least 1 hour. Pressure-cook with 2 cups (480ml) water for 20 to 25 minutes using high pressure and medium heat. Let the pressure release naturally, drain and rinse the chickpeas, and use them in the recipe.

Per serving: Calories 192, Total Fat 4g, Saturated Fat 1g, Sodium 329mg, Total Carbs 35g, Fiber 5g, Sugars 16g, Protein 7g

Quinoa-Mushroom Burgers

If you love mushrooms, you will love these juicy quinoa-mushroom burgers. Use a variety of mushrooms—like shiitake, portobello, white, and cremini—for added flavor. These patties might be on the softer side depending on the moisture content in the mushrooms, so adjust accordingly. Use other nuts, sunflower seeds, or pepitas instead of almonds, if you prefer. If desired, top with nondairy cheese slices of your choice when the patties are just about done. Dress the burgers with ketchup, mustard, or a creamy dressing. Top them with Caramelized Onions (page 242), if you like, and serve in burger buns or over a salad.

Prep time: 10 minutes
Active time: 30 minutes
Inactive time: 20 minutes
soy free, gluten-free option, nut-free option
Makes 6 patties

3 teaspoons organic safflower or other neutral oil, divided

2 cups (150g) sliced or coarsely chopped mushrooms

1/2 cup (60g) coarsely chopped onion

1/4 cup (20g) old-fashioned oats (gluten-free if necessary)

1/2 cup (80g) almond meal or raw almonds

1/2 teaspoon salt, or more to taste

1/2 teaspoon dried sage, or more to taste

1/2 teaspoon cayenne, or more to taste

1/2 teaspoon garlic powder

1 to 2 tablespoons nutritional yeast

2 tablespoons (16g) ground flax seed

2 cups (370g) cooked quinoa (see note), divided

2 teaspoons extra-virgin olive oil

2 to 4 tablespoons (10 to 20g) dry breadcrumbs or flour (gluten-free, if necessary)

1. Heat 2 teaspoons of the safflower oil in a medium skillet over medium heat. Add the mushrooms, onion, and a pinch salt and cook, stirring occasionally, for 5 to 8 minutes, or until the mushrooms are golden. Remove the skillet from the heat and allow the mushroom mixture to cool slightly.

2. In a food processor, combine the mushrooms, oats, and almond meal, processing in 5-second intervals, until a coarse mixture is formed. Add the salt, sage, cayenne, garlic powder, nutritional yeast, flax seed, and 1 cup (185g) of the quinoa and pulse a few times. Transfer the mixture to a bowl. Add the remaining 1 cup (185g) quinoa and the olive oil. Add the breadcrumbs if the mixture is too wet. Taste and adjust the seasonings. Chill the mixture for at least 15 minutes.

3. Divide the mixture into 6 equal portions and shape into tightly packed patties. Heat the remaining 1 teaspoon safflower oil in a large skillet over medium heat. Add the patties and cook for 4 to 6 minutes on each side.

Note: When a recipe calls for quinoa, it helps to remember that 3/4 cup (130g) dry quinoa will yield 2 heaping cups (370g) cooked. Rinse the quinoa well. Combine the quinoa with 1 3/4 cups (420ml) water and a pinch salt in a medium saucepan over medium heat. Bring the quinoa to a rolling boil. Reduce the heat to low. Cover the saucepan and cook for 15 minutes. Let the quinoa stand for another few minutes. Fluff the quinoa and drain if needed.

Per serving: Calories 258, Total Fat 15g, Saturated Fat 2g, Sodium 211mg, Total Carbs 24g, Fiber 5g, Sugars 2g, Protein 8g

Samosa Sliders with Tamarind Chutney and Mango

Samosa Potatoes make a great addition to practically anything. Add some to wraps or bowls, roll them up in a pinwheel, or pack them into a burger patty. Serve these potato-stuffed sliders with or without the bun and top them with mango, Tamarind Chutney, baby greens, and cilantro.

Prep time: 10 minutes + Samosa Potatoes
Active time: 20 minutes
Inactive time: 10 minutes
soy-free, gluten-free option, nut-free
Makes 5 to 7 patties

1 recipe Samosa Potatoes (page 239), chilled for at least 15 minutes

1 small green chile, finely chopped (optional)

1 cup (185g) cooked quinoa (see note)

2 to 4 tablespoons (10 to 20g) dry breadcrumbs (gluten-free if necessary)

2 teaspoons organic safflower or other neutral oil, divided

Slider buns or burger buns (optional)

Tamarind Chutney (page 240), for serving

Coarsely chopped mango, for serving

Finely chopped fresh cilantro, for serving

Baby greens, for serving

1. Combine the samosa potatoes, chile, and quinoa in a large bowl. Add the breadcrumbs and mix well. Shape the mixture into large or small patties, depending on the size of your burger buns. If the mixture is too crumbly, mash it well to stick, or sprinkle it with a little water. If the mixture is too moist, add more breadcrumbs.

2. Heat 2 teaspoons of the oil in a large skillet over medium-high heat. Place the patties in the skillet and cook 3 to 5 minutes per side, or until the burgers are golden brown on each side.

3. Serve the burgers on buns (if using) and topped with the tamarind chutney, mango, cilantro, and baby greens.

Note: When a recipe calls for quinoa, it helps to remember that 1/3 heaping cup (60g) dry quinoa will yield 1 cup (185g) cooked quinoa. Rinse the quinoa well. Combine the quinoa with 3/4 cup (180ml) water and a pinch salt in a medium saucepan over medium heat. Bring the quinoa to a rolling boil. Reduce the heat to low. Cover the saucepan and cook for 15 minutes. Let the quinoa stand for another few minutes. Fluff the quinoa and drain if needed.

Per serving: Calories 208, Total Fat 4g, Saturated Fat 1g, Sodium 390mg, Total Carbs 38g, Fiber 6g, Sugars 3g, Protein 7g

Kidney Bean and Black Bean Harissa Burgers

Kidney beans can feel left out among all these chickpea and black bean burgers. But they are delicious and filling and they make a toothsome bean burger. These spicy burgers use two different kind of beans and harissa mix made from scratch (see note). Serve the patties with Caramelized Onions (page 242) and a creamy dressing.

Prep time: 15 minutes
Active time: 25 minutes
Inactive time: 20 minutes
soy-free, gluten-free option, nut-free
Makes 6 to 7 patties

Harissa Mix

1 teaspoon red pepper flakes
1 teaspoon smoked paprika
1/4 teaspoon cayenne
1 teaspoon ground cumin
1 teaspoon ground coriander
2 teaspoons extra-virgin olive oil
1/4 cup (30g) finely chopped onion
5 cloves garlic, finely chopped

Burgers

1/3 cup (30g) old-fashioned oats
   (gluten-free if necessary)
1 1/2 tablespoons ground flax seed
1 (15-ounce [425g]) can kidney beans
   or 1 1/2 cups (250g) cooked kidney
   beans, drained and rinsed
1 (15-ounce [425g]) can black beans
   or 1 1/2 cups (250g) cooked black
   beans, drained and rinsed
1/2 teaspoon salt, or to taste
1/2 teaspoon garlic powder
1 teaspoon fresh lemon juice
2 teaspoons ketchup
1 tablespoon chopped fresh mint
   (optional)
1/4 teaspoon toasted caraway seeds
   (optional)
2 to 4 tablespoons (10 to 20g) flour or
   dry breadcrumbs (or gluten-free)
1 teaspoon organic safflower or other
   neutral oil, or more as needed

1. Harissa Mix: To make the harissa mix, heat a small skillet over medium heat. Add the red pepper flakes and toast them until they start to change color or you start sneezing. Add the paprika, cayenne, cumin, and coriander and stir for a few seconds. Add the oil and stir to combine. Add the onion and garlic and a pinch salt. Cook for 3 minutes, stirring occasionally. If the spices start to burn or stick, add a splash of water and stir to scrape the bottom of the skillet.

2. Burgers: Transfer the harissa mix to a food processor. Add the oats and flax seed and process until the onion breaks down. Add approximately three-quarters of the kidney beans and black beans, salt (if using unsalted beans), garlic powder, lemon juice, ketchup, mint (if using), and caraway seeds (if using) and pulse a few times so most of the beans break down.

3. Transfer the mixture to a large bowl and add the remaining quarter of the kidney beans and black beans. Taste and adjust the seasonings. Add the flour if needed and mix. Chill the burger mixture for 15 minutes.

4. Divide the mixture into 6 to 7 equal portions and shape them into large patties. Heat the oil in a large skillet over medium heat. Place the patties in the skillet and cook 4 to 6 minutes on each side, or until the burgers are browned. Brush the patties with more oil if needed.

Note: If you are using prepared harissa paste, use 2 tablespoons (30ml) paste (or more, to taste) and omit the red pepper flakes, paprika, cayenne, cumin, and coriander. Instead, heat the oil in a small skillet over medium heat. Add the onion and garlic and cook until the onion is translucent. Add the prepared harissa paste and cook for 1 minute. Transfer the mixture to a food processor and proceed with the directions. Adjust the spiciness of the mixture later as needed.

Per serving: Calories 178, Total Fat 3g, Saturated Fat 0g, Sodium 200mg, Total Carbs 29g, Fiber 8g, Sugars 3g, Protein 9g

Quinoa Carrot Barbecue Burgers

Most patties use beans or nuts for the texture or protein. Some people have allergy issues with either or both. These patties use seeds and quinoa and lots of barbecue sauce for a moist and filling burger. Use my Barbecue Sauce or your favorite tangy or smoky barbecue sauce. (If you like, you can add other vegetables, like mushrooms or cauliflower, for variation. Cook the vegetables before adding them to the burger mixture.)

Prep time: 15 minutes
Active time: 25 minutes
Inactive time: 15 minutes + chilling time
soy-free, gluten-free option, nut-free
Makes 6 patties

1/2 cup (60g) pepitas or raw sunflower seeds

2/3 cup (60g) old-fashioned oats (gluten-free if necessary)

1 1/2 tablespoons chia seeds

2/3 cup (80g) finely chopped carrots or 1/2 cup (60g) packed shredded carrots

1 (1/2-inch [1cm]) knob fresh ginger, peeled and minced

2 teaspoons organic safflower or other neutral oil, plus more for pan-frying

3/4 cup (90g) finely chopped onion

3 cloves garlic, finely chopped

1 1/2 cups (280g) tightly packed cooked quinoa (see note)

3/4 teaspoon salt, or more to taste

1/2 teaspoon garlic powder

1/4 to 1/2 teaspoon cayenne

1/2 teaspoon ground cumin

1/2 teaspoon dried oregano

2 tablespoons (6g) finely chopped fresh cilantro or basil

3 to 4 tablespoons (45 to 60ml) Barbecue Sauce (page 241) or store-bought barbecue sauce, plus more for serving

4 to 6 tablespoons (20 to 30g) flour or dry breadcrumbs (gluten-free if necessary)

1. Heat a medium skillet over medium heat. Add pepitas and oats and toast for 5 to 7 minutes. Add the chia seeds, stir, and toast for another minute. Take the skillet off the heat and allow the mixture to cool slightly. Transfer the mixture to a food processer and pulse to make a coarse meal. Add the carrots and ginger and process until evenly shredded, then transfer the mixture to a bowl. Alternatively, use grated carrot and ginger and combine with the oat mixture in a bowl.

2. Heat the oil in the same skillet over medium heat. Add the onion and garlic and cook, stirring occasionally, for 5 to 6 minutes, or until the onion is translucent. Transfer the onion mixture to the bowl with the pepita mixture. Add the quinoa, salt, garlic powder, cayenne, cumin, oregano, cilantro, and barbecue sauce and mix well.

3. Chill the mixture for 30 minutes. Taste and adjust the seasonings. Add the flour and mix, making sure that the mixture is not too moist (add more flour if needed). Mash the mixture a bit if needed. Divide the mixture into 6 equal portions and shape them into patties.

4. Heat the additional oil in a large skillet over medium heat. Cook the patties for 4 to 6 minutes per side.

5. Alternatively, to bake the burgers, preheat the oven to 400°F (200°C). Place the patties on a medium baking sheet lined with parchment paper. Bake the patties for 15 minutes, flip, and bake another 10 minutes, or until the burgers are golden. Serve the burgers with more barbecue sauce and your favorite burger fixings.

Note: When a recipe calls for quinoa, it helps to remember that 1/2 cup (85g) dry quinoa will yield 1 1/2 cups (270g) cooked quinoa. Rinse the quinoa well. Combine the quinoa with 1 cup (240ml) plus 2 tablespoons (30ml) water and a pinch salt in a medium saucepan over medium heat. Bring the quinoa to a rolling boil. Reduce the heat to low. Cover the saucepan and cook for 15 minutes. Let the quinoa stand for another few minutes. Fluff the quinoa and drain if needed.

Per serving: Calories 249, Total Fat 8g, Saturated Fat 1g, Sodium 345mg, Total Carbs 36g, Fiber 5g, Sugars 6g, Protein 8g

Whopper Mushroom, Pecan, and Lentil Burgers

Earthy lentils and mushrooms, buttery pecans, and lively spices make this a very satisfying burger patty. I like to make big patties of this burger mix to make a hearty burger. To reduce the active time, I use a food processor to chop the onion and garlic. The mushrooms will be cooked down and processed later anyway, so they don't need to be sliced precisely. Just roughly chop them and add them to the pan. These are the most burger-like veggie burgers for entertaining guests.

Prep time: 10 minutes
Active time: 25 minutes
Inactive time: 12 minutes
soy-free, gluten-free option
Makes 6 to 7 large patties

2 teaspoons organic safflower or other neutral oil, divided, plus more as needed

1/2 cup (60g) coarsely chopped onion

5 cloves garlic, finely chopped

1/2 cup (40g) coarsely chopped mushrooms

1/2 to 3/4 cup (55 to 80g) raw pecans

1/4 cup (30g) pepitas

2 tablespoons (16g) ground flax seed

1 1/2 cups (300g) cooked lentils, drained and rinsed, divided

1 cup (200g) cooked brown rice

1 teaspoon ground cumin

1 teaspoon ground coriander

1 teaspoon Old Bay Seasoning

1 teaspoon soy sauce

2 teaspoons ketchup or tomato paste

1/4 teaspoon black pepper

1/2 teaspoon cayenne (optional)

1/4 teaspoon baking powder

Zest of 1 small lime

3/4 teaspoon salt

1/4 cup (30g) oat flour or dry breadcrumbs (gluten-free if necessary), plus more as needed

1. Heat 1 teaspoon of the oil in a medium skillet over medium heat. Add the onion and garlic and cook for 2 minutes. Add the mushrooms and a pinch salt and cook for 4 to 5 minutes or until golden.

2. In a food processor, process the pecans and pepitas until they are a coarse mixture. Add the onion-mushroom mixture and flax seed and pulse in 5-second intervals until the mixture is evenly chopped. Add 1 cup (200g) of the lentils, the brown rice, cumin, coriander, Old Bay Seasoning, soy sauce, ketchup, pepper, cayenne (if using), and baking powder and process in 5-second intervals to combine thoroughly and to mash most of the rice and lentils.

3. Transfer the mixture to a large bowl. Add the lime zest and the remaining 1/2 cup (100g) lentils. Add the flour and mix until the mixture is not too pasty. Chill for 20 minutes. If the mixture is too sticky, add more flour. Divide the mixture into 6 or 7 equal portions and shape them into large patties using your hands or a cookie cutter. Heat the remaining 1 teaspoon oil in a large skillet over medium heat. Place the patties in the skillet and cook 4 to 6 minutes on each side. Brush more oil on the patties if needed.

4. Alternatively, to bake the burgers, preheat the oven to 400°F (200°C). Place the patties on a medium baking sheet lined with parchment paper. Bake the patties for 15 minutes, flip, and bake for another 10 minutes, or until the burgers are golden.

Per serving: Calories 224, Total Fat 10g, Saturated Fat 1g, Sodium 364mg, Total Carbs 27g, Fiber 6g, Sugars 2g, Protein 9g

Chickpea Barbecue Loaf

The vegan world has fallen in love with aquafaba (canned-chickpea brine), and sometimes this means that the chickpeas themselves become the by-products of all the experimentation. This loaf is an excellent way to use them up. This Chickpea Barbecue Loaf, just like the Lentil-Quinoa Loaf with Spicy Glaze (page 118), is great as a loaf or as burger patties. The baked loaf can be sliced, frozen, and reheated in a skillet for a quick and easy dinner. Serve the loaf or patties with cranberry sauce, gravy, mashed potatoes, or other sides of choice.

Prep time: 10 minutes
Active time: 20 minutes
Inactive time: 35 minutes
soy-free option, gluten-free option, nut-free
Serves 4

Loaf

1 teaspoon organic safflower or other neutral oil

3/4 cup (90g) finely chopped red onion

4 cloves garlic, finely chopped

1/2 cup (40g) finely chopped celery

1/4 cup (40g) finely chopped red bell pepper

1/4 cup (30g) finely chopped carrots

2 tablespoons (20g) dried cranberries (optional)

1 (15-ounce [425g]) can chickpeas or 1 1/2 cups (250g) cooked chickpeas, drained and rinsed

1 (15-ounce [425g]) can cannellini beans or 1 1/2 cups (250g) cooked cannellini beans, drained and rinsed

2 tablespoons (6g) finely chopped fresh cilantro

2 tablespoons (6g) finely chopped fresh parsley

1 tablespoon ground chia seed or 1 1/2 tablespoons (12g) ground flax seed

2 to 4 tablespoons (30 to 60ml) Barbecue Sauce (page 241), or more if needed

1 1/2 teaspoons fresh lemon juice

1 tablespoon tahini (optional)

1 teaspoon ground cumin

1/4 to 1/2 teaspoon ground black pepper

1. Loaf: Heat the oil in a large skillet over medium heat. Add the onion, garlic, and a pinch salt. Cook for 5 minutes, stirring occasionally, or until the onion is translucent. Add the celery, bell pepper, carrots, and cranberries (if using) and cook for 3 minutes.

2. In a food processor, combine the chickpeas, beans, cilantro, parsley, and half of the onion mixture. Process until the mixture is half mashed but still has texture.

3. Transfer the mixture to a large bowl. In a small bowl, whisk together the ground chia seed, barbecue sauce, and lemon juice. Let this mixture sit for 1 minute. Add the chia mixture, tahini (if using), cumin, pepper, cayenne, thyme, sage, salt, and the remaining onion mixture to the large bowl. Mix well. Add the breadcrumbs and combine thoroughly. If the loaf mixture is too wet, add more breadcrumbs. If it is too dry, add the additional barbecue sauce. Taste the mixture and adjust the seasonings.

4. Transfer the mixture to a 9-inch (23cm) loaf pan lined with parchment paper. (Be sure that the parchment sheet is hanging over the sides to make it easy to remove the loaf.) Smooth the top of the mixture in the loaf pan and press it down well. (If you don't have a loaf pan, use a medium baking sheet lined with parchment paper and shape the mixture into a rectangular log.) Preheat the oven to 400°F (200°C).

5. Glaze: Whisk together the barbecue sauce, hot sauce, maple syrup, ketchup, pepper, and paprika in a small bowl. Brush or spread the glaze over the loaf.

6. Cover the loaf with parchment paper or foil and bake for 20 minutes. Remove the cover and continue to bake for another 15 to 25 minutes, or until a toothpick inserted into the center comes out clean. Bake longer for a taller loaf or if you want crispier edges. Let the loaf cool for 15 minutes, then remove it from the pan. Let it cool almost completely and slice it with a serrated knife.

7. Alternatively, to make patties, preheat the oven to 400°F (200°C). Shape the loaf mixture into 8 to 10 patties and place them on a medium baking sheet lined with parchment paper. Bake the patties for 15 minutes, flip, and bake for another 10 to 15 minutes. Brush the glaze on the patties during the last 5 minutes of baking.

1/4 to 1/2 teaspoon cayenne or chipotle chili powder

1 teaspoon dried thyme or rosemary or 2 teaspoons finely chopped fresh thyme or rosemary

1/2 teaspoon dried sage

1/2 to 3/4 teaspoon salt, or to taste

1/2 cup (40g) or more dry breadcrumbs (gluten-free if necessary) or coarsely ground oats

Glaze

3 tablespoons (45ml) Barbecue Sauce (page 241)

1 teaspoon hot sauce

1 tablespoon maple syrup

2 teaspoons ketchup

Dash black pepper

1/4 teaspoon smoked paprika

Variation: Add 1/2 cup (40g) finely chopped mushrooms to the skillet with the onions. Add 1/4 cup (30g) walnuts or 1/4 cup (50g) cooked rice with the beans in the processor for added texture.

Per serving: Calories 326, Total Fat 5g, Saturated Fat 1g, Sodium 458mg, Total Carbs 60g, Fiber 12g, Sugars 18g, Protein 13g

Lentil-Quinoa Loaf with Spicy Glaze

Lentils and quinoa work well together to make this hearty loaf. This loaf can be the main attraction of your holiday spread as well as fit in seamlessly with the everyday meal. It is delicious, simple, and versatile. Brush on the glaze and use the foil to make a tent over the loaf prior to baking. The loaf is pictured opposite for a U.S. Thanksgiving meal.

Prep time: 20 minutes
Active time: 25 minutes
Inactive time: 45 minutes
soy-free option, gluten-free option, nut-free
Serves 4

Loaf

1/2 cup (50g) brown lentils, picked over, rinsed, and drained (see variation)

1 dried bay leaf

2 1/4 cups (540ml) water

1/3 cup (60g) quinoa or millet, well rinsed (see variation)

2 teaspoons organic safflower or other neutral oil

3/4 cup (90g) finely chopped onion

3 cloves garlic, finely chopped

1 small jalapeño, finely chopped (optional)

1/2 cup (40g) finely chopped celery

1/2 cup (60g) thinly sliced or shredded carrots

1/2 teaspoon dried thyme

1/2 teaspoon dried oregano

2 to 4 tablespoons (20 to 40g) raisins or dried currants, to taste

2 tablespoons (16g) ground flax seed or chia seed

1 tablespoon vegan Worcestershire sauce (see note)

2 to 3 tablespoons (30 to 45ml) ketchup

1 to 2 tablespoons tamari (or coconut aminos to make soy-free)

2 tablespoons (30ml) tahini

1 to 2 tablespoons nutritional yeast

1/4 teaspoon coarsely ground fennel seed

1/2 to 3/4 cup (40 to 60g) dry bread-

1. Loaf: Combine the lentils, bay leaf, and water in a medium saucepan over medium heat. Bring the lentils to a boil. Partially cover the saucepan and cook for 20 minutes. Add the quinoa to the saucepan. Partially cover the saucepan and continue to cook, stirring occasionally, for 10 to 15 minutes, or until the lentils and quinoa are very tender. (The lentils should be slightly overcooked; this helps prevent a crumbly loaf.) Drain any excess water and transfer the lentils and quinoa to a large bowl.

2. Preheat the oven to 375°F (190°C). Heat the oil in a large skillet over medium heat. Add the onion, garlic, and jalapeño and cook for 5 minutes, or until the onion is translucent. Add the celery, carrots, thyme, and oregano, and stir to combine. Cook for 5 minutes, or until the vegetables are al dente. Add the raisins, stir, and cook for 2 minutes. Take the skillet off the heat.

3. Add the onion mixture and flax seed to the large bowl and combine. Mash the mixture using a potato masher or your hands, so that at least half the mixture is thoroughly mashed while still having some texture. (Mashing thoroughly is important to prevent a crumbly loaf.) Add the Worcestershire sauce, ketchup, tamari, tahini, nutritional yeast, and fennel seed and mix well. Taste and adjust the seasonings.

4. Add the breadcrumbs and mix. (To check if the mixture is the right consistency, form a burger patty. If the mixture is too sticky or pasty, add more breadcrumbs to create the consistency of a slightly wet dough. If it is too crumbly and doesn't stick easily, add additional Worcestershire sauce, ketchup, or tamari.)

5. Line a 9-inch (23cm) loaf pan with parchment paper, ensuring that some of the parchment sheet is hanging over the sides to make the loaf easier to remove. Press the loaf mixture into the pan, packing it down well and evening it out. (If you don't have a loaf pan, use a medium baking sheet lined with parchment paper and shape the loaf into a tightly packed 1-inch [3cm] thick rectangle.)

6. Glaze: Whisk together the ketchup, hot sauce, maple syrup, and Worcestershire sauce in a small bowl. Spread or brush the glaze over the top of the loaf.

7. Cover the loaf with foil and bake for 25 to 30 minutes. Remove the foil and bake for 5 to 10 minutes. Let the loaf rest for 15 minutes before slicing.

crumbs (gluten-free if necessary) or coarsely ground oats, plus more as needed

Glaze

1/4 cup (60ml) ketchup or Barbecue Sauce (page 241)

1 teaspoon hot sauce, or more to taste

2 teaspoons maple syrup, or to taste

1 teaspoon vegan Worcestershire sauce

Per serving: Calories 367, Total Fat 9g, Saturated Fat 1g, Sodium 537mg, Total Carbs 61g, Fiber 9g, Sugars 16g, Protein 15g

8. Alternatively, to make burger patties, divide the loaf mixture into 5 or 6 equal portions. Shape them into burger patties using your hands or a cookie cutter. Heat a large skillet over medium heat. Pan-fry the patties with or without oil for 4 to 6 minutes, or until they are golden brown on both sides. Brush the glaze over the burger patties during the last 2 minutes of cooking or just before serving.

9. Store the loaf or patties in the refrigerator for up to 3 days. The patties can be frozen and the loaf can be frozen in slices. Reheat them in the oven or in a skillet.

Variation: If you would like to save time while preparing this recipe, use 1 1/4 cups (250g) cooked brown lentils and 1 cup (185g) cooked quinoa and proceed with the directions.

Note: If you do not have access to vegan Worcestershire sauce, you can substitute it by whisking together 1/2 teaspoon tamarind paste, 1 teaspoon molasses, 1/2 to 1 teaspoon distilled white vinegar, and 1/2 teaspoon ground mustard.

6

Bowls & Hands

This chapter features food served in bowls, such as soups, and food held in your hands, such as wraps. Certain bowl recipes have multiple components, which can be made faster by making some of those components ahead of time. To quickly dress and serve these bowls, make the Tahini Garlic Sauce (page 123) and store it in a squeeze bottle in the refrigerator. These recipes are versatile in how you can serve them. Make tacos, wraps, and burritos to use your hands or serve the recipes in a bowl for less mess.

Try the warming Winter Mushroom Soup with Spinach and Chickpeas (page 127), the flavor-packed Chickpea Vegetable Stew with Baharat (page 130), and the Buddha Bowl with Nacho-Spiced Sweet Potatoes (page 136), tasty enough to replace all previous Buddha bowls. When you feel like eating with your hands, Cauliflower Shawarma Wraps (page 140) and Tempeh Broccoli Wraps with Jalapeño Popper Cream (page 138) are great for breakfast or lunch.

Smoky Crisped Lentils over Creamy Greens (page 143)

Tinga Sauce

This is a great Mexican sauce that can be used to cook beans or jackfruit for the Tinga-Spiced Jackfruit Chickpea Bowl (page 125) or used in a soup, like the Tinga Black Bean Soup (page 126). I make variations of this for taco nights and add different types of beans, lentils, vegetables, shredded jackfruit, or vegan chicken to it. This sauce can get hot depending on the chipotle peppers. Remove the seeds of the peppers to control the heat if needed. Store the rest of the peppers and adobo sauce by freezing one or two peppers plus some sauce in an ice cube tray. Once frozen, transfer the chipotle cubes to a zip-top bag and freeze for up to three months.

Prep time: 5 minutes
Active time: 15 minutes
soy-free, gluten-free, nut-free
Makes 1 1/4 to 1 3/4 cups (300 to 420ml)

6 to 7 cloves garlic, divided
1 teaspoon organic safflower or other neutral oil
3/4 cup (90g) finely chopped red or white onion
2 large tomatoes
2 chipotle chiles in adobo sauce
1 tablespoon adobo sauce
1/2 teaspoon dried oregano
1/4 teaspoon dried thyme
1/2 teaspoon paprika
Dash black pepper
1/4 teaspoon salt, or to taste
Cayenne pepper, to taste (optional)

1. Finely chop 1 of the garlic cloves. Heat the oil in a medium skillet over medium heat. Add the onion, chopped garlic, and a pinch salt. Cook, stirring occasionally, until the onion is translucent, 4 to 5 minutes.

2. Meanwhile, blend the remaining 5 to 6 garlic cloves, tomatoes, chipotles, adobo sauce, oregano, thyme, paprika, pepper, and salt in a blender until smooth. Add this mixture to the skillet and cook for 5 to 7 minutes, or until the garlic does not smell raw and the sauce has thickened a bit. Taste and adjust the seasonings, adding the cayenne for extra heat (if using). Use the tinga sauce immediately or store it in the refrigerator for up to 4 days.

Variation: Add 1/4 cup (60ml) dark beer along with the blended ingredients and proceed with the directions.

Per 1 1/4 cups: Calories 236, Total Fat 8g, Saturated Fat 1g, Sodium 772mg, Total Carbs 40g, Fiber 7g, Sugars 15g, Protein 6g

Tahini Garlic Sauce

This sauce goes well with almost everything—or maybe I am partial. This sauce is heaven in a bottle. Thin it as you like for dressing the Turmeric Lentil Fritters Bowl (page 134), Cauliflower Shawarma Wraps (page 140), or a Turmeric Cauliflower Rice and Spiced Chickpea Bowl (page 131). You can also slather it on the Chickpea Jackfruit Burgers (page 104) and Baharat Chickpea Burgers (page 103).

Prep time: 5 minutes
Active time: 10 minutes
soy-free, gluten-free, nut-free
Makes 3/4 cup (180ml)

- 1/3 cup (90g) tahini
- 1 clove garlic (see variation)
- 2 to 3 tablespoons (30 to 45ml) fresh lemon juice
- 1/3 cup (80ml) warm water, plus more as needed
- 1/2 teaspoon dried parsley or 2 teaspoons finely chopped fresh parsley
- 1/4 teaspoon salt
- 1/4 teaspoon garlic powder (optional)

Add the tahini, garlic, lemon juice, water, parsley, and salt to a small blender and blend until the mixture is white and creamy (see note). Taste and adjust the seasonings. Add the garlic powder for stronger garlic flavor, if desired. Add more water, if needed, to reach the preferred consistency. Refrigerate the sauce for up to 1 week. Freeze it for up to 1 month. To use frozen sauce, thaw it completely, whisk it well, and use.

Variation: Add a sweetener to taste if you like. If you are averse to raw garlic, gently cook chopped garlic over medium-low heat in 1/2 teaspoon oil until it is fragrant and use.

Note: If you don't have a small blender, double the recipe, process it in a larger blender, and freeze the leftover sauce. Alternatively, mince the garlic and mix with other ingredients in a bowl until smooth and use.

Per 3/4 cup: Calories 441, Total Fat 39g, Saturated Fat 5g, Sodium 672mg, Total Carbs 19g, Fiber 7g, Sugars 2g, Protein 13g

Tinga-Spiced Jackfruit Chickpea Bowl

This bowl has many flavors and textures. Each of the components can be used individually or in combination with other recipes. Make the all or some components and serve as a bowl, taco, or burrito.

Prep time: 10 minutes + Tinga Sauce
Active time: 25 minutes
soy-free, gluten-free, nut-free
Serves 3 to 4

Jackfruit

1 recipe Tinga Sauce (page 122, see note)
20 ounces (568g) jackfruit or hearts of palm, drained
1/2 cup (120ml) water

Chickpeas

1 teaspoon organic safflower or other neutral oil
1 (15-ounce [425g]) can chickpeas or 1 1/2 cups (250g) cooked chickpeas, drained and rinsed
1/4 teaspoon salt, or to taste
1/2 teaspoon dried oregano
1/2 teaspoon ancho or chipotle chili powder
1/2 teaspoon ground cumin
2 tablespoons (30ml) Tinga Sauce
2 tablespoons (30ml) water
Dash fresh lemon juice

For serving

3 to 4 cups (90 to 120g) baby spinach or coarsely chopped lettuce
Spanish Rice (see sidebar) or plain cooked rice
Salsa
Fresh or thawed frozen corn
Finely chopped fresh cilantro
Nondairy sour cream or guacamole

1. Jackfruit: Bring the tinga sauce to a simmer in a medium saucepan over medium heat. Wrap the jackfruit in paper towels and squeeze out as much excess moisture as possible. Chop the jackfruit into thin strips or shred it using a food processor. Add the jackfruit to the tinga sauce. Add the water and cook for 10 to 15 minutes, or until the sauce thickens and coats the shredded jackfruit. Taste and adjust the seasonings.

2. Chickpeas: Heat the oil in a medium skillet over medium heat. Add the chickpeas and toss to coat them in the oil. Add the salt, oregano, ancho chili powder, and cumin and toss to coat. Add the tinga sauce and water and stir to combine. Cover the skillet and cook for 4 to 5 minutes, until the chickpeas soften and the sauce dries up and sticks to the chickpeas. Taste and adjust the seasonings. Add the lemon juice, toss, and add the chickpeas to the serving bowls.

3. For serving: Layer the bowls with the spinach, Spanish rice, salsa, corn, cilantro, and jackfruit. Dress each serving with the sour cream.

Note: When making this recipe, simply reserve 2 tablespoons (30ml) of Tinga Sauce for the chickpeas. Using slightly less than 1 recipe of sauce will not adversely affect the jackfruit.

Per serving: Calories 327, Total Fat 6g, Saturated Fat 1g, Sodium 427mg, Total Carbs 63g, Fiber 11g, Sugars 35g, Protein 11g

Spanish Rice

Combine 1 large tomato, 1/4 cup (30g) finely chopped onion, 1 teaspoon ground cumin, 1 teaspoon chili powder blend or taco seasoning, 1/2 teaspoon salt, and 1 tablespoon pickled jalapeño in a blender. Blend until smooth. Combine the puree with 1 cup (180g) uncooked and rinsed rice and 1 3/4 cups (420ml) water in a medium saucepan over medium-low heat. Cover the saucepan and cook for 16 to 18 minutes, or until the rice is done. Stir in 2 to 3 tablespoons (30 to 45ml) chunky salsa and 2 tablespoons (6g) coarsely chopped fresh cilantro and fluff.

Tinga Black Bean Soup

This is a simple and quick soup with a homemade tinga sauce. Even with the time it takes to prepare the tinga sauce, the soup is ready within half an hour. While this is a black bean soup, feel free to use other beans, such as pinto, kidney, or white beans (or a combination).

Prep time: 10 minutes + Tinga Sauce
Active time: 30 minutes
Inactive time: 20 minutes
soy-free, gluten-free, nut-free
Serves 4

- 2 teaspoons organic safflower or other neutral oil
- 1 1/2 cups (140g) finely chopped green bell pepper
- 1 1/2 cups (140g) finely chopped red bell pepper
- 1 recipe Tinga Sauce (page 122)
- 2 (15-ounce [425g]) cans black beans or 3 cups (500g) cooked black beans, drained and rinsed
- 2 cups (180g) frozen or fresh corn
- 1 teaspoon ground cumin
- 2 tablespoons (32g) tomato paste
- 3 cups (720ml) water
- 1 teaspoon salt, or more to taste (if using unsalted black beans)
- 1 teaspoon fresh lime juice, or more to taste
- 1 cup (32g) crushed tortilla chips, for garnish
- 1/4 cup (10g) finely chopped fresh cilantro, for garnish
- 1 ripe Hass avocado, pitted, peeled, and finely chopped, for garnish (optional)

Heat the oil in a large saucepan over medium heat. Add the bell peppers and cook until they brown on some sides, 6 to 7 minutes. Add the tinga sauce, beans, corn, cumin, and tomato paste, stirring to combine. Add the water and salt (if using unsalted beans) and cook, partially covered, for 15 minutes. Add the lime juice and stir to combine. Taste and adjust the seasonings. Simmer for a few minutes longer or until the soup reaches the desired consistency. Pour the soup into bowls and garnish with the tortilla chips, cilantro, and avocado (if using).

Per serving: Calories 370, Total Fat 8g, Saturated Fat 1g, Sodium 778mg, Total Carbs 64g, Fiber 1g, Sugars 10g, Protein 16g

Winter Mushroom Soup with Spinach and Chickpeas

This brothy soup has vegetables, chickpeas, and a ton of flavor from garlic, mushrooms, and spices, such as cinnamon (yes, it works). I like this soup extra brothy so I can sip it slowly while sitting near the fireplace during the chilly months—it is a mushroom soup for the soul.

Prep time: 10 minutes
Active time: 40 minutes
Inactive time: 25 minutes
soy-free option, gluten-free, nut-free
Serves 4

1 teaspoon organic safflower or other neutral oil
3/4 cup (90g) finely chopped onion
5 cloves garlic, finely chopped
1 1/2 cups (110g) sliced white or cremini mushrooms
2 teaspoons grated fresh ginger
3/4 to 1 cup (90 to 120g) finely chopped or thinly sliced carrots
2 cups (200g) thinly sliced bell peppers or celery or cubed sweet potato or winter squash
1 1/2 cups (250g) cooked chickpeas, drained and rinsed (see variation)
1/2 teaspoon ground cumin
1/2 teaspoon black pepper
1/4 teaspoon white pepper
1/4 teaspoon ground cinnamon
1/4 teaspoon cayenne, or to taste
2 teaspoons soy sauce or tamari (or coconut aminos for soy-free)
2 teaspoons rice vinegar
1 to 1 1/2 teaspoons sugar
2 cups (480ml) vegetable broth or water
1 1/2 cups (360ml) water
1/2 teaspoon salt, or more to taste
1 1/2 cups (45g) chopped spinach
2 teaspoons cornstarch (optional)
2 tablespoons (30ml) cold water (optional)
Finely chopped scallions, for garnish

1. Heat the oil in a large saucepan over medium heat. Add the onion, garlic, and a pinch salt and cook, stirring occasionally, for 3 minutes or until the onion is almost translucent.

2. Add the mushrooms and cook for 4 minutes, or until they start to become golden. Add the ginger, carrots, and bell peppers and cook for 1 minute. Add the chickpeas, cumin, black pepper, white pepper, cinnamon, and cayenne and cook for 2 minutes. Add the soy sauce, vinegar, sugar, broth, and water. Partially cover the saucepan and cook for 20 minutes. Add the salt and stir to combine. Taste and adjust the seasonings. Reduce the heat to medium-low. Continue to simmer for another 10 minutes. Add the spinach during the last 2 minutes of cooking.

3. Alternatively, for a thicker soup, whisk together the cornstarch and cold water until well combined. Stir the mixture into the soup just before adding the spinach. Garnish the soup with the scallions and serve hot.

Variation: Use cooked lentils or tofu instead of chickpeas.

Per serving: Calories 168, Total Fat 3g, Saturated Fat 0g, Sodium 443mg, Total Carbs 29g, Fiber 8g, Sugars 8g, Protein 9g

Laksa Curry Soup

This Laksa Curry Soup is super flavorful and anti-inflammatory. The laksa paste can be made at home and used whenever you want a bowl of the soup, or it can be used in a quick stir-fry.

Prep time: 20 minutes
Active time: 40 minutes
Inactive time: 20 minutes
soy-free, gluten-free, nut-free option
Serves 4

1 teaspoon organic safflower or other neutral oil

1 recipe Laksa Curry Paste (recipe opposite)

2 cups (150g) sliced white mushrooms

3/4 cup (90g) thinly sliced carrots

1 cup (100g) finely chopped bell peppers, zucchini, or broccoli

3 cups (720ml) vegetable broth or water

1 (13.5-ounce [400ml]) can full-fat coconut milk, plus more as needed

6 to 8 ounces (170 to 227g) brown rice noodles

1 cup (30g) coarsely chopped spinach or chard

Salt and cayenne, to taste

Dash fresh lime juice, if needed

1/4 teaspoon raw sugar or other sweetener, if needed

1/4 cup (10g) finely chopped fresh cilantro or mint, for garnish

1/2 cup (50g) fresh bean sprouts (optional)

1 cup (250g) Crisped Tofu (page 243, optional)

Heat the oil in a large saucepan over medium heat. Add the curry paste and fry for 3 minutes, stirring occasionally. Add the mushrooms and cook for 2 minutes. Add the carrots, bell peppers, broth, and milk and bring to a boil, about 10 minutes. Reduce the heat to medium-low. Add the rice noodles and let the mixture simmer for 10 minutes. Add the spinach. Taste and adjust the seasonings, adding the salt and cayenne to taste. Add the lime juice and sugar if needed. Add more milk if needed. Simmer for another few minutes. Garnish with the cilantro, bean sprouts, and crisped tofu and serve.

Per serving (includes Laksa Curry Paste): Calories 293, Total Fat 5g, Saturated Fat 2g, Sodium 199mg, Total Carbs 55g, Fiber 7g, Sugars 5g, Protein 10g

Laksa Curry Paste

Laksa soups can be made from a variety of soup bases or pastes. This paste is used to make curry laksa. The flavorful paste can also be used in any recipe that calls for red curry paste. Make the paste ahead and freeze it for up to two months. To use the paste, roast it in a bit of oil to release the flavors and continue with your desired recipe.

Prep time: 10 minutes
Active time: 5 minutes
soy-free, gluten-free, nut-free option
Makes about 1/2 cup

2 teaspoons coriander seeds

1/2 teaspoon fennel or cumin seeds

1 (1-inch [3cm]) fresh turmeric root, peeled, or 1 teaspoon ground turmeric, or to taste

1 (1-inch [3cm]) knob fresh ginger, peeled

1 hot green chile, seeded if desired

1/2 teaspoon cayenne (or a combination of paprika and cayenne for a milder version)

1 stalk lemongrass (see note)

3 cloves garlic

2 tablespoons (14g) raw cashews or almonds, soaked for 15 minutes (or pepitas for nut-free)

1/2 cup fresh cilantro with tender stems

1 teaspoon fresh lime juice

Water, as needed

1. Heat a small skillet over medium heat. Add the coriander seeds and fennel seeds and toast them for 2 to 3 minutes, or until fragrant. Add the seeds to a blender and grind to a coarse mixture.

2. Add the turmeric, ginger, chile, cayenne, lemongrass, garlic, cashews, cilantro, and lime juice to the blender and blend until a paste is formed. Add a tablespoon or so water if needed to help the mixture blend. The paste can be refrigerated for up to 1 week and frozen for up to 1 month.

Note: To prepare lemongrass, peel away the thick outer layer of the stalk and chop off the hard root end. Chop the stalk into small pieces and use.

Per 1/2 cup: Calories 127, Total Fat 8g, Saturated Fat 1g, Sodium 6mg, Total Carbs 13g, Fiber 3g, Sugars 2g, Protein 4g

Chickpea Vegetable Stew
with Baharat

This is a flavorful Lebanese- and Turkish-inspired stew for fall and winter. Use seasonal and local vegetables with beans or lentils of your choice. Serve the soup in a bowl with crusty garlic bread or over some rice. Like any soup or stew with many spices, the flavor gets stronger as it sits. The Baharat Spice Blend is potent in this soup. You will want to slurp the entire helping.

Prep time: 15 minutes
Active time: 40 minutes
Inactive time: 20 minutes
soy-free, gluten-free, nut-free
Serves 4

1 teaspoon organic safflower or other
   neutral oil
1 cup (120g) finely chopped onion
3 cloves garlic, finely chopped
1 tablespoon Baharat Spice Blend
   (page 100), or more to taste
1/4 teaspoon cayenne, or more to taste
2 large tomatoes, crushed or pureed
1 tablespoon tomato paste (optional)
2 1/2 cups (350g) coarsely chopped
   mixed vegetables, such as potatoes,
   green beans, zucchini, cauliflower,
   and bell peppers (any color)
2 cups (330g) cooked chickpeas,
   drained and rinsed
3/4 to 1 teaspoon salt
2 3/4 cups (660ml) water or low-sodium
   vegetable broth, plus more as
   needed
Fresh lime juice, for garnish
Finely chopped fresh cilantro or mint,
   for garnish

1. Heat the oil in a large saucepan over medium heat. Add the onion, garlic, and a pinch salt and cook, stirring occasionally, for 4 to 5 minutes, or until the onion is translucent. Add the baharat spice blend and cayenne and stir to combine. Cook for 30 seconds. Add the tomatoes and tomato paste (if using) and cook for 3 to 4 minutes.

2. Add the mixed vegetables, chickpeas, salt, and water. Partially cover the saucepan and cook for 15 minutes. Taste and adjust the seasonings. Continue to simmer for another 10 to 15 minutes, until the vegetables are tender (add more water if too much liquid evaporates). Garnish with an extra dash baharat spice blend, the lime juice, and cilantro.

Per serving: Calories 240, Total Fat 4g, Saturated Fat 1g, Sodium 467mg, Total Carbs 44g, Fiber 11g, Sugars 10g, Protein 10g

Turmeric Cauliflower Rice and Spiced Chickpea Bowl

Spiced lightly with turmeric and lemon until it reaches a golden hue and served with Moroccan spiced chickpeas, this is one of my favorite ways to eat cauliflower rice. Add up to 1 cup of vegetables, such as sweet potatoes, to the chickpeas and cook until the sweet potatoes are tender. Dress with Tahini Garlic Sauce or thinned hummus.

Prep time: 15 minutes + Tahini Garlic
Sauce
Active time: 25 minutes
soy-free, gluten-free, nut-free
Serves 4

1 recipe Tahini Garlic Sauce (page 123)
1/4 cup (60ml) water

Turmeric Cauliflower Rice
1 medium head cauliflower, chopped
1 teaspoon organic safflower oil
3/4 cup (90g) chopped onion
2 teaspoons ground turmeric
1/2 teaspoon salt
1/4 teaspoon cayenne
1 tablespoon fresh lemon or lime juice

Spiced Chickpeas
1 teaspoon organic safflower oil
2 1/2 cups (415g) cooked chickpeas,
    drained and rinsed
1 1/2 teaspoons ground cumin
1 1/2 teaspoons ground coriander
1 teaspoon paprika
1 teaspoon garlic powder
1/2 teaspoon ground cinnamon
1/2 teaspoon ground cardamom
1/2 teaspoon cayenne
1/2 teaspoon black pepper
1/2 teaspoon salt, or to taste
1 cup (120g) thinly sliced carrots
1/4 cup (60ml) water
1 teaspoon fresh lemon juice
3 cups (100g) baby greens or lettuce
2 cups (250g) sliced zucchini

1. In a small bowl, combine the tahini garlic sauce and water, stirring to blend. Set aside.

2. Turmeric Cauliflower Rice: Process the cauliflower in a food processor in 2- to 3-second intervals until the cauliflower is evenly shredded. Alternatively, shred the whole cauliflower using a large box grater. Heat the oil in a large skillet over medium heat. Add the onion and a pinch salt and cook until the onion is translucent, 4 minutes. Add the turmeric and stir for a few seconds. Add the cauliflower, salt, and cayenne. Toss and stir to combine. Cover the skillet and cook for 6 to 7 minutes. The cauliflower will steam and cook through. Add the lemon juice and fluff the cauliflower. Taste and adjust the seasonings. Cover the skillet and let sit for 1 to 2 minutes before serving.

3. Spiced Chickpeas: Heat the oil in a large skillet over medium heat. Add the chickpeas, cumin, coriander, paprika, garlic powder, cinnamon, cardamom, cayenne, pepper, and salt and toss to coat the chickpeas. Cook for 2 minutes. Add the carrots and water. Cover the skillet and cook for 7 to 8 minutes, or until the carrots are cooked to your preference. Add the lemon juice and stir to combine. Cover the skillet and let sit for 1 minute. To serve, add a layer of baby greens to each bowl. Add a generous helping of the chickpeas, turmeric cauliflower rice, and zucchini. Drizzle the tahini garlic sauce over the bowls. Garnish each serving with a sprinkle of lemon juice and black pepper.

Variation: To make Turmeric Lemon Rice instead of cauliflower rice, omit the cauliflower and add 1 tablespoon water and 1 1/2 tablespoons fresh lemon juice after adding the turmeric, stirring to combine. Add 2 1/2 cups (500g) cooked rice, salt, and cayenne and toss well. Cover and cook for 3 minutes. Fluff the rice, taste and adjust the seasonings, and serve.

Per serving: Calories 358, Total Fat 17g, Saturated Fat 2g, Sodium 612mg, Total Carbs 50g, Fiber 16g, Sugars 13g, Protein 17g

Baharat Chickpea Avocado Bowl

I love this bowl with the Baharat Spice Blend. The Mediterranean dressing is fabulous with the peppery baharat. This is another customizable bowl—try using my Shawarma Spice Blend (page 140), Garam Masala (page 244), or Curry Powder (page 245) with the chickpeas—that is satisfying, delicious, and easily transformed into wraps for lunch.

Prep time: 20 minutes
Active time: 20 to 25 minutes
soy-free, gluten-free, nut-free
Serves 4

Dressing

1 to 2 cloves garlic, pressed, or 1/2 teaspoon garlic powder
1/4 teaspoon black pepper
1/4 to 1/2 teaspoon dried oregano
3 tablespoons (45ml) extra-virgin olive oil
2 tablespoons (30ml) fresh lemon juice, or more to taste
1/4 teaspoon salt

Baharat Chickpeas

2 teaspoons organic safflower or other neutral oil
2 1/2 cups (415g) cooked chickpeas, drained and rinsed
1 to 2 tablespoons Baharat Spice Blend (page 100)
1/4 to 3/4 teaspoon salt, to taste
1/4 teaspoon black pepper
1 teaspoon garlic powder
1/2 teaspoon onion powder

For serving

4 to 5 cups (200 to 250g) chopped lettuce or baby kale (see note)
1 medium zucchini, thinly sliced
2 1/2 to 3 cups (550 to 650g) roasted vegetables, such as eggplant, zucchini, or sweet potato (optional)
2 ripe Hass avocados, pitted, peeled, and chopped
Salt and black pepper, as needed
2 tablespoons (6g) chopped mint (optional)

1. Dressing: Whisk together the garlic, pepper, oregano, oil, lemon juice, and salt in a small bowl. Alternatively, combine the ingredients in a small mason jar, close the lid, and shake the jar vigorously to combine.

2. Baharat Chickpeas: Heat the oil in a medium skillet over medium heat. Add the chickpeas, baharat spice blend, salt, pepper, garlic powder, and onion powder and mix well. Cover the skillet and cook for 3 minutes. Add a splash of water to deglaze the skillet, stir, and continue to cook for another 3 minutes, or until the spices stick to the chickpeas and some chickpeas start to break down. Taste and adjust the seasonings.

3. For serving: Arrange the lettuce, zucchini, and roasted vegetables (if using) in each bowl. Add a serving of the chickpeas, some of the avocado, salt and pepper, and a good drizzle of the dressing. Top with the mint (if using) and serve.

Note: To make this bowl with baby kale, place the kale in a medium bowl and drizzle it with 1 tablespoon fresh lemon juice, 1 tablespoon extra-virgin olive oil, and 1 teaspoon maple syrup. Massage the kale for 1 to 2 minutes to soften it, then proceed with the directions.

Variation: Try this dish with caramelized-onion chickpeas. Heat the oil in a medium skillet over medium heat. Add 1 1/2 cups (180g) finely chopped onion and 3 cloves finely chopped garlic. Add a pinch salt and sugar and stir to combine. Cook for 7 to 9 minutes, stirring occasionally, until the onion and garlic are golden. Add the chickpeas, baharat spice blend, salt, pepper, garlic powder, and onion powder and stir. Cook for 4 to 5 minutes, deglazing with a splash of water if needed.

Per serving: Calories 490, Total Fat 30g, Saturated Fat 4g, Sodium 399mg, Total Carbs 42g, Fiber 18g, Sugars 8g, Protein 13g

Turmeric Lentil Fritters Bowl

These fritters come together quickly. They're like a lighter, more versatile falafel with red lentils, turmeric, and seeds. Cook the lentils, use a cookie scoop to quickly scoop the fritters onto a baking sheet, bake, and serve in a bowl. These fritters also are great in wraps, in warm pita bread, or served as a snack with the Tahini Garlic Sauce.

Prep time: 10 minutes
Active time: 30 minutes
Inactive time: 40 minutes
soy-free, gluten-free option, nut-free

Serves 4

1 teaspoon organic safflower or other neutral oil
1 cup (120g) finely chopped onion
7 cloves garlic, finely chopped
1 teaspoon ground cumin
1 teaspoon ground coriander
1 1/2 teaspoons ground turmeric
3/4 teaspoon ground cardamom
1/2 teaspoon cayenne, or to taste
1 cup (190g) red lentils (masoor dal), picked over, rinsed, and drained (see sidebar, page 4)
3 cups (720ml) water
1 teaspoon salt
1 1/2 cups (45g) tightly packed chopped spinach
2 tablespoons (6g) chopped fresh parsley
2 teaspoons fresh lemon juice
2 tablespoons (16g) chia seeds
2 tablespoons (16g) ground flax seed
2 tablespoons (20g) toasted sesame seeds or hemp seeds
1/4 cup (20g) dry breadcrumbs (gluten-free if necessary)
1/2 teaspoon dried dill or 1 teaspoon finely chopped fresh dill
Tahini Garlic Sauce (page 123)
3 cups (90g) baby greens or chopped lettuce; 1 cucumber, chopped, or dill pickles; 2 tomatoes, chopped, or cherry tomatoes, halved

1. Heat the oil in a large saucepan over medium heat. Add the onion, garlic, and a pinch salt. Cook, stirring occasionally, until the onion is translucent, 5 minutes. Add the cumin, coriander, turmeric, cardamom, cayenne, and lentils. Stir to combine and cook for 1 minute. (At this point, other spices or blends, like 1/2 teaspoon Garam Masala [page 244] or Shawarma Spice Blend [page 140] can be added.)

2. Add the water and salt and cook for 11 minutes, partially covered. Uncover the saucepan, add the spinach, parsley, and lemon juice and cook for 3 to 4 minutes, or until the lentils are cooked and all the liquid is absorbed. The mixture will be soft. Taste and adjust the seasonings. Let the mixture sit for 2 minutes. If there is too much liquid, drain the lentils for a few seconds, then transfer the mixture to a large bowl. Add the chia seeds, flax seed, and sesame seeds and mix. Chill the lentil mixture for 30 minutes.

3. Preheat the oven to 425°F (220°C). Add the breadcrumbs to the lentil mixture. If the mixture is too sticky, add more breadcrumbs. The mixture will be soft but should be able to easily be shaped into soft balls without making a sticky mess.

4. Use a 1 1/2-tablespoon cookie scoop to scoop the lentil mixture onto a large baking sheet lined with parchment paper. Spray oil on the balls. Bake for 20 minutes. If the fritters are soft to the touch, bake a few minutes longer, until they are firm to the touch but soft and moist inside.

5. Add the dill to the tahini garlic sauce and stir to combine. Taste and adjust the seasonings, and thin the sauce with water until it reaches the desired consistency.

6. Assemble bowls with the greens, cucumber, tomatoes, and as many fritters as you like. Drizzle them generously with the tahini garlic sauce dressing. Alternatively, warm pita bread and layer the fritters, greens, tomatoes, cucumber, and dressing and serve immediately.

Per serving: Calories 472, Total Fat 18g, Saturated Fat 2g, Sodium 784mg, Total Carbs 55g, Fiber 15g, Sugars 6g, Protein 20g

Buddha Bowl with Nacho-Spiced Sweet Potatoes

We eat Buddha bowls not just for the daily amounts of vegetables and beans but for the amazing combination of flavors and textures. Barbecue chickpeas, nacho-spiced vegetables, greens, and ranch or barbecue dressing. What's not to love?

Prep time: 20 minutes
Active time: 10 minutes
Inactive time: 30 minutes
soy-free option, gluten-free, nut-free option
Serves 4

Chickpeas

2 1/2 cups (415g) cooked chickpeas, drained and rinsed
1/2 teaspoon smoked paprika
1/4 teaspoon cayenne
1/2 teaspoon salt, or more to taste
1/2 teaspoon dried oregano
1/3 cup (90ml) Barbecue Sauce (page 241) or store-bought

Nacho Seasoning

1/4 cup (32g) nutritional yeast
2 teaspoons sweet paprika
2 teaspoons onion powder
1 teaspoon garlic powder
1/2 to 3/4 teaspoon cayenne
1/4 teaspoon salt
1/8 teaspoon kala namak (Indian sulphur black salt, optional)
1 teaspoon dried parsley
1/4 teaspoon black pepper

Vegetables

14 ounces (400g) sweet potatoes, cut into 1/2-inch (1cm) cubes
2 cups (200g) coarsely chopped green beans or cauliflower
1 tablespoon organic safflower or other neutral oil
4 cups (120g) baby greens
Sliced cucumber or radish
1 recipe Ranch Dressing (page 87)
1/4 cup (60ml) Barbecue Sauce (page 241)
1/4 cup (30g) pepitas or hemp seeds

1. Chickpeas: Preheat the oven to 400°F (200°C). Line a 9 x 9-inch (23 x 23cm) or larger baking dish with parchment paper. Combine the chickpeas, smoked paprika, cayenne, salt, oregano, and barbecue sauce in the dish and toss to coat the chickpeas. Spread out the chickpeas evenly so that there is only 1 or 2 layers of chickpeas. Spray oil on top, if desired.

2. Nacho Seasoning: Combine the nutritional yeast, sweet paprika, onion powder, garlic powder, cayenne, salt, kala namak, parsley, and pepper in a small bowl.

3. Vegetables: In a large bowl, combine the sweet potatoes, green beans, and oil. Toss the vegetables to coat them evenly. Add the nacho seasoning and toss to coat. Spread the vegetables on a large baking sheet lined with parchment paper. Salt the vegetables lightly.

4. Bake the vegetables and chickpeas for 20 minutes. Stir the vegetables and chickpeas and bake for another 8 to 10 minutes, or until the vegetables are cooked to your preference.

5. Assemble the bowls by layering the baby greens, a generous serving of the chickpeas and roasted vegetables, and cucumber. Drizzle each serving with the ranch dressing or barbecue sauce (or both). Top the bowls with the pepitas and serve.

Variations: Use black beans or 21 ounces (596g) cubed tofu instead of the chickpeas. Use broccolini or Brussels sprouts instead of the green beans or cauliflower.

Notes: Paprika can be mild to hot, depending on the type and brand. This might determine the extra heat or lack thereof in the seasoning. Taste the seasoning with a tortilla chip and adjust before using it on the vegetables. To make nut-free, use the Nut-Free Ranch Dressing.

Per serving: Calories 531, Total Fat 20g, Saturated Fat 3g, Sodium 180mg, Total Carbs 62g, Fiber 16g, Sugars 13g, Protein 22g

Nacho Chips

To make Doritos-style nacho chips, spray oil on plain tortilla chips in a large bowl. Add the prepared Doritos nacho seasoning and toss to coat the chips evenly. Spread the chips on a large baking sheet and bake at 350 °F (180°C) for 5 to 7 minutes or microwave for 1 to 1 1/2 minutes to warm. Serve.

Tempeh Broccoli Wraps with Jalapeño Popper Cream

This tempeh scramble is a smoky, crumbly scramble that works well paired with the creamy jalapeño popper spread in a wrap, burrito, or taco. These wraps will get your appetite going. If using cashews for the popper dip, you can also make quesadillas. Layer the scramble, thinly sliced broccoli, and a drizzle of the dip and grill.

Prep time: 15 minutes
Active time: 25 minutes
gluten-free option, nut-free option
Makes 2 large or 4 small wraps

1 teaspoon organic safflower or other neutral oil

1/2 cup (60g) chopped onion

3 cloves garlic, minced

1 cup (150g) chopped red and green bell peppers

1 teaspoon Quick Italian Herb Blend (page 163) or 1/2 teaspoon dried thyme, dash dried oregano, dash dried basil, and dash dried rosemary

1/2 teaspoon smoked paprika

1/4 teaspoon chipotle chili powder

1/2 teaspoon ground mustard

Pinch kala namak (Indian sulphur black salt, optional)

1/2 teaspoon ground turmeric (optional)

8 ounces (227g) tempeh, steamed for 10 minutes and crumbled

1 tablespoon nutritional yeast

1/2 teaspoon salt, or to taste

3 tablespoons (45ml) water (omit if using tofu)

Dash black pepper

Jalapeño Popper Cream (opposite)

Tortillas or taco shells

1/4 cup (65g) chopped pickled jalapeños

1 cup (100g) small broccoli florets, blanched for 2 minutes

2 cups (60g) chopped lettuce

1. Heat the oil in a large skillet over medium heat. Add the onion and garlic and cook for 5 minutes, or until the onion is translucent. Add the bell peppers and cook for 3 minutes. Add the quick Italian herb blend, paprika, chili powder, mustard, kala namak (if using), and turmeric (if using) and cook for 2 minutes. Add the tempeh, nutritional yeast, salt, and water and stir to combine. Cover the skillet and cook until all the water is absorbed and the mixture starts to dry a bit, 6 to 7 minutes. Taste and adjust the seasonings. Garnish liberally with the pepper.

2. Make the Jalapeño Popper Cream.

3. Warm the tortillas. Spread some of the jalapeño popper cream on each tortilla. Spread some chopped pickled jalapeños on the cream. Add a generous layer of tempeh scramble, a layer of broccoli, and a layer of lettuce. Fold the tortillas into wraps or serve as tacos.

Note: For quick pickled jalapeños, mix chopped dill pickles with chopped fresh jalapeños. Let the mixture sit for 10 minutes and use.

Variation: Replace the tempeh with 14 ounces (400g) firm tofu (drained, pressed for 5 minutes, and crumbled).

Per serving: Calories 304, Total Fat 17g, Saturated Fat 3g, Sodium 639mg, Total Carbs 22g, Fiber 7g, Sugars 6g, Protein 19g

Jalapeño Popper Cream

In addition to serving with the Tempeh Broccoli Wraps, this versatile cream also makes a terrific dip using the variation below. It can be made ahead and refrigerated for up to three days.

Prep time: 5 minutes
Active time: 5 minutes
Inactive time: 1 hour (soaking time)
soy free, gluten free
Makes about 1 cup

1/2 cup (60g) raw cashews, soaked for 1 hour, or 4 to 5 ounces (113 to 142g) silken tofu, drained

1/2 teaspoon apple cider vinegar

1/2 teaspoon fresh lemon juice

1/4 teaspoon salt, or more to taste

1 teaspoon raw sugar

1/4 teaspoon garlic powder

2 teaspoons extra-virgin olive oil

1 tablespoon nutritional yeast, or more to taste

4 slices pickled jalapeños or 1/2 whole pickled jalapeño (see note opposite)

2 to 4 tablespoons (30 to 60ml) water, as needed

Combine the cashews, vinegar, lemon juice, salt, sugar, garlic powder, oil, nutritional yeast, jalapeños, and the water in a blender and blend into a smooth, spreadable consistency. Taste and adjust the seasonings.

Variation: To make the jalapeño popper cream as a dip, chop the pickled jalapeños and mix them into the dip mixture. Top with dry breadcrumbs mixed with salt, pepper, and nutritional yeast.

Per 1 cup: Calories 524, Total Fat 38g, Saturated Fat 6.3g, Sodium 693mg, Total Carbs 31g, Fiber 6g, Sugars 8g, Protein 21g

Cauliflower Shawarma Wraps

Mediterranean spice blends work wonders with anything you put them on. You will want to make a bottle full of this shawarma blend to rub on roasted vegetables or chickpeas or beans. These wraps are served with hummus and Tahini Garlic Sauce. For additional protein, use cooked beans, chickpeas, or tofu instead of cauliflower.

Prep time: 15 minutes
Active time: 30 minutes
soy-free, gluten-free option, nut-free
Serves 4

4 heaping cups (420g) cauliflower
  florets
1/4 cup (60ml) water
1/2 teaspoon salt
1/4 to 1/2 teaspoon cayenne
1/2 teaspoon dehydrated minced garlic
  or 1 teaspoon garlic paste
2 tablespoons (12g) Shawarma Spice
  Blend (see sidebar) or Baharat Spice
  Blend (page 100)
2 teaspoons organic safflower or other
  neutral oil

For serving
Pita bread or tortillas
1 cup (250g) hummus
2 medium tomatoes, chopped
1/2 cup (100g) dill pickle slices or
  thinly sliced cucumbers
1 1/2 cups (75g) chopped lettuce
1 recipe Tahini Garlic Sauce (page
  123)
Finely chopped fresh cilantro or parsley, for garnish

1. Combine the cauliflower, water, and salt in a large skillet over medium heat. Cover the skillet and cook for 12 to 14 minutes, or until the cauliflower is al dente, stirring halfway through. Add the cayenne, garlic, shawarma spice blend, and oil, stirring to combine. Cook, uncovered, for 2 to 4 minutes, until the cauliflower is cooked through and the spices start to smell roasted. Stir occasionally. Taste and adjust the seasonings. (Alternatively, to bake the cauliflower, preheat the oven to 425°F [220°C]. In a large bowl, combine the cauliflower and oil and toss to coat. Add the salt, cayenne, garlic, and shawarma spice blend and toss again. Transfer the cauliflower to a large baking sheet lined with parchment paper and bake for 25 to 30 minutes, or until the cauliflower is tender.)

2. **For serving:** Warm the pita bread in a skillet or over a gas flame. Add a layer of hummus. Add the warm cauliflower, tomatoes, pickles, and lettuce. Drizzle the tahini garlic sauce over each serving. Garnish with the cilantro and serve.

Variation: To make this with 2 1/2 cups (415g) cooked chickpeas or other beans, heat the oil in a large skillet. Add the shawarma spice blend and cook for a few seconds. Add the cooked chickpeas, salt, cayenne, garlic, and a splash water. Toss to coat, cover the skillet, and cook for 4 minutes.

Per serving: Calories 327, Total Fat 19g, Saturated Fat 3g, Sodium 774mg, Total Carbs 32g, Fiber 11g, Sugars 9g, Protein 13g

Shawarma Spice Blend

1 1/2 teaspoons ground cumin	1/2 teaspoon ground cardamom
1 1/2 teaspoons ground coriander	1/8 teaspoon ground cloves
1 teaspoon paprika	1/8 teaspoon ground nutmeg
1/4 to 1/2 teaspoon black pepper	1/8 teaspoon ground allspice
1/2 teaspoon ground cinnamon	1 1/2 teaspoons garlic powder

Combine the cumin, coriander, paprika, pepper, cinnamon, cardamom, cloves, nutmeg, allspice, and garlic powder in a small bowl.

Smoky Crisped Lentils over Creamy Greens

Greens lightly cooked in creamy masala sauce make an amazing dip. In this bowl, the greens are saturated with sauce and topped with crispy, smoky, puffy lentils. Serve this greens dip bowl with warm pita bread. Use lentils that are cooked to a bit al dente so they don't get mushy while cooking in the skillet. If you are using frozen greens, thaw them and squeeze out excess water before using.

Prep time: 15 minutes
Active time: 20 minutes
soy-free, gluten free, nut-free option
Serves 4

Crisped Lentils

2 cups (400g) cooked brown lentils, drained and rinsed
1 tablespoon organic safflower or other neutral oil
3/4 teaspoon salt, or to taste (if using unsalted lentils)
1/2 to 1 teaspoon ground cumin
1/2 teaspoon Garam Masala (page 244)
1 teaspoon smoked paprika, or more to taste
1 teaspoon garlic powder
1/2 teaspoon onion powder
1/2 teaspoon cayenne or black pepper

Creamy Greens

2 teaspoons organic safflower or other neutral oil
4 cloves garlic, minced
1/4 cup (30g) finely chopped onion
5 cups (150g) tightly packed finely chopped collard greens, spinach, chard, or baby kale or 10 ounces (284g) frozen greens
1/4 teaspoon salt, or more to taste
1 recipe Creamy White Masala Sauce (page 52) or White Garlic Sauce (page 85)
1/2 cup (120ml) water, if needed
Pita bread, for serving

1. Crisped Lentils: Drain the lentils well in a strainer for 10 to 15 minutes. Use a paper towel to lightly press them and absorb any excess liquid.

2. Heat half of the oil in a large skillet over medium-high heat. Add half the lentils and spread them out evenly. Cook for 2 to 4 minutes, stirring occasionally. (The lentils will feel like they are sticking or getting mushy, but they will start to get crispy and puffy all over.) Add half of the salt, cumin, garam masala, paprika, garlic powder, onion powder, and cayenne and toss well. Continue to cook for 1 minute to toast the spices, tossing frequently. Transfer the lentils to a bowl. Repeat this process for the remaining lentils and transfer them to the bowl. Let the lentils cool for 10 minutes, then taste and adjust the seasonings.

3. Creamy Greens: Heat the oil in a large skillet over medium heat. Add the garlic and onion and cook until the onion is translucent, stirring occasionally, 3 to 4 minutes. Add the collard greens and stir to combine. Add the salt and a splash water, stir, cover the skillet, and cook for 4 to 5 minutes, or until the greens are almost wilted. Add the creamy white masala sauce and stir to combine. Bring the mixture to a boil. Add the water to thin the sauce, if needed. Take the skillet off the heat. Let the mixture sit, covered, for a few minutes for the flavors to infuse. Serve the greens topped with a generous helping of the lentils and some warmed pita bread.

Per serving: Calories 336, Total Fat 17g, Saturated Fat 2g, Sodium 693mg, Total Carbs 37g, Fiber 9g, Sugars 5g, Protein 15g

Crispy Lentil Snack

Use the crisped lentils to make an evening or between-meal snack. Mix in some chopped onion, tomato, fresh cilantro, and a dash lemon juice and serve with chips or pappadam.

7

Deep-Dishing

In this chapter, you'll find your favorite deep-dish recipes, such as lasagna, bakes, casseroles, and pizza. These are simple, flavorful recipes that you can build up to add more toppings or layers. Start with the simple and much-loved Margherita Pizza (page 155) or Deep-Dish Pizza (page 148), versatile Vegetable Lasagna (page 162), and the testers' favorite: Spinach-Artichoke Lasagna with Cauliflower Alfredo (page 164).

There are many traditional and creative pizza options in this chapter. I make my own Easy Pizza Dough (page 230) which works perfectly while prepping the toppings. The pizza is usually in the oven within twenty to thirty minutes, then it's a wait to get to the amazing result. Most of the pizzas in this chapter can be made into quesadillas or wraps. Make the Mushroom-Jalapeño White Pizza (page 151) or the Alfredo Spinach Pizza (page 156) into a melt sandwich or a quesadilla.

Deep-Dish Pizza (page 148)

Red Pizza Sauce

This is a super quick and delicious pizza sauce that takes five minutes and makes great pizzas. Use it on the Margherita Pizza (page 155), Deep-Dish Pizza (page 148), or any other pizza you can think up.

Prep time: 5 minutes
Active time: 5 minutes
soy-free, gluten-free, nut-free
Makes 1 3/4 cups (420ml)

1 (6-ounce [170g]) can unsalted tomato
   paste
1 cup (240ml) water
2 teaspoons extra-virgin olive oil
3 cloves garlic, minced
2 teaspoons dried oregano
2 teaspoons dried basil
1/2 teaspoon dried thyme or rosemary
1/4 teaspoon onion powder
1/4 teaspoon salt (optional)
1/4 teaspoon black pepper
1/4 teaspoon sugar or maple syrup
   (optional)

In a medium bowl, combine the tomato paste, water, oil, garlic, oregano, basil, thyme, onion powder, salt (if using), pepper, and sugar (if using). Taste and adjust the seasonings. Refrigerate the sauce for a few hours before using so the flavors can marry. Refrigerate the sauce for up to 5 days. Freeze in individual jars for up to 2 months.

Per 1 3/4 cups: Calories 250, Total Fat 10g, Saturated Fat 2g, Sodium 698mg, Total Carbs 40g, Fiber 9g, Sugars 22g, Protein 9g

Cauliflower Alfredo Sauce

Awesome Sauce

Cauliflower makes a great base for a nut-free white sauce or alfredo. Cook the cauliflower, blend it with herbs, and use the sauce with your favorite pasta, the Spinach-Artichoke Lasagna with Cauliflower Alfredo (page 164), or the Alfredo Spinach Pizza (page 156).

Prep time: 10 minutes
Active time: 25 minutes
Inactive time: 10 minutes
soy-free option, gluten-free option, nut-free
Makes 2 cups (480ml)

1 tablespoon plus 1 teaspoon extra-virgin olive oil, divided

3 cloves garlic, finely chopped

3 heaping cups (315g) 1 1/2-inch (4cm) cauliflower florets

1/2 cup (120ml) water

1/2 teaspoon salt

3/4 cup (180ml) plain unsweetened nondairy milk

1/2 teaspoon onion powder

1/4 teaspoon dried thyme

1/4 teaspoon dried basil or 1 tablespoon fresh basil leaves

3 tablespoons (18g) nutritional yeast

Dash black pepper

2 teaspoons fresh lemon juice

1 tablespoon unbleached all-purpose flour (or rice flour or arrowroot starch to make gluten-free)

1. Heat 1 teaspoon of the oil in a large skillet over medium heat. Add the garlic and cook for 2 minutes, or until the garlic is fragrant. Add the cauliflower, water, and salt. Cover the skillet and cook for 10 minutes, or until the cauliflower is tender.

2. Cool slightly, partially covered, and transfer the cauliflower mixture (including the water) to a blender. Add the milk, onion powder, thyme, basil, nutritional yeast, pepper, lemon juice, the remaining 1 tablespoon oil, and flour. Blend to a smooth puree. Taste and adjust the seasonings. Add more milk for thinner sauce, if needed.

3. Refrigerate the sauce for up to 3 days and freeze it for up to 1 month. (The frozen sauce might get chunky.) Thaw the sauce, whisk, and use.

Note: For a richer, creamier version, add another tablespoon extra-virgin olive oil and 3 tablespoons soaked cashews.

Per 2 cups : Calories 430, Total Fat 23g, Saturated Fat 3g, Sodium 1451mg, Total Carbs 41g, Fiber 17g, Sugars 10g, Protein 24g

Deep-Dish Pizza

This is the simple deep-dish pizza that I love to make as is or customize depending on what I have on hand. The garlicky peppers and greens, loads of red sauce, nondairy mozzarella or alfredo, and fresh basil make a pizza that's simple and perfect. This pizza can be made nut-free with the Cauliflower Alfredo Sauce (page 147), Nut-Free White Garlic Sauce (page 86), or a store-bought nondairy shredded mozzarella. To make this gluten-free, see the Gluten-Free Pizza Crust on VeganRicha.com.

Prep time: 15 minutes + Easy Pizza Dough + Vegan Mozzarella + Red Pizza Sauce
Active time: 25 minutes
Inactive time: 25 minutes
soy-free option, nut-free option
Serves 8

Filling

1 teaspoon organic safflower or other neutral oil
1 cup (120g) chopped onion
6 cloves garlic, finely chopped
2 large red bell peppers, thinly sliced (or jarred sliced roasted red bell pepper)
10 ounces (284g) baby spinach or thawed frozen spinach, drained and squeezed
1/4 cup (10g) finely chopped fresh basil
1 teaspoon dried thyme
3/4 teaspoon salt
1/2 teaspoon red pepper flakes

Pizza

1 recipe Easy Pizza Dough (page 230) or store-bought pizza dough
1 teaspoon extra-virgin olive oil
1 recipe Vegan Mozzarella (page 152) or White Garlic Sauce (page 85)
1 recipe Red Pizza Sauce (page 146)
3 tablespoons (30g) sliced pitted brine-cured black or green olives
1/4 cup (10g) chopped fresh basil
1 teaspoon red pepper flakes

1. Filling: Heat the oil in a large skillet over medium heat. Add the onion and garlic and cook until the onion is translucent, 4 to 5 minutes. Add the red bell peppers and cook for 4 minutes. Add the spinach, basil, thyme, salt, and red pepper flakes and stir to combine. Cook until the spinach is wilted and the mixture is not wet.

2. Pizza: Meanwhile, preheat the oven to 435°F (225°C). Grease 2 (8- or 9-inch [20- to 23cm]) springform pans or iron skillets (or line them with parchment paper).

3. Prepare the pizza dough according to instructions. Once the dough has sat for 15 minutes, drizzle the oil over the pizza dough and spread it over the dough. Punch the dough down. Divide it into 2 equal pieces using a pizza cutter. Shape each into a somewhat smooth ball. Using your hands or a rolling pin and flour as needed, shape the dough into an 11-inch (28cm) diameter circle. Repeat this process with the second ball of dough. Place the rolled-out dough in the pans, making sure to pull some of the dough above the pans' edges. (Keep the bottoms thick; otherwise, the pizzas might not support the heavy toppings.) Bake in the oven for 5 minutes. Remove the crusts from the oven.

4. To assemble the pizzas, add a layer of the vegan mozzarella to each crust. Divide half the pizza sauce between each crust, then add a generous layer of the filling mixture (see variation). Add the olives, the remaining half of the red pizza sauce, half the basil, another generous layer of mozzarella, and half of the red pepper flakes. Bake the pizzas for 25 to 30 minutes. Add the remaining basil and red pepper flakes. Let the pizzas rest for 5 to 10 minutes before slicing.

Variation: You can add some other sauteed or roasted, thinly sliced vegetables, such as mushrooms, zucchini, and so on over the filling, then add a layer of pizza sauce and continue.

Per serving: Calories 337, Total Fat 10g, Saturated Fat 2g, Sodium 824mg, Total Carbs 53g, Fiber 5g, Sugars 6g, Protein 10g

Place the rolled-out dough in the pan.

Add a generous layer of the filling mixture.

Add a generous layer of Vegan Mozzarella.

Cut the pizza into wedges.

Mushroom-Jalapeño White Pizza

Caramelized onions and mushrooms make a fantastic topping on this pizza. The white sauce is thickened so you can use it like mozzarella. Add other toppings of your choice, such as thinly sliced vegetables, sliced vegan sausage, or more mushrooms. Three different peppers add a dimension of heat and flavor. For a kid-friendly version, omit the red pepper flakes and use thinly sliced bell pepper instead of jalapeño.

Prep time: 10 minutes + Easy Pizza
   Dough + White Garlic Sauce
Active time: 50 minutes
Inactive time: 35 minutes
soy-free, gluten-free option, nut-free option
Serves 8

Mushrooms

2 teaspoons extra-virgin olive oil
1 small onion, finely chopped
6 cloves garlic, finely chopped
8 ounces (227g) sliced white or cremini
   mushrooms
1/4 teaspoon salt, or more to taste
1/2 teaspoon dried oregano
1/4 teaspoon dried thyme
1/4 teaspoon red pepper flakes, or
   more to taste

Pizza

1 recipe Easy Pizza Dough (page 230),
   Gluten-Free Pizza Crust (page 232),
   or store-bought pizza dough
1 recipe White Garlic Sauce (page
   85) or Nut-Free White Garlic Sauce
   (page 86)
1 small jalapeño, seeded, if desired,
   and thinly sliced
1/2 cup (100g) thinly sliced red onion
Toppings of your choice (optional)
Black pepper, to taste

1. Mushrooms: Heat the oil in a medium skillet over medium heat. Add the onion, garlic, a pinch salt, and a pinch sugar and stir to combine. Cook until the onion is translucent, 4 to 5 minutes. Add the mushrooms, stir, and cook for 10 minutes. Add the salt, oregano, thyme, and red pepper flakes and continue to cook, stirring occasionally, until the mushrooms are brown on most edges, 10 to 20 minutes.

2. Pizza: Meanwhile, preheat the oven to 425°F (220°C) and shape the pizza dough into 2 (12-inch [30cm]) or larger thin pizza crusts. Heat the white garlic sauce in a small saucepan over medium-low heat. Stir frequently and take the saucepan off the heat as soon as the sauce has reached a thick, creamy consistency. (The nut-free sauce might already be thick enough, in which case it will not need to be heated.)

3. Spread some of the sauce on the crusts, reserving some for topping. Layer the mushrooms, jalapeño, and onion on the sauce. Add the toppings of your choice (if using). Add dollops of the reserved sauce on top of the mushrooms. Add the black pepper. Bake the pizzas for 17 to 19 minutes. Broil for 1 minute if needed to brown the tops. Slice the pizzas and serve.

Per serving: Calories 290, Total Fat 9g, Saturated Fat 1g, Sodium 540mg, Total Carbs 45g, Fiber 3g, Sugars 2g, Protein 9g

An Alternative to Pizza

Not into pizza? Make a grilled melt sandwich. Use your favorite sandwich bread instead of pizza crust and spread the thickened white sauce on the bread. Layer the mushrooms, jalapeño, and onion on the sauce. Add dollops of leftover sauce on top of the mushrooms. Add black pepper to taste, place another slice of bread on top, and grill until melty.

Vegan Mozzarella

Getting vegan cheese just right is a tough task and chefs keep working to make a nondairy mozzarella that is true to the dairy-based version in terms of texture, flavor, spreadability, and browning ability. I use this mozzarella not to compete with the dairy version but just to have a great topping to use with pizzas, lasagnas, quesadillas, and the like. Adapted from the many versions by Miyoko Schinner and Somer McCowan, this is a soft, mouthy mozzarella that is sturdy, spreadable, and melty. I use a combination of potato starch and tapioca starch for the texture of this cheese. For sturdier cheese slices, use 2 tablespoons (22g) potato starch and 2 teaspoons tapioca starch. Play around with the ratio of the starches for the texture that works best for you.

Prep time: 5 minutes + soaking time
Active time: 15 minutes
soy-free option, gluten-free
Makes about 2 cups (480ml)

- 1/2 cup (60g) raw cashews, soaked for 1 hour and drained (or macadamia nuts to make cashew-free)
- 1 1/4 cups (300ml) water
- 1/4 cup (60g) plain unsweetened nondairy yogurt (see note)
- 1 tablespoon + 1 teaspoon potato starch
- 1 tablespoon + 1 teaspoon tapioca starch
- 2 teaspoons extra-virgin olive oil
- 1 tablespoon refined coconut oil or additional extra-virgin olive oil
- 1 clove garlic
- 3/4 to 1 teaspoon salt (use 3/4 teaspoon if using miso)
- 1 teaspoon fresh lemon juice
- Pinch onion powder
- 1/2 teaspoon white miso (or chickpea miso to make soy-free, optional)

1. Combine the cashews, water, yogurt, potato starch, tapioca starch, olive oil, coconut oil, garlic, salt, lemon juice, onion powder, and miso (if using) in a blender. Blend for at least 3 (30-second) intervals to ensure a very smooth consistency. Scrape the sides of the blender between intervals.

2. Add the mixture to a medium skillet or saucepan and cook over medium heat until the mixture starts to get lumpy, stirring occasionally. Taste the mixture and adjust the seasonings.

3. Once the mixture has started to get lumpy, stir it frequently and cook until it becomes custard-like, 6 to 8 minutes. Continue to cook for another 2 minutes, stirring occasionally. Transfer the mozzarella to a greased container. Use the mozzarella immediately or refrigerate it. (Note that this cheese does not keep its texture after freezing.)

4. To make slices, spread the mixture evenly, while still hot, on parchment paper into a 1/8-inch [3mm] thick rectangle with a spatula, or by placing another sheet of parchment papper on the mixture and pressing to spread (see photo). Refrigerate it for 30 minutes, cut it into slices, and store the slices between layers of parchment paper in a sealed container for up to 5 days.

5. To make mozzarella balls, drop balls of the mixture into a large bowl of ice water. Remove the balls from the water after 10 minutes. Brush the balls with olive oil and refrigerate them in an airtight container for up to 5 days.

Note: I prefer Kite Hill almond plain yogurt in this cheese, but you can use any other plain unsweetened nondairy yogurt.

Per 2 cups: Calories 663, Total Fat 52g, Saturated Fat 8g, Sodium 1976mg, Total Carbs 42g, Fiber 5g, Sugars 6g, Protein 14g

1. Cook the mixture until it becomes custard-like.

2. To make slices, transfer the mixture to a sheet of parchment paper.

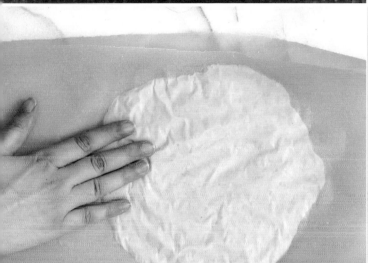

3. Cover with a second sheet of parchment paper, press it into a 1/8-inch thick sheet, and chill.

4. Cut the cheese into rectanglular slices.

5. The cheese is now ready to use in various recipes.

6. The cheese melts nicely
The stringiness will depend on the starches used.

Margherita Pizza

This is just an amazing pizza. I've never loved overly cheesy and greasy pizza, but the Vegan Mozzarella (page 152) makes the process of making this pizza a lot of fun (without the heaviness of dairy-laden pizza). It also doesn't hurt that this comes together so quickly once you have the mozzarella ready. To make this nut-free, use my Nut-Free White Garlic Sauce (page 86) instead of the mozzarella. To make this gluten-free, use my Gluten-Free Pizza Crust (page 232) and bake the pizza according to the crust's recipe.

Prep time: 5 minutes + Easy Pizza Dough + Red Pizza Sauce + Vegan Mozzarella
Active time: 15 minutes
Inactive time: 15 minutes
soy-free option, gluten-free option, nut-free option
Serves 4

1 recipe Easy Pizza Dough (page 230) or store-bought pizza dough
1 recipe Red Pizza Sauce (page 146) or 1 1/4 cups (300ml) store-bought pizza sauce
1/4 cup (10g) tightly packed, coarsely chopped fresh basil
2 medium tomatoes, thinly sliced
1/2 recipe Vegan Mozzarella (page 152), cooled
1 tablespoon extra virgin olive oil (see variation)
1 teaspoon dried oregano
1 teaspoon red pepper flakes

1. Preheat the oven to 450°F (230°C). Shape the dough into 2 (12-inch [30cm]) or larger circles or rectangles. Keep the crust thin, as it doubles in thickness and can get bready. Spread the pizza sauce on the crusts. Add 1 tablespoon of the basil. Arrange the tomato slices on the pizzas.

2. Add dollops of the mozzarella. Drizzle the oil on the pizza. Add a dash salt and the oregano and red pepper flakes. Bake the pizzas for 14 to 15 minutes. Broil for 1 minute to brown if needed. Sprinkle the remaining basil over the hot pizzas. Let sit for 1 minute. Slice and serve.

Variation: Add 2 minced cloves garlic to the olive oil before drizzling it over the pizzas.

Per serving: Calories 579, Total Fat 19g, Saturated Fat 4g, Sodium 873mg, Total Carbs 89g, Fiber 7g, Sugars 8g, Protein 15g

Veggie Pizza

To make this a veggie pizza, arrange thinly sliced raw or grilled vegetables of your choice (such as bell peppers, mushrooms, zucchini, and olives) and vegan sausage on the pizza sauce. Add the mozzarella and bake.

Alfredo Spinach Pizza

Garlic, greens, and creamy cheesy sauce = love. This pizza doubles as a great quesadilla for a quicker meal. Use my Gluten-Free Pizza Crust (page 232) to make this gluten-free and the Nut-Free White Garlic Sauce (page 86) to make it nut-free.

Prep time: 10 minutes + Easy Pizza Dough + White Garlic Sauce
Active time: 20 minutes
soy-free, gluten-free option, nut-free option
Serves 4

1 teaspoon organic safflower or other neutral oil
10 to 12 cloves garlic, minced
12 to 14 ounces (340 to 400g) chopped spinach, thawed and squeezed if frozen
1/4 teaspoon salt, or more to taste
Dash black pepper
1 recipe Easy Pizza Dough (page 230) or store-bought pizza dough
1 recipe White Garlic Sauce (page 85), Cauliflower Alfredo Sauce (page 147), or Creamy White Masala Sauce (page 52)
Toppings of your choice (see note)
Nondairy shredded cheese (optional)
2 teaspoons extra-virgin olive oil
1 teaspoon red pepper flakes, or to taste

1. Heat the safflower oil in a medium skillet over medium heat. Add the garlic and cook until it is golden. Add the spinach, salt, and pepper and stir to combine. Cook, uncovered, until the spinach wilts, 4 to 5 minutes, stirring halfway through the cooking time. If there is too much liquid, lightly squeeze the spinach mixture before spreading it on the pizza.

2. Preheat the oven to 425°F (220°C). Shape the pizza dough into 2 thin-crust 12-inch (30cm) or larger pizzas. Spread some of the white garlic sauce on the dough.

3. Spread the spinach mixture on the pizzas in a thin, even layer. Drizzle some of the white garlic sauce over the spinach. Add other toppings of your choice (if using). Add the nondairy cheese (if using). Drizzle 1 teaspoon olive oil over each pizza. Sprinkle with the red pepper flakes and bake the pizzas for 17 to 18 minutes. Slice and serve.

Note: Other toppings that go well on this pizza are sliced olives, sautéed mushrooms, and sliced artichoke hearts.

Per serving: Calories 589, Total Fat 20g, Saturated Fat 3g, Sodium 846mg, Total Carbs 86g, Fiber 7g, Sugars 2g, Protein 19g

Makhani Vegetable Pizza

This is a one of the pizzas that my dad loves because of the fusion of flavors. This pizza doesn't need any cheese, but you can add some vegan shreds if you like. To make this soy-free, use more vegetables or 1 cup (165g) cooked chickpeas. This is also great made with the Tikka Masala Sauce (page 54) or the Creamy White Masala Sauce (page 52).

Prep time: 15 minutes + Makhani Sauce + Easy Pizza Dough
Active time: 20 minutes
Inactive time: 18 minutes
soy-free option, gluten-free option, nut-free option
Serves 4

Pizza

1 recipe Easy Pizza Dough (page 230), Gluten-Free Pizza Crust (page 232), or store bought pizza dough
1 recipe Makhani Sauce (page 54)
1/2 cup (100g) thinly sliced onion
1/2 cup (50g) thinly sliced bell peppers (any color)
Nondairy shredded mozzarella (optional)

Topping

7 to 8 ounces (200 to 227g) firm or extra-firm tofu, drained, pressed for 10 minutes (page 243), and cut into small cubes
1 cup (100g) finely chopped cauliflower, broccoli, zucchini, or mushrooms (or more tofu)
2 teaspoons organic safflower or other neutral oil
1 1/2 tablespoons cornstarch
1 teaspoon ground coriander
1 teaspoon Garam Masala (page 244)
1/2 teaspoon ground turmeric
1/2 teaspoon paprika, or more to taste
1/4 teaspoon coarsely crushed fennel seeds (optional, see note)
1/2 teaspoon salt
Finely chopped fresh cilantro and red pepper flakes, for garnish

1. Pizza: Preheat the oven to 425°F (220°C). Shape the pizza dough into 2 12-inch (30cm) or larger pizzas with a thick edge to hold the sauce. Spread a thin layer of the makhani sauce on the crusts. Depending on the size of the crust, you might have some sauce remaining.

2. Topping: In a medium bowl, combine the tofu and cauliflower. Drizzle the oil over the mixture and toss to coat. In a small bowl, combine the cornstarch, coriander, garam masala, turmeric, paprika, fennel seeds, and salt. Sprinkle the spice mixture all over the tofu and vegetables. Toss to coat.

3. Spread the tofu mixture on the pizzas. Add the onion and bell peppers. Add the mozzarella (if using). Bake the pizzas for 16 to 18 minutes. Garnish with the cilantro and red pepper flakes. Slice and serve.

Note: To make coarsely crushed fennel seeds, coarsely chop them or use a mortar and pestle to crush them.

Per serving: Calories 586, Total Fat 16g, Saturated Fat 2g, Sodium 765mg, Total Carbs 93g, Fiber 8g, Sugars 8g, Protein 20g

Barbecue Pizza
with Jerk Beans and Vegetables

This pizza is a tangy, flavorful pizza with jerk beans over barbecue sauce and vegetables. I love the combination of barbecue sauce, red onion, jerk seasonings, and cilantro. If you prefer, substitute the black beans with pinto beans or black-eyed peas.

Prep time: 10 minutes + Easy Pizza Dough
Active time: 10 minutes
Inactive time: 15 minutes
soy-free option, gluten-free option, nut-free
Serves 4

1 recipe Easy Pizza Dough (page 230) or store-bought pizza dough

1 recipe Barbecue Sauce (page 241) or 3/4 cup (180ml) store-bought barbecue sauce

2 large tomatoes, sliced paper thin

1 (15-ounce [425g]) can black beans or 1 1/2 cups (250g) cooked black beans, drained and rinsed

1 1/2 tablespoons (15g) Jamaican Jerk Seasoning (recipe following)

1 teaspoon fresh lime juice

Salt, to taste

1 small red onion, sliced paper thin

Thinly sliced bell peppers or zucchini, to taste

Red pepper flakes, to taste

Nondairy shredded cheese (optional)

1/4 cup (10g) chopped fresh cilantro

1. Preheat the oven to 425°F (220°C). Shape the pizza dough into 2 12-inch (30cm) or larger pizzas.

2. Spread a thin layer of the barbecue sauce on the crusts. Add a layer of tomato slices on the sauce.

3. In a medium bowl, combine the beans with the Jamaican jerk seasoning and lime juice, stirring to coat. Add salt to taste if using unsalted beans. Spread the bean mixture over the 2 crusts. Add the onion and bell peppers. Add the red pepper flakes and cheese (if using).

4. Bake the pizzas for 15 to 18 minutes. Let the pizzas cool for 1 minute. Sprinkle the pizzas with the cilantro and more red pepper flakes. Slice and serve.

Per serving: Calories 575, Total Fat 5g, Saturated Fat 1g, Sodium 622mg, Total Carbs 114g, Fiber 12g, Sugars 21g, Protein 18g

Jamaican Jerk Seasoning

1 1/2 teaspoons garlic powder

1 teaspoon onion powder

1 teaspoon dried thyme

1 teaspoon dried parsley

1 teaspoon dried paprika

1/2 teaspoon cayenne

1/4 teaspoon black pepper

1/4 teaspoon ground cinnamon

1/4 teaspoon ground nutmeg

Pinch ground allspice

1/4 teaspoon sugar

Combine all the ingredients in a small bowl with a tight-fitting lid. Stir to mix well. Cover and set aside until needed.

Makes about 2 tablespoons

Vegetable Lasagna

This is a tall lasagna with several layers of deliciousness. Herbed mushrooms, luscious sauces, earthy greens, tofu thyme ricotta, and mozzarella come together to form simple perfection. To make this soy-free, use almond-based nondairy ricotta by brands such as Kite Hill. Crumble the ricotta and mix it with my Quick Italian Herb Blend (see sidebar). You can also use my Vegan Mozzarella and sprinkle the herb blend over it. If using gluten-free lasagna noodles, bake the lasagna depending on the noodle times mentioned on the package.

Prep time: 15 minutes + Vegan Mozzarella or White Garlic Sauce (if using)
Active time: 20 minutes
Inactive time: 60 minutes
soy-free option, gluten-free option, nut-free option
Serves 4 to 6

Ricotta
1 (14-ounce [400g]) package firm tofu, drained and pressed lightly (page 243, see headnote to make soy-free)
1 teaspoon garlic powder
1 1/2 to 2 teaspoons dried thyme
1 teaspoon Quick Italian Herb Blend (see sidebar)
1 tablespoon extra-virgin olive oil
2 teaspoons apple cider vinegar
1/2 teaspoon salt, or to taste

Mushrooms
2 cups (480g) sliced mushrooms
1 tablespoon extra-virgin olive oil
1/2 teaspoon garlic powder
2 teaspoons Quick Italian Herb Blend
Salt and black pepper, to taste

Lasagna
1 (32-ounce [908g]) jar tomato-basil marinara sauce or 1 recipe Red Pizza Sauce (page 146)
12 to 18 no-boil lasagna noodles (gluten-free if necessary)
Nondairy cheese slices, Vegan Mozzarella slices (page 152), White Garlic Sauce (page 85), or Nut-Free White Garlic Sauce (page 86)

1. Ricotta: In a medium bowl, combine the tofu, garlic powder, thyme, quick Italian herb blend, oil, vinegar, and salt and mash with a fork until the mixture is crumbly and thoroughly combined. Taste and adjust the seasonings and set aside.

2. Mushrooms: In another medium bowl, combine the mushrooms, oil, garlic powder, quick Italian herb blend, and salt and pepper and toss well.

3. Lasagna: Preheat the oven to 400°F (200°C). Spread a ladle of marinara on the bottom of a 9 x 9-inch (23 x 23cm) baking pan and spread it out into an even layer. Place a single layer of lasagna noodles to cover the bottom of the pan.

4. Add another ladle of marinara sauce and spread it over the noodles. Add all the mushrooms and spread them out over the marinara. Add another layer of noodles, a ladle of marinara, and half of the cheese slices. Add another layer of noodles and a ladle of marinara, spreading the sauce out evenly.

5. Distribute the baby spinach across the marinara. Add all the ricotta and spread it evenly on the greens to press them down. Add another layer of noodles, marinara, and cheese. Place the tomato slices on top. Season with the salt and pepper and Quick Italian Herb Blend. Pour the water along the edges of the pan. Cover the pan lightly with foil or parchment paper and bake for 50 to 60 minutes.

6. Uncover the pan, let the lasagna sit for a few minutes, then slice and serve. Refrigerate the lasagna for up to 3 days. Freeze it for up to 1 month.

Per serving (with cheese): Calories 425, Total Fat 13g, Saturated Fat 2g, Sodium 671mg, Total Carbs 53g, Fiber 7g, Sugars 10g, Protein 18g

1 cup (100g) tightly packed sautéed
　　baby spinach, chard, or kale
1 large tomato, sliced
Salt and black pepper, to taste
1 teaspoon Quick Italian Herb Blend,
　　or to taste
1/4 cup (60ml) water

Quick Italian Herb Blend

1 teaspoon dried basil
1 teaspoon dried oregano
1 teaspoon dried parsley
1 teaspoon dried thyme
1/2 teaspoon dried rosemary
1/2 teaspoon garlic powder
1/4 teaspoon black pepper

In a small bowl, combine the
basil, oregano, parsley, thyme,
rosemary, garlic powder, and
pepper.

Deep-Dishing 163

Spinach-Artichoke Lasagna with Cauliflower Alfredo

This lasagna has everything you would want to eat in a day: amazing creamy alfredo, spinach, artichoke, and other additions of choice, all layered up to make a hearty, comforting lasagna. This recipe is a favorite of many of the recipe testers and blog readers. Use gluten-free lasagna sheets to make this gluten-free.

Prep time: 10 minutes + Cauliflower Alfredo
Active time: 15 minutes
Inactive time: 50 minutes
soy-free, nut-free, gluten-free option
Serves 6

1 (32-ounce [908g]) jar marinara sauce
14 to 18 no-boil lasagna noodles, or as needed
1 cup (30g) tightly packed fresh spinach or 3/4 cup (143g) frozen spinach, thawed and squeezed
1 recipe Cauliflower Alfredo Sauce (page 147) or 2 cups (480ml) other nondairy Alfredo sauce
1 large zucchini, thinly sliced or 6 ounces (170g) mushrooms, thinly sliced
1/2 teaspoon salt
Black pepper, to taste
5 to 6 canned artichoke hearts, drained, rinsed, and finely chopped
1 to 2 tablespoons nutritional yeast or Vegan Parmesan (page 233)
1/3 cup (80ml) water
1/2 teaspoon red pepper flakes
2 teaspoons Quick Italian Herb Blend (page 163)

1. Preheat the oven to 400°F (200°C). Spread 3/4 cup (180ml) of the marinara sauce in the bottom of a 9 x 9-inch (23 x 23cm) baking pan, then add lasagna noodles in a single layer to cover the marinara. Add a thin layer of spinach on the noodles, then drizzle 3/4 cup (180ml) of the cauliflower alfredo all over the spinach. Add another layer of noodles, then spread 3/4 cup (180ml) marinara sauce on them. Arrange the zucchini over the marinara. Season with the salt and pepper.

2. Add another layer of noodles and spread 3/4 cup (180ml) cauliflower alfredo sauce evenly over them. Arrange the artichoke hearts on the cauliflower alfredo. Sprinkle the nutritional yeast on the artichoke hearts.

3. Add another layer of noodles. Pour the water all around the edges. Add about 1 to 1 1/2 cups (240 to 360ml) marinara on the top layer. Drizzle some cauliflower alfredo on the marinara. Sprinkle some more nutritional yeast on the marinara. Sprinkle the top of the lasagna with the red pepper flakes, quick Italian herb blend, and some additional salt.

4. Cover the pan lightly with foil and bake for 50 minutes. Let the lasagna cool slightly, slice, and serve hot. Refrigerate the lasagna for up to 3 days. Slice and freeze for up to 1 month.

Per serving: Calories 385, Total Fat 5.2g, Saturated Fat 1g, Sodium 563mg, Total Carbs 70g, Fiber 13g, Sugars 11g, Protein 19g

Black Pepper Cheesy Mac and Broccoli

Potato-carrot cheese sauce is the thing these days. My version of this sauce is creamy, filled with vegetables, and loaded with black pepper. What makes this sauce different, you may ask? It's the black pepper: add black pepper and then, when you think that should be enough, add some more.

Prep time: 10 minutes
Active time: 35 minutes
Inactive time: 15 minutes
soy-free option, gluten-free option, nut-free option

Serves 4

2 1/2 cups (600ml) water
1 medium potato, peeled and cubed
1/3 cup (50g) chopped carrots
4 cloves garlic, chopped, or 1 teaspoon garlic powder
3 tablespoons chopped onion or 1/2 teaspoon onion powder
1/2 small green chile (optional)
1 small tomato, chopped
1/4 cup (30g) raw cashews or macadamias (or 1/4 cup pepitas to make nut-free)
2 1/2 cups (225g) chopped broccoli
3/4 teaspoon prepared mustard
2 teaspoons soy sauce or tamari (or coconut aminos to make soy-free)
4 tablespoons nutritional yeast
2 teaspoons fresh lemon juice
2 tablespoons extra-virgin olive oil (omit to make oil-free)
1/2 teaspoon paprika
1/2 teaspoon sriracha sauce (optional)
3/4 teaspoon salt, or more to taste
1/4 teaspoon white pepper
1 1/2 teaspoons freshly ground black pepper, or to taste, divided
10 to 12 ounces cooked elbow pasta (gluten-free if necessary)

1. In a medium skillet over medium-high heat, combine the water, potato, carrots, garlic, onion, chile (if using), tomato, and cashews. Cover the skillet and cook 18 to 20 minutes, or until the potato is very tender. Let the mixture cool slightly.

2. Meanwhile, bring a medium saucepan of water to a boil over high heat. Add the broccoli and cook for 2 minutes. Drain the broccoli and set aside. Alternatively, you can add the broccoli to the cooking pasta pot in the last two minutes.

3. Combine the potato mixture (along with its liquid), mustard, soy sauce, nutritional yeast, lemon juice, oil, paprika, and sriracha (if using) in a blender. Blend for 1 minute, let the mixture rest for 1 minute, and blend again until smooth.

4. Transfer the mixture to the saucepan over medium heat. Add the salt, white pepper, and 1/2 teaspoon of the black pepper, stirring to combine. Add some additional water to adjust the consistency if the sauce is too thick.

5. Bring the sauce almost to a boil. Taste and adjust the seasonings. Add the elbow pasta and broccoli. Stir to combine, cover the saucepan, and cook for 3 minutes. Let the mixture sit for 2 minutes. Add the remaining 1 teaspoon black pepper. Sprinkle some more pepper on each serving, if desired.

Per serving: Calories 307, Total Fat 12g, Saturated Fat 2g, Sodium 582mg, Total Carbs 40g, Fiber 7g, Sugars 4g, Protein 13g

Broccoli Casserole with Baharat

This is another great way to eat broccoli, or any vegetable for that matter. The creamy sauce bursts with flavor from the Baharat Spice Blend (clearly, I like this blend). The baharat has a strong flavor; hence, there is a range mentioned in the ingredients. To make this a macaroni casserole, substitute half of the broccoli with 2 heaping cups cooked pasta.

Prep time: 15 minutes
Active time: 15 minutes
Inactive time: 30 minutes
soy-free, gluten-free option, nut-free option
Serves 4

2 teaspoons extra-virgin olive oil, divided
3/4 cup (90g) finely chopped onion
4 cloves garlic, finely chopped
1 1/2 to 2 teaspoons Baharat Spice Blend (page 100), divided
1/2 teaspoon ground mustard
Dash cayenne (optional)
1/2 teaspoon salt, or more to taste
1/4 teaspoon garlic powder
1/4 to 1/3 cup (30 to 40g) raw cashews, soaked for 15 minutes (or Nut-Free White Garlic Sauce [page 86] to make nut-free, see note)
2 tablespoons (16g) unbleached all-purpose flour (or rice flour or arrowroot starch to make gluten-free)
2 cups (480ml) plain, unsweetened nondairy milk
1 large bunch broccoli, crowns and stems finely chopped
1 cup (165g) cooked chickpeas, drained and rinsed (optional)
Dash paprika or black pepper

Optional Toppings
2 tablespoons (15g) Vegan Parmesan (page 233)
1/4 cup (20g) dry breadcrumbs (gluten-free if necessary) + 1 teaspoon extra-virgin olive oil + 1 clove garlic, minced

1. Preheat the oven to 400°F (200°C). Heat 1 teaspoon of the oil in a medium skillet over medium heat. Add the onion and garlic and cook, stirring occasionally, until the onion is translucent, 4 minutes. In a blender, combine half of the onion mixture, 1/2 to 1 teaspoon of the baharat spice blend, mustard, cayenne (if using), salt, garlic powder, cashews, flour, and milk and blend for 1 minute. Let the mixture rest 1 minute, then blend again for 1 minute. Taste and adjust the salt if needed.

2. Grease an 8 x 8-inch (20 x 20cm) baking pan with the remaining 1 teaspoon oil. Place the broccoli in the pan and top it with the remaining onion mixture. Pour the sauce all over the broccoli. Add the chickpeas (if using). Sprinkle the remaining 1/2 to 1 teaspoon baharat spice blend and the paprika evenly over the top of the casserole. (If using the chickpeas, be generous with the baharat spice blend, as the chickpeas will need the seasoning.)

3. Cover the pan lightly with foil and bake for 20 minutes. Uncover the pan, add the desired toppings, and bake for another 10 to 15 minutes.

Variation: Instead of the Baharat Spice Blend, use the Shawarma Spice Blend (page 140), Garam Masala (page 244), or Jamaican Jerk Seasoning (page 160).

Note: For a nut-free option, blend the Nut-Free White Garlic Sauce with 1 cup (240ml) nondairy milk, half of the cooked onion mixture, and 1/2 teaspoon Baharat Spice Blend and proceed with the directions.

Per serving: Calories 182, Total Fat 8g, Saturated Fat 1g, Sodium 428mg, Total Carbs 22g, Fiber 6g, Sugars 4g, Protein 7g

Smoky Mac Bake

This mac bake takes some of the things I like about the macs I have eaten in restaurants in and around Seattle: smoky, creamy, sharp flavors combined with a crumb topping. Add whatever vegetables you like. The spiciness of paprika can vary depending on the brand. If you are using a hot paprika, reduce the cayenne and red pepper flakes to half the amounts or less.

Prep time: 10 minutes
Active time: 20 minutes
Inactive time: 20 minutes
soy-free option
Serves 4

Casserole

2 to 2 1/2 cups (200 to 250g) **finely chopped broccoli, cauliflower, mushrooms, or zucchini (optional)**

6 to 8 ounces (170 to 227g) **cooked elbow macaroni or other small pasta, rinsed with cold water**

1 recipe **Smoky Cheese Sauce (recipe opposite)**

Breadcrumb Topping

1/3 cup (27g) **panko breadcrumbs or dry breadcrumbs**

1/2 teaspoon **smoked paprika**

2 cloves **garlic, minced, or 1/4 teaspoon garlic powder**

1/4 teaspoon **salt**

1/4 teaspoon **dried oregano**

1 teaspoon **extra-virgin olive oil**

Nut-Free Option

To make this nut-free, use Nut-Free White Sauce (page 86), and add 1 teaspoon smoked paprika and more nutritional yeast and cayenne to taste. Thin the sauce with some nondairy milk if needed.

1. Casserole: Preheat the oven to 425°F (220°C). Place the broccoli (if using) on the bottom of a greased 1 1/2-quart (1.4-L) casserole dish. Add the macaroni. Pour the cheese sauce over the macaroni and stir gently so the sauce coats the pasta and some of the broccoli.

2. Breadcrumb Topping: Combine the panko, paprika, garlic, salt, oregano, and oil in a small bowl. Sprinkle the topping mixture all over the casserole. Bake for 20 to 25 minutes. Let the casserole cool for 5 minutes before serving.

Per serving: Calories 352, Total Fat 13g, Saturated Fat 2g, Sodium 765mg, Total Carbs 49g, Fiber 5g, Sugars 4g, Protein 11g

Smoky Cheese Sauce

Awesome Sauce

This Cheesy sauce is your basic vegan cheese sauce with cashews, elevated with amazing flavor from smoked paprika, herbs and spices. It works great poured over almost anything. Simmer the sauce to bring to a boil to thicken and pour over roasted vegetables, baked sweet potato, dress burritos, Nachos, toss into pasta and what not. To make this gluten-free use 2 tablespoons of cornstarch or arrowroot starch.

Prep time: 10 minutes
Active time: 5 minutes
soy-free option gluten-free option
Makes 1 1/2 to 1 3/4 cups sauce

1 1/4 cups (300ml) almond milk or other nondairy milk

1/3 cup (40g) raw cashews, soaked for 15 minutes

2 tablespoons (16g) unbleached all-purpose flour

1/2 medium tomato, chopped

1 1/2 tablespoons soy sauce (or coconut aminos to make soy-free)

2 teaspoons prepared mustard

1 clove garlic

1 teaspoon smoked paprika

1 teaspoon fresh lemon juice

1/4 to 1/2 teaspoon cayenne

1/2 teaspoon garlic powder

1/2 teaspoon onion powder

1/2 teaspoon dried oregano

1/4 teaspoon dried thyme

1/4 cup (32g) nutritional yeast

1/2 teaspoon salt, or to taste

1 tablespoon extra-virgin olive oil

1/4 teaspoon red pepper flakes

In a blender, combine the milk, cashews, flour, tomato, soy sauce, mustard, garlic, paprika, lemon juice, cayenne, garlic powder, onion powder, oregano, thyme, nutritional yeast, salt, oil, and red pepper flakes and blend for 1 minute. Let the mixture sit for 2 minutes, then blend for 1 to 2 minutes, until very smooth. Taste and adjust the seasonings.

Per 1/2 cup: Calories 155. Total Fat 11g, Saturated Fat 1g, Sodium 793mg, Carbs 12g, Fiber 2g, Sugars 2g, Protein 4.5g

8

Breakfast for Lunch

Breakfast in our home is often savory, and filling enough to be a satisfying meal. Breakfast is the first and most important meal of the day. In our home, we usually make time to sit and eat a plateful, cooked fresh in the morning. The rotation usually includes some Indian breakfast options, soy-free frittatas, fritter patties, tofu scrambles, avocado or hummus toast topped with spiced sprouted lentils or beans, breakfast loaves such as banana bread, or a quick vegetable hash.

This chapter features savory Zucchini, Carrot, and Chickpea Fritters (page 185), Stuffed Flatbread (page 186), Samosa-Stuffed French Toast (page 182), and a Chickpea Flour Vegetable Frittata (page 177). All of these recipes are easy to make and can be enjoyed any time of day.

On days when we rush out the door in a hurry, a premade breakfast loaf, muffin, or snack bar works to satisfy and start up the day. (You'll find some sweet breakfast options in chapter 9.)

Chickpea Chilaquiles (page 174)

Chickpea Chilaquiles

This is a simple breakfast with a Mexican-inspired sauce, tortilla chips, and chickpeas. To make ahead, make the chilaquiles without the tortilla chips. When you are ready to serve, top warm tortilla chips with the chilaquiles.

Prep time: 10 minutes
Active time: 17 minutes
soy-free, gluten-free option, nut-free
Serves 3 to 4

Chilaquiles

1 teaspoon organic safflower or other neutral oil
1 small onion, finely chopped
5 cloves garlic, finely chopped
1/3 cup (50g) chopped carrots
1 (15-ounce [425g]) can chickpeas or 1 1/2 cups (250g) cooked chickpeas, drained and rinsed (see variation)
3/4 teaspoon ground cumin
1 teaspoon ground coriander
1/2 teaspoon paprika
1/2 teaspoon dried oregano
1/2 teaspoon garlic powder
1/4 teaspoon cayenne
Dash cinnamon
1/4 teaspoon salt, or to taste

Red Sauce

1/4 cup (65g) tomato paste
1 medium tomato, chopped
1 cup (240ml) water or vegetable broth
1 chipotle chile in adobo sauce or 1/4 teaspoon chipotle chili powder
1/2 teaspoon ground cumin
1/4 teaspoon salt, or more to taste
1 1/2 cups (50g) tortilla chips (see note)

Garnish

2 tablespoons (20g) chopped red onion
2 tablespoons (6g) chopped fresh cilantro
Fresh lime juice

1. Chilaquiles: Heat the oil in a medium skillet over medium heat. Add the onion, garlic, carrots, and a pinch salt and cook, stirring occasionally, until the vegetables are golden, 4 to 6 minutes. Transfer half of the onion mixture to a small bowl and set aside.

2. Add the chickpeas, cumin, coriander, paprika, oregano, garlic powder, cayenne, cinnamon, and salt to the skillet. Stir to combine, cover the skillet, and cook for 4 to 5 minutes. Mash some of the chickpeas if you like.

3. Red Sauce: Combine the tomato paste, tomato, water, chipotle, cumin, salt, and the reserved onion mixture in a blender. Blend until smooth and set aside.

4. Add the tortilla chips to the skillet. Pour the sauce over the chickpeas and chips. Stir gently and bring the mixture to a boil. Taste and adjust the seasonings. Serve immediately, garnished with the onion, cilantro, and lime juice.

Variations: Use pinto beans, black beans, cooked lentils, or crumbled tofu instead of chickpeas. Use less or more cayenne and chipotle chiles to taste. You can also use 1 tablespoon taco seasoning or chili powder instead of the spices and herbs.

Note: If you'd prefer not to use store-bought tortilla chips, you can make your own crisp tortillas. Sear 2 tortillas over an open flame until the edges are dark and the tortillas are slightly crispy. Slice the tortillas into triangles and proceed with the directions. You can also pan-fry or bake the tortilla strips until crisp.

Per serving: Calories 208, Total Fat 5g, Saturated Fat 0.5g, Sodium 812mg, Total Carbs 36g, Fiber 8g, Sugars 8g, Protein 8g

Chickpea Flour Vegetable Frittata

This is a filling, savory frittata made with chickpea flour, kala namak, and vegetables. The batter is very versatile and pairs well with any vegetables or greens. The batter also makes quick pancakes to serve with a variety of sauces (see note). If omitting the kala namak (or if you desire additional flavor), add 1/4 teaspoon garlic powder and 1/4 teaspoon onion powder to the batter. Feel free to add any of the spice blends—like the Baharat Spice Blend (page 100), Garam Masala (page 244), or Jamaican Jerk Seasoning (page 160)—to the batter. This frittata can be made ahead and served cold. Serve it with some sriracha or your favorite sauce.

Prep time: 15 minutes
Active time: 15 minutes
soy-free, gluten-free, nut-free option
Makes 1 (9-inch [23cm]) frittata

Vegetables

2 cups (200g) finely chopped broccoli, cauliflower, mushrooms, bell peppers (any color), or zucchini (or a combination)
1/4 cup (30g) finely chopped red onion
1 cup (30g) tightly packed finely chopped greens
1/4 teaspoon salt

Batter

1 1/2 cups (135g) chickpea flour
1 1/2 cups (360ml) water
1/4 cup (60g) plain unsweetened or lightly sweetened yogurt or thick cashew cream
1/2 teaspoon salt
1/4 heaping teaspoon kala namak (Indian sulphur black salt)
1/2 teaspoon ground turmeric
1/4 teaspoon cayenne
1/4 teaspoon black pepper, or to taste
1 tablespoon organic safflower or other neutral oil
1/2 cup (15g) chopped fresh cilantro or parsley
1/4 teaspoon dried thyme
1/2 teaspoon dried dill

1. Preheat the oven to 375°F (190°C). Grease a 9-inch (23cm) pie pan (or line it with parchment paper).

2. **Vegetables:** In a large bowl, combine the broccoli, onion, greens, and salt. Toss to combine.

3. **Batter:** In a blender, combine the flour, water, yogurt, salt, kala namak, turmeric, cayenne, pepper, and oil. Blend until smooth. (Alternatively, whisk the ingredients together in a large bowl until smooth.)

4. Add the broccoli mixture to the batter. Add the cilantro, thyme, and dill and mix well. Pour the frittata mixture into the prepared pie pan and bake for 45 to 50 minutes, or until a toothpick inserted in the center comes out almost clean. The top will crack and get golden. Spray or brush some oil on the top of the frittata while it is still hot. Let it sit for 10 minutes before serving. Store refrigerated for up to 3 days.

Note: To make chickpea flour pancakes, heat a medium skillet over medium heat. Add a few drops oil and spread it all over the skillet. Spread a ladle of the prepared frittata mixture in the skillet in an even layer. Cook the pancakes for 4 to 6 minutes per side, or until they are speckled with golden-brown spots. Serve with condiments of your choice.

Variation: For richer vegetable flavor, heat 1 teaspoon oil in a medium skillet over medium heat. Add the broccoli, onion, and salt and cook for 4 to 5 minutes. Add the greens and cook for 1 minute, or until they are just wilted.

Per serving: Calories 205, Total Fat 8g, Saturated Fat 1g, Sodium 498mg, Total Carbs 26g, Fiber 7g, Sugars 5g, Protein 10g

Lentil-Vegetable Frittata

This frittata looks more complicated than the Chickpea Flour Vegetable Frittata (page 177), but the main ingredients are similar. The batter features almond flour for volume, but this can be omitted for a nut-free dish. (Add an additional 1/4 cup [48g] lentils to make nut-free.) And do not worry about the fact that there are lentils in your frittata—the herbs and spices mask the lentil flavor. Use the seasonings listed in the recipe or mix and match to make your own flavor profile.

Prep time: 20 minutes
Active time: 20 minutes
Inactive time: 40 minutes
soy-free, gluten-free, nut-free option
Serves 4

Vegetables

1 teaspoon organic safflower or other neutral oil
1/2 cup (60g) finely chopped onion
3 cloves garlic, finely chopped
2 cups (200g) chopped cauliflower
1/2 cup (15g) packed baby spinach
1/4 teaspoon salt, or to taste
1/4 teaspoon chipotle chili powder
Dash black pepper
1/4 to 1/2 teaspoon dried oregano
1/4 to 1/2 teaspoon dried thyme
1/3 cup (40g) nondairy shredded cheese (optional)

Lentils

1/2 cup (95g) red lentils, rinsed, drained, and soaked for 20 minutes
1 cup (240ml) water
1/4 cup (28g) almond flour
2 teaspoons cornstarch or arrowroot starch
1 teaspoon baking powder
1/2 teaspoon salt
1/2 teaspoon garlic powder
1/4 teaspoon ground turmeric
1/4 teaspoon chipotle chili powder or cayenne
1/4 teaspoon Garam Masala (page 244) or other spice blend
2 teaspoons extra-virgin olive oil
2 tablespoons (12g) nutritional yeast
1/8 teaspoon kala namak (Indian sulphur black salt, optional)

1. Grease a 9-inch (23cm) pie pan (or line it with parchment paper). Preheat the oven to 365°F (185°C).

2. **Vegetables:** Heat the oil in a large skillet over medium heat. Add the onion and garlic and cook until the onion is translucent, 3 to 4 minutes. Add the cauliflower and stir to combine. Cover the skillet and cook for 2 minutes. Add the spinach, salt, chili powder, pepper, oregano, and thyme. Cover the skillet and cook for 2 to 4 minutes, or until the spinach is wilted. Take the skillet off the heat and let the mixture sit, covered, for 1 minute.

3. **Lentils:** Drain the soaked lentils and add them to a blender along with the water. Blend for at least 1 minute. Add the almond flour, cornstarch, baking powder, salt, garlic powder, turmeric, chili powder, garam masala, oil, nutritional yeast, and blend until smooth.

4. Transfer the vegetables to the pie pan. Add the cheese (if using) and stir gently to combine. Top the vegetables with the lentil mixture and spread it out with a spatula. Tap the bottom of the pan once or twice on the work surface so the mixture settles on the vegetables.

5. Bake the frittata for 40 to 50 minutes, until a toothpick inserted in the center comes out almost clean. Cool the frittata in the pan for 10 minutes, then remove it from the pan and cool it on a cooling rack for another 10 minutes before slicing. Serve the frittata with the chutney, sauce, or dressing of your choice.

Variation: Instead of (or in addition to) the cauliflower, use asparagus, green beans, carrots, or broccoli.

Tip: To reduce browning, arrange some tomato slices on top of the frittata before baking.

Per serving: Calories 277, Total Fat 8g, Saturated Fat 1g, Sodium 819mg, Total Carbs 40g, Fiber 8g, Sugars 6g, Protein 13g

Baked Vegetable Pakoras

These vegetable pakoras make a delicious and quick snack. Chop up the vegetables, fold in the chickpea flour and spices, and bake. And then comes the hardest part—waiting. Serve these pakoras with ketchup or chutneys of your choice. They can also be served in tacos with slaw and chutney or baked into flat patties for sandwiches or burgers.

Prep time: 15 minutes
Active time: 15 minutes
Inactive time: 22 minutes
soy-free, gluten-free option, nut-free
Makes 15 to 18 pakoras

1 heaping cup (110g) 1-inch (3cm) cauliflower florets

3/4 cup (90g) finely chopped onion

3/4 cup (75g) 1-inch (3cm) broccoli florets

1/3 cup (50g) chopped carrots

1/3 cup (50g) chopped raw or cooked potato

1 small green chile, seeded if desired

1 (1/2-inch [1cm]) knob fresh ginger, peeled

1/4 cup (10g) tightly packed chopped fresh cilantro

1 tablespoon fresh mint leaves (optional)

1/4 teaspoon carom seeds (ajwain) or toasted cumin seeds, or to taste

1/2 teaspoon ground turmeric, or to taste

1/4 teaspoon cayenne, or to taste

1/2 teaspoon to 3/4 teaspoon salt

1 teaspoon chaat masala or amchur (dried mango powder), divided

2 tablespoons (16g) semolina flour (or brown or white rice flour to make gluten-free)

1/4 teaspoon baking soda

2/3 cup (60g) chickpea flour, or more

2 teaspoons organic safflower or other neutral oil, or more

1 to 2 teaspoons water, or more

1. Add the cauliflower, onion, broccoli, carrots, potato, chile, ginger, cilantro, and mint (if using) to a food processor. Pulse in 5-second intervals a few times to finely chop the vegetables.

2. Transfer the vegetable mixture to a large bowl. Add the carom seeds, turmeric, cayenne, salt, 1/2 teaspoon of the chaat masala, and the semolina flour.

3. In a small bowl, combine the baking soda and chickpea flour. Add the chickpea flour mixture to the vegetables and stir to combine. Add 1 tablespoon or so more chickpea flour, if needed. You need just a light coating of flour on all the vegetables. Let the mixture sit for 2 to 3 minutes so the vegetables can transfer some of their moisture to the flour. Preheat the oven to 425°F (220°C). Line a medium baking sheet with parchment paper.

4. Add the oil and water to the pakora mixture and mix. Depending on the moisture content of the vegetables, you might or might not need more water. The mixture should not be a batter, but should easily form balls in your hands. Add water 1 teaspoon at a time until the mixture just starts to stick. Using your hands, a tablespoon, or an ice cream scoop, place scoops of the pakora mixture on the baking sheet. (To ensure even cooking, keep the scoops small, around 1 1/2 inches [4cm]). Spritz or brush additional oil on the pakoras.

5. Bake the pakoras for 22 to 25 minutes, or until golden brown and crispy on the outside. (Alternatively, air-fry the pakoras at 400°F [200°C] for 12 to 14 minutes. Note that the texture will be a bit different from the baked pakoras.) Cool for 1 minute. Sprinkle the remaining 1/2 teaspoon chaat masala over the pakoras.

Serving suggestion: Serve them with Tamarind Chutney (page 240), Mint-Cilantro Herb Sauce (page 183), ketchup, or other sauces of your choice.

Per serving: Calories 146, Total Fat 4g, Saturated Fat 1g, Sodium 407mg, Total Carbs 24g, Fiber 4g, Sugars 5g, Protein 6g

Samosa-Stuffed French Toast

This is a modified version of a favorite snack that my mom makes. Bread is stuffed with spiced potatoes, then dipped in chickpea batter and pan-fried (although my mom deep-fries it). It's a comfort-food breakfast, snack, or light lunch. To make it a meal, mix some cooked quinoa into the Samosa Potatoes. Or use other fillings, such as jerk black beans (page 160), baharat chickpeas (page 133), any lentil or chickpea burger mixture that is not crumbly, or liberally spiced mashed sweet potatoes. (Photo opposite.)

Prep time: 15 minutes + Samosa Potatoes
Active time: 25 minutes
Inactive time: 10 minutes
soy-free, nut-free
Makes 4 to 6 stuffed sandwiches

1 cup (90g) chickpea flour or besan

1 1/4 to 1 1/2 cups (300 to 360ml) water, as needed

3/4 teaspoon salt

1/4 teaspoon ground turmeric

1/4 teaspoon cayenne

1 loaf bakery sandwich bread or 1 loaf pre-sliced sandwich bread

1/2 to 1 recipe Samosa Potatoes (page 239)

1 to 2 tablespoons organic canola or safflower oil, divided

1 recipe Mint-Cilantro Herb Sauce, optional (recipe opposite)

1. In a shallow bowl, combine the flour, 1 1/4 cups (300ml) of the water, salt, turmeric, and cayenne. Add the remaining 1/4 cup (60ml) water to make a thin pancake batter consistency, if needed.

2. If using bakery bread, cut it into 8 to 10 thick slices. Carve out a bit of bread from each slice to create a pouch for the samosa stuffing. Stuff the bread with the samosa potatoes. Alternatively, if using thinner pre-sliced bread, use 8 to 10 slices to make samosa sandwiches: Press the samosa potatoes on one slice. Press the other slice on top to form a sandwich.

3. Heat 1 teaspoon of the oil in a large skillet over medium heat. Dip the stuffed French toast in the batter and place it in the skillet. Cook 4 to 6 minutes, carefully flip, and cook another 4 to 6 minutes. Add 1/2 to 1 teaspoon of the oil to the skillet before cooking the next batch of French toast. Serve hot with the Mint-Cilantro Herb Sauce (if using), ketchup, or sriracha.

Note: To make these gluten-free, make thin pancakes with the chickpea flour batter in a skillet over medium heat. Serve the Samosa Potatoes stuffed into the folded pancakes.

Per serving (not including the sauce): Calories 371, Total Fat 11g, Saturated Fat 1g, Sodium 849mg, Total Carbs 56g, Fiber 6g, Sugars 6g, Protein 12g

Mint-Cilantro Herb Sauce

1/4 teaspoon ground cumin

1 clove garlic

1/2 teaspoon salt

1/2 teaspoon sugar or maple syrup

2 to 4 tablespoons (30 to 60ml) water, or as needed

1 cup (40g) tightly packed fresh mint

1 cup (40g) tightly packed fresh cilantro (or more mint)

1 teaspoon extra-virgin olive oil

1 tablespoon fresh lime juice, or more to taste

In a blender, combine the cumin, garlic, salt, sugar, water, mint, cilantro, oil, and lime juice and process until well blended. Taste and adjust the seasonings.

Makes 1 cup (240ml)

Zucchini, Carrot, and Chickpea Fritters

These fritters are another popular recipe from the blog because they are easy to make and boast a bold flavor profile thanks to the peppery Turkish blend of spices. They come together quickly if you have the spices ready. You can also use your own spice blend, garam masala, baharat spice, or just cumin and coriander in these. Pan-fried and crispy, these fritters are a filling breakfast or snack. Serve them with Tamarind Chutney (page 240), Tahini Garlic Sauce (page 123), Ranch Dressing (page 87), sriracha, or ketchup.

Prep time: 15 minutes
Active time: 30 minutes
Inactive time: 10 minutes
soy-free, gluten-free option, nut-free
Makes 8 to 9 large fritters

1 large zucchini, shredded

3/4 cup (120g) shredded carrots

3 cloves garlic, minced

1 (1/2-inch [1cm]) knob fresh ginger, peeled and minced

1 small green chile, minced, or cayenne, to taste

1 (15-ounce [425g]) can chickpeas or 1 1/2 cups (250g) cooked chickpeas, drained and rinsed

1/2 teaspoon cumin seeds

1/2 teaspoon coriander seeds

1/2 teaspoon black peppercorns or ground black pepper

1/2 teaspoon organic safflower or other neutral oil, plus more as needed

1/4 teaspoon ground cinnamon

1/4 teaspoon ground cardamom

1/2 to 3/4 teaspoon salt (if using unsalted chickpeas)

1 tablespoon ground flax seed or chia seed

1/4 cup (30g) oat flour or other flour

1 to 2 tablespoons dry breadcrumbs or more flour, if needed

1. Lightly press the shredded zucchini in a paper towel if it is very moist. Add the zucchini to a large bowl and add the carrots, garlic, ginger, and chile and stir to combine.

2. Process the chickpeas in a food processor until they are coarsely blended, but not fully a paste. Add the chickpeas to the bowl and stir to combine.

3. Using a mortar and pestle or spice grinder, crush or grind the cumin seeds, coriander seeds, and peppercorns. Heat the oil in a small skillet. Add the cumin mixture and cook until it is fragrant. (Alternatively, dry-roast the spices without the oil.) Add the cumin mixture to the bowl. Add the cinnamon, cardamom, salt, flax seed, and flour and mix well. Add the breadcrumbs if the mixture is too wet.

4. Form the mixture into large, flat, pancake-like patties and cook them in a lightly oiled skillet over medium heat for 5 to 6 minutes per side. Alternatively, to bake the fritters, preheat the oven to 400°F (200°C). Line a large baking sheet with parchment paper, place the fritters on the baking sheet, and bake for 20 to 25 minutes. Broil for 1 minute to make the fritters crispy.

Variation: Add 1 to 2 tablespoons sesame seeds.

Per serving: Calories 184, Total Fat 3g, Saturated Fat 1g, Sodium 336mg, Total Carbs 31g, Fiber 8g, Sugars 7g, Protein 9g

Stuffed Flatbread

A breakfast chapter wouldn't be complete without a paratha recipe. I grew up eating flatbreads stuffed with various simple fillings—shredded or roasted vegetables or beans. This simple, hearty, savory breakfast is where it is at.

Prep time: 20 minutes
Active time: 35 minutes
soy-free, gluten-free option, nut-free
Makes 7 to 8 stuffed flatbreads

1 recipe **Wheat Flatbread dough (page 236) or Gluten-Free Flatbread dough (page 237)**
1 recipe **Samosa Potatoes (page 239) or any of the burger mixtures from chapter 5**
Flour (any variety), as needed

1. Divide the dough into 8 to 9 balls. Divide the samosa potatoes into an equal number of balls (uneven balls are okay). Roll out each dough ball using some flour into an approximately 5-inch (13cm) circle.

2. Place a ball of the samosa potatoes in the center of the dough circle. Fold the flatbread over the filling and press around the edges to seal it like a dumpling. Dust each stuffed flatbread with flour and roll it lightly to a 6- to 7-inch (15- to 18cm) size.

3. Heat a medium skillet over medium-high heat. Place a stuffed flatbread in the skillet and cook for 1 to 2 minutes. Flip the flatbread and cook the other side for 1 to 2 minutes. Spray or brush each side with a little oil and continue to cook until both sides have some brown spots. Repeat this process for all the stuffed flatbreads.

4. Store the stuffed flatbreads in a kitchen towel or paper towel–lined container on the counter for a few hours. Serve the stuffed flatbreads with dips or chutneys of your choice, or as a side with soups, curries, and so on. These flatbreads can be made ahead and refrigerated for up to 3 days or frozen for a month. Reheat in a skillet or microwave.

Variation: Add 1/2 teaspoon toasted cumin seeds or carom seeds to the dry ingredients while making the flatbread dough.

Per serving: Calories 240, Total Fat 4g, Saturated Fat 1g, Sodium 450mg, Total Carbs 45g, Fiber 6g, Sugars 2g, Protein 8g

9

On a Sweet Note

Amazing meals need some equally amazing sweet options to follow them (or sometimes we just need a between-meal snack).

Vegan baking can get tricky when trying to navigate substitutes to achieve similar tastes and textures. And vegan gluten-free baking has its own sets of rules. I bake very intuitively just like I cook, keeping an eye on the dough or batter and adjusting it before it bakes. Different flours (even the same types of flour from different brands) and substituted liquids all eventually behave differently during baking. Try to stick with the given ingredients in these recipes. I and the recipe testers have tested several variations with options for both regular and gluten-free flours and those are mentioned within the recipes.

Start with the easy and addictive Chocolate Chip Cookie Dough Bars (page 194), make some classic brownies (page 213), indulge in the One-Bowl Pumpkin Bread (page 217), and definitely try the Salted Date Caramel Chocolate Pie (page 197). One-Bowl Banana Apple Bread (page 201), Lemon Chia Coconut Muffins (page 222), and Ginger Tahini Cookies (page 198) make amazing breakfasts or snacks.

Richa's Brownies (page 213)

Chocolate Peanut Butter Ganache Cake

This super moist chocolate layer cake comes together quickly—the key is to not overbake the cakes to keep them moist. The cakes are layered with a smooth chocolate nut butter ganache glaze and a layer of seedless fruit preserves. This cake keeps well—store it in the refrigerator for up to five days or freeze individual slices for up to a month.

Prep time: 10 minutes
Active time: 30 minutes
Inactive time: 45 minutes
soy-free, nut-free option
Serves 12

Cake

1 cup (120g) whole-wheat flour

1 cup (120g) unbleached all-purpose flour

1/2 cup (40g) unsweetened cocoa powder

1 1/2 teaspoons baking soda

1 1/4 cups (150g) confectioners' sugar

1/2 scant teaspoon salt

1 1/2 cups (360ml) nondairy milk, divided

1/3 cup (80g) nondairy semisweet chocolate chips

1/4 cup (60ml) organic safflower or other neutral oil

1 teaspoon apple cider vinegar or distilled white vinegar

1 1/2 teaspoons vanilla extract

3 tablespoons (45ml) maple syrup

Ganache

1/2 cup (120ml) nondairy milk

1/3 to 1/2 cup (40 to 60g) confectioners' sugar

2/3 cup (160g) nondairy semisweet chocolate chips

1/2 teaspoon vanilla extract

1/4 cup (65g) smooth peanut butter or almond butter (see note)

Raspberry, apricot, or cherry preserves (optional)

1. Cake: Preheat the oven to 350°F (180°C). Grease 2 (8-inch [20cm]) cake pans (or line them with parchment paper). In a medium bowl, whisk together the whole-wheat flour, all-purpose flour, cocoa, baking soda, confectioners' sugar, and salt. In a large microwave-safe bowl, combine 1 cup (240ml) of the milk and the chocolate chips. Microwave until the milk is almost hot (or heat the milk and chocolate chips in a large saucepan over medium-low heat). Whisk until the chocolate chips melt. Add the remaining 1/2 cup (120ml) milk, oil, vinegar, vanilla, and maple syrup and whisk until smooth. Add the flour mixture to the milk mixture and stir until smooth. Transfer the batter to the cake pans.

2. Bake for 32 to 34 minutes, or until a toothpick inserted in the center comes out clean. Do not overbake. Cool the cakes for 10 minutes, then remove them from the pans and cool completely on a cooling rack. Cover the cakes with a towel while they are cooling to prevent them from drying out. To shorten the cooling time, cover the cakes with a towel and refrigerate for 15 to 20 minutes.

3. Ganache: Heat the milk and confectioners' sugar in a small saucepan over medium heat until the milk is almost hot. Stir well to combine. Add the chocolate chips, stir once, then remove from the heat. Keep stirring until the chocolate is melted and smooth, 1 to 2 minutes. Add the vanilla and peanut butter. Stir until smooth. Chill the ganache in the refrigerator for 20 to 30 minutes to thicken.

4. Pour some of the ganache on 1 cake layer and spread it evenly using a spatula. Return this layer to the refrigerator for 20 minutes so the ganache can harden. Add a thin, even layer of fruit preserves, if using, to the other cake layer (warm the preserves to make them easier to spread if needed). Place this cake layer on top of the layer with the ganache. Pour the rest of the ganache over the top of the cake, using a spatula to spread it evenly. Refrigerate the cake for 30 minutes, then cover and chill for 3 hours before serving.

Notes: For a sweeter cake, add an additional 2 tablespoons (16g) confectioners' sugar to the dry ingredients. To make nut-free, omit the nut butter and add 1/4 cup (60g) more chocolate chips to the milk prior to heating.

Per serving: Calories 340, Total Fat 13g, Saturated Fat 4g, Sodium 200mg, Total Carbs 52g, Fiber 5g, Sugars 28g, Protein 7g

Gluten-Free Baking

Gluten-free baking is tricky on its own. Vegan gluten-free baking gets tougher. Here are my six tips for better chances of success:

1. **Bake small.** Because there is no gluten to hold the rising loaf structure, loaves need a lot of air and many other elements to rise up and stay. Muffins, on the other hand, are much more predictable. When in doubt, bake one or two muffins of the batter to see if they work in terms of rise and texture. If they turn out dry, adjust the batter with additional moisture (like oil, fruit puree, or nondairy yogurt). If they fall, add more volume (like oats and similar dry ingredients for thicker batter).

2. **Add starch.** Starch helps add a fluffy texture and some sticky hold.

3. **Use gums.** Xanthan gum is not always necessary, but if you are a beginner, use it to get a handle on gluten-free baking.

4. **Look to seeds.** Chia seeds, psyllium husk, and other sticky seed-based ingredients help with binding. Too much, though, will yield gummy results.

5. **Keep failed results.** Bake them into biscotti or croutons or crumbs to top oatmeal.

6. **Try again!** Gluten-free baking can be a bit unpredictable. But do not be intimidated—trials and errors are your best friends. (This philosophy also applies to baking in general. Stuff happens.)

Lemon Chia Pudding

This pudding is a refreshing breakfast or snack. It's like lemon pie in chia pudding form. Loads of lemon juice, lemon zest, and coconut milk make this is a runny pudding compared to other chia puddings. But it is worth it—the higher ratio of lemony coconut milk to chia seeds packs a bigger flavor punch. For a thicker pudding, use 1 to 2 tablespoons more chia seeds. If the pudding doesn't turn out to your preference, turn it into the Lemon Chia Coconut Muffins (page 222): add the dry ingredients and some sweetener to make a muffin-like batter and bake. (Photo opposite.)

Prep time: 5 minutes
Active time: 10 minutes
Inactive time: chilling time
soy-free, gluten-free, nut-free
Serves 4

1 1/2 cups (360ml) full-fat coconut
   milk, divided
2 to 3 teaspoons lemon zest, plus more
   for garnish
Juice of 2 lemons, about 1/3 cup (80 ml)
3 tablespoons (36g) raw sugar or 3
   tablespoons (45ml) maple syrup
Pinch salt
1/4 teaspoon ground turmeric, or more
   to taste
1/4 cup (40g) plus 1 to 2 tablespoons
   chia seeds
Whipped coconut cream, for garnish

1. In a blender, combine 1/2 cup (120ml) of the milk, lemon zest, lemon juice, sugar, and salt and blend until well combined (alternatively, combine the ingredients in a medium bowl and whisk to combine).

2. In a small saucepan, heat the remaining 1 cup (240ml) coconut milk and turmeric until the mixture is almost boiling. Take the saucepan off the heat and add the chia seeds. After 2 minutes, combine with the lemon milk mixture and let the pudding sit for 10 minutes to cool.

3. Whisk the mixture vigorously to distribute the chia seeds. Taste and adjust the seasonings. Pour the pudding into serving glasses or individual bowls. Chill the pudding for a few hours or overnight in the refrigerator. Garnish with additional lemon zest and the whipped coconut cream and serve.

Variation: Use Key lime juice and zest for Key lime pudding.

Per serving: Calories 212, Total Fat 13g, Saturated Fat 9g, Sodium 17mg, Total Carbs 21g, Fiber 5g, Sugars 13g, Protein 4g

Chocolate Chip Cookie Dough Bars

These bars are dangerous, as they come together in five minutes. The dough often does not make it to the bar or truffle state—it goes from bowl to scoop to mouth.

Prep time: 5 minutes
Active time: 5 minutes
Inactive time: chilling time
soy-free, gluten-free
Makes 16 to 18 small bars

2 tablespoons (24g) solid or semisolid coconut oil (use refined for a neutral flavor)

1 tablespoon almond milk or other nondairy milk

3 tablespoons (45ml) maple syrup

1 tablespoon pure vanilla extract (use 2 teaspoons for a milder flavor)

1/4 cup (50g) coconut sugar or fine brown sugar

1/4 teaspoon salt

1 cup (120g) oat flour or finely ground rolled oats (certified gluten-free if needed), divided (see note)

3/4 cup (85g) fine almond flour

1 tablespoon fine cane sugar (optional)

1/3 to 1/2 cup (80 to 120g) nondairy mini chocolate chips

1. Melt the oil in the microwave in a small microwave-safe bowl or on the stove in a small saucepan. Add the milk, maple syrup, and vanilla and whisk to combine. Add the coconut sugar and stir (no need for the sugar to combine with the other ingredients fully).

2. Add the salt, 3/4 cup (90g) of the oat flour, the almond flour, and sugar and mix. Add the remaining 1/4 cup (30g) oat flour in small increments just until the mixture is a stiff batter or soft dough consistency. The dough stiffens more on chilling. Add the chocolate chips, stirring to combine. Refrigerate the dough for 30 minutes, then shape it into balls using a cookie scoop. Alternatively, pat the dough onto parchment paper, refrigerate it another 15 minutes, then slice and store.

Note: I like this dough with an oat and fine almond flour combination for a neutral, pleasing flavor and some texture. You can use other flours as well—any mild-tasting grain flour will do. Be sure to test out a bit of the flour before moving forward with the recipe, though. Mix the flour with maple syrup and taste it to see if you like the flavor profile of the raw dough. The flour also can be toasted by cooking it in a skillet over medium-low heat for 4 to 5 minutes. Some flours taste better toasted (e.g., wheat flour) while some don't (e.g., oat or nut flours).

Variations:

Truffles: To make truffles, shape the cookie dough into balls. Melt 1/2 cup (120g) nondairy chocolate chips and 2 teaspoons refined coconut oil in a double boiler (or microwave the mixture in a microwave-safe bowl in 30-second intervals, whisking between each interval) until smooth and shiny. Dip the cookie dough balls in the melted chocolate using a fork or spoon. Coat the balls evenly and place them on a parchment paper-lined baking sheet. Chill the truffles in the refrigerator to harden the chocolate.

Cookie Dough Blizzard: To make a cookie dough blizzard, blend 1 1/2 cups almond milk ice cubes, 4 pitted dates, and 3 tablespoons of the cookie dough, and serve immediately. (To make almond milk ice cubes, freeze 2 cups almond milk in an ice cube tray.)

Per serving: Calories 124, Total Fat 7g, Saturated Fat 3g, Sodium 46mg, Total Carbs 15g, Fiber 2g, Sugars 8g, Protein 3g

Salted Date Caramel Chocolate Pie

This is a no-bake frozen pie. This is also an insanely delicious pie: fudgy salted caramel sweetened with dates, thick chocolate ganache, and a chocolatey almond coconut crust. This is what should be in your freezer for the weekend!

Prep time: 20 minutes
Active time: 20 minutes
Inactive time: 5 to 6 hours
soy-free, gluten-free
Serves 8

Crust

1/2 cup (80g) plus 2 tablespoons (21g) raw almonds

1 cup (60g) unsweetened dried shredded coconut

2 tablespoons ground flax seed

1/8 teaspoon salt

1 1/2 tablespoons unsweetened cocoa powder

8 to 9 soft Medjool dates, pitted

1 1/2 teaspoons vanilla extract

2 tablespoons (30ml) maple syrup

1 tablespoon almond milk, if needed

Salted Caramel

12 large Medjool dates, pitted and soaked in hot water for 15 minutes

2 tablespoons smooth almond butter or other nut butter

2 tablespoons solid coconut oil

1/2 cup (120ml) almond milk or other nondairy milk

1/4 teaspoon fine sea salt

Chocolate Ganache

1/2 cup (120ml) full-fat coconut milk

3 ounces (85g) nondairy 70% dark chocolate or 2/3 cup (160g) nondairy semisweet chocolate chips

2 tablespoons (32g) smooth almond butter

2 tablespoons (27g) solid coconut oil

2 teaspoons vanilla extract

1/4 cup (60ml) maple syrup

1. Crust: Process the almonds in a food processor or blender to form a coarse meal. Add the coconut, flax seed, salt, and cocoa and pulse a few times so the coconut becomes a coarse meal. Add the dates, vanilla, and maple syrup and process until doughy. Add the almond milk if needed to make a soft, somewhat sticky dough. Press the dough into a 9-inch (23cm) pie pan.

2. Salted Caramel: Drain the soaked dates. In a blender, combine the dates, almond butter, oil, almond milk, and salt. Blend for 1 minute, let the mixture rest for 1 minute, and blend again. Repeat this process until the mixture is smooth. Taste and adjust the seasonings. Spread the caramel on the prepared crust. Refrigerate or freeze until the chocolate ganache is ready.

3. Chocolate Ganache: Heat the coconut milk in a small saucepan over medium heat until it just starts to bubble. Take the saucepan off the heat. Add the chocolate and whisk to melt it in the milk. Add the almond butter, oil, vanilla, and maple syrup, whisking briskly. Pour the ganache onto the caramel layer. Tap the bottom of the pie pan against the work surface to spread the layers evenly.

4. Freeze the pie until set, 5 to 6 hours. Let it thaw for a few minutes prior to slicing and serving. The pie can be frozen for up to 1 month. Cover the pie pan and freeze so that the top layer does not dry out.

Note: I like to slice the pie once frozen into bite-size bars for a quick snack or dessert, as a whole slice of this pie is quite decadent. To make it more like a Snickers candy bar, sprinkle some roasted peanuts over the caramel layer.

Per serving: Calories 534, Total Fat 30g, Saturated Fat 16g, Sodium 116mg, Total Carbs 68g, Fiber 9g, Sugars 54g, Protein 7g

Ginger Tahini Cookies

Love tahini? Then you will love these cookies. Ginger and tahini go so well together in these cookies. The sweet, sharp ginger takes the edge off the tahini's bitterness and the combination works magically. Tahini also makes these cookies shortbread-soft.

Prep time: 10 minutes
Active time: 15 minutes
Inactive time: 10 to 11 minutes
soy-free, gluten-free option, nut-free
Makes 26 to 28 cookies

1/2 cup (71g) tahini

1/4 cup (60ml) maple syrup

1/4 cup (60ml) organic safflower or other neutral oil

1/4 cup (50g) fine cane sugar

1 teaspoon vanilla extract

2 1/2 tablespoons (40ml) nondairy milk

1 1/2 teaspoons ground ginger

1 teaspoon ground cinnamon

Pinch ground cloves

Pinch ground nutmeg

2 teaspoons baking powder

1/2 teaspoon baking soda

1 1/2 to 1 3/4 cups (180 to 210g) whole-wheat pastry flour or whole-wheat flour (or Gluten-Free Flour Blend [page 231] to make gluten-free), plus more as needed

1/4 teaspoon salt

3 tablespoons (40g) finely chopped candied ginger

1 tablespoon granulated sugar, for topping

1. Preheat the oven to 350°F (180°C). In a large bowl, combine the tahini, maple syrup, oil, sugar, vanilla, and milk, stirring until the mixture is smooth and the sugar has dissolved. Add the ginger, cinnamon, cloves, nutmeg, baking powder, and baking soda and stir to combine. Add the flour, salt, and candied ginger and use your hands to make a smooth dough. If the mixture is too wet, add additional flour, 1 tablespoon at a time.

2. Divide the dough into 26 to 28 portions and shape them into 1 1/2-inch (4cm) flat discs. Press one side of the discs into the granulated sugar and place them on a large baking sheet lined with parchment paper.

3. Bake the cookies for 10 to 11 minutes. Let them cool completely and serve. For softer cookies, bake 1 minute less. For crispier cookies, bake 1 minute longer. Store the cookies in an airtight container for up to 3 days.

Variation: Try other spices and additions, such as 1/2 teaspoon Baharat Spice Blend (page 100) or Garam Masala (page 244) with 1/2 teaspoon ground cinnamon.

Per serving: Calories 93, Total Fat 5g, Saturated Fat 0.5g, Sodium 92mg, Total Carbs 12g, Fiber 2g, Sugars 5g, Protein 2 g

Almond Butter Snickerdoodles

The almond butter in these snickerdoodles keeps them soft and crumbly. These cookies are double-rolled in cinnamon for an amazing cinnamon punch. For variation, use other spice blends and other nut butters, such as hazelnut, cashew, or pecan. The dough consistency depends on the nut butter. Smooth, drippy nut butter works best. Adjust the dough using additional oil or nondairy milk if using a more solid nut butter.

Prep time: 10 minutes
Active time: 20 minutes
Inactive time: 1 hour + baking time
soy-free, gluten-free option
Makes 12 cookies

- 3/4 cup (90g) **unbleached all-purpose flour or spelt flour (or Gluten-Free Flour Blend [page 231] to make gluten-free)**
- 1 tablespoon **cornstarch or arrowroot starch**
- 1/3 cup (65g) plus 2 tablespoons (24g) **fine cane sugar or finely ground raw sugar, divided**
- 1/4 teaspoon **baking powder**
- 1/8 teaspoon **baking soda**
- 1/8 teaspoon **salt**
- 2 teaspoons **ground flax seed**
- 2 tablespoons (30ml) **almond milk or other nondairy milk**
- 3 tablespoons (48g) **almond butter**
- 3 tablespoons (45ml) **organic safflower or other neutral oil**
- 1/2 teaspoon **vanilla extract**
- 3 1/4 teaspoons **ground cinnamon, divided**

1. In a medium bowl, whisk together the flour, cornstarch, 1/3 cup (65g) of the sugar, baking powder, baking soda, and salt. In another medium bowl, combine the flax seed and the milk. Add the almond butter, oil, vanilla, and 1/4 teaspoon of the cinnamon and stir to combine. (It will take a minute for the almond butter to mix in.) Add the milk mixture to the flour mixture and knead in the bowl to form a dough. It will feel crumbly at first, but will come together. (If it doesn't come together, knead a few drops of water into the dough.) Wrap the dough in plastic wrap and refrigerate for 1 hour.

2. Preheat the oven to 375°F (190°C). Line a medium baking sheet with parchment paper. Combine 2 teaspoons of the cinnamon and the remaining 2 tablespoons (24g) sugar in a small bowl. Put the remaining 1 teaspoon cinnamon in another small bowl.

3. Make balls with the chilled dough that measure 1 to 1 1/2 inches (3 to 4cm). Roll the balls first in the cinnamon then in the cinnamon sugar. Place the balls on the baking sheet. Press them down with a fork. Bake the cookies for 11 to 12 minutes. Cool completely. The cookies will be soft out of the oven but will firm up. Store them in an airtight container.

Per serving: Calories 119, Total Fat 6g, Saturated Fat 0.4g, Sodium 61g, Total Carbs 16g, Fiber 1g, Sugars 8g, Protein 2g

One-Bowl Banana Apple Bread

This loaf comes together very easily and is also simple to adjust to your preferences. Add 1/4 cup (19g) unsweetened dried shredded coconut for a caramelized, coconutty flavor profile. Add 1/4 cup (65g) peanut butter or almond butter for a nut butter banana bread. I use generous amounts of cinnamon, nutmeg, and cardamom for a warming, fragrant loaf.

Prep time: 15 minutes
Active time: 65 minutes
Inactive time: 50 minutes
soy-free, gluten-free option, nut-free option
Serves 8

- 2 1/2 cups (300g) white whole-wheat flour or unbleached all-purpose flour (or Gluten-Free Flour Blend [page 231] to make gluten-free, see note)
- 2 1/4 teaspoons baking powder
- 1/4 teaspoon baking soda
- 1 1/4 teaspoons pumpkin pie spice (see note)
- 1/4 teaspoon ground cardamom
- 1/4 teaspoon salt
- 3 to 4 tablespoons (24 to 32g) confectioners' sugar, coconut sugar, or other sweetener
- 2 large or 3 medium very ripe bananas
- 1/2 cup (120ml) nondairy milk
- 1 tablespoon blackstrap molasses or maple syrup
- 2 tablespoons (32g) smooth almond butter or other nut butter (or coconut oil to make nut-free)
- 1 teaspoon vanilla extract
- 1 cup (180g) shredded Fuji or Gala apple
- 4 tablespoons (32g) toasted walnuts or pecans (or unsweetened dried shredded coconut to make nut-free)
- 3 tablespoons (30g) nondairy semi-sweet chocolate chips or chopped dried fruit

1. Preheat the oven to 365°F (185°C). Line a 9 x 5-inch (23 x 13cm) loaf pan with parchment paper. In a large bowl, whisk together the flour, baking powder, baking soda, pumpkin pie spice, cardamom, salt, and confectioners' sugar. (Use 3 tablespoons [24g] confectioners' sugar if the bananas are very sweet; use 4 tablespoons [32g] if they are not very sweet.)

2. In a small blender, combine the bananas, milk, molasses, almond butter, and vanilla. Blend until smooth and add the puree to the flour mixture. (Alternatively, mash the banana in a medium bowl until smooth, then add the milk, molasses, almond butter, and vanilla, stirring to combine.) Stir until the dry and wet ingredients are well combined and form a stiff batter. Add the apple, walnuts, and chocolate chips and stir to combine. Transfer the batter to the loaf pan. Top with additional chocolate chips, if desired.

3. Bake the bread for 40 minutes. Reduce the heat to 350°F (180°C). Bake for 10 to 15 minutes, or until a toothpick inserted in the center comes out almost clean. Cool the loaf for 10 minutes in the pan. Remove the loaf from the pan and transfer it to a cooling rack. Let it cool completely before slicing. Store the loaf on the counter for the day and refrigerate for up to 5 days.

Notes: If you decide to make this recipe gluten-free, it is best to make muffins rather than a loaf. To make muffins, bake them at 375°F (190°C) for 18 to 22 minutes.

If you don't have pumpkin pie spice, use a combination of 3/4 teaspoon ground cinnamon, 1/4 teaspoon ground cardamom, 1/4 teaspoon ground nutmeg, and a pinch ground cloves.

Per serving: Calories 228, Total Fat 9g, Saturated Fat 1g, Sodium 267mg, Total Carbs 40g, Fiber 4g, Sugars 15g, Protein 8g

Seedy Chocolate Snack Bars

These seedy bars, filled with sunflower, sesame, and chia seeds, are easy to put together and very filling. Chop these into bite-size bars and keep them handy to snack on. I like the chewy candied ginger in these, but any dried or candied fruit will work. Add seeds and nuts according to your preference. You can also add some protein powder to these bars.

Prep time: 5 minutes
Active time: 20 minutes
Inactive time: 15 minutes
soy-free, gluten-free
Makes 10 to 12 snack bars

1 cup (80g) old-fashioned oats

1/4 cup (30g) pepitas or raw sunflower seeds

2 tablespoons (20g) sesame seeds or hemp seeds

2 tablespoons (16g) chia seeds

3 tablespoons (25g) raw cashews, coarsely chopped

1/4 cup (30g) raw walnuts or pecans, coarsely chopped

3 tablespoons (40g) finely chopped candied ginger (optional)

1/4 teaspoon ground cinnamon

2 to 3 tablespoons (14 to 21g) vegan protein powder (optional)

3/4 cup (180g) nondairy semisweet chocolate chips

2 teaspoons solid coconut oil

2 tablespoons (32g) smooth peanut butter, almond butter, or sunflower seed butter

1. Line a 9 x 5-inch (23 x 13cm) loaf pan with parchment paper and set aside.

2. Toast the oats in a medium skillet over medium heat, stirring occasionally, until the color changes slightly, 5 to 7 minutes. Remove the oats from the skillet and set them aside in a medium bowl. Add the pepitas and sesame seeds to the skillet and toast until they start to change color, about 4 minutes. Add the chia seeds and continue to toast for 1 minute. Add the pepita mixture to the bowl with the oats. Add the cashews, walnuts, candied ginger (if using), cinnamon, and protein powder (if using) to the bowl and stir to combine.

3. In a double boiler over medium-low heat, melt the chocolate chips and coconut oil, stirring until most of the chocolate chips are melted. Take the chocolate mixture off the heat and continue to whisk until it is smooth. Let it sit for 1 minute. Add the peanut butter to the warm chocolate mixture and stir to combine. (It will take a minute to mix in.)

4. Add the oat mixture to the chocolate mixture and mix well.

5. Transfer the snack bar mixture to the loaf pan. Place another piece of parchment paper on top and press the mixture evenly. Chill the mixture for 30 minutes, or until it is fully firm. Then slice it into 10 to 12 bars and serve or store, refrigerated, for up to 2 weeks.

Per serving: Calories 239, Total Fat 15g, Saturated Fat 6g, Sodium 4mg, Total Carbs 23g, Fiber 4g, Sugars 9g, Protein 5g

Nut Butter Blondies

These blondies are a fudgy, nutty treat with just the right amount of chocolate thrown in. They are like a nut butter chocolate chip cookie bar, but fudgier. Nut butters vary in moisture; flours also vary in terms of absorption. The batter may be wet or stiff depending on these two factors, but the blondies should bake fine. If you are feeling festive, make these using fall flavors, such as pumpkin pie spice or gingerbread spices.

Prep time: 5 minutes
Active time: 20 minutes
Inactive time: 24 minutes
soy-free, gluten-free option, nut-free option
Serves 4 to 6

1/4 cup (60ml) plus 2 tablespoons (30ml) nondairy milk

2 tablespoons (30ml) maple syrup

1/2 cup (100g) coconut sugar or other sugar

1 tablespoon ground flax seed

1 1/2 to 2 teaspoons vanilla extract

3/4 cup (195g) smooth almond butter or peanut butter, or use sunbutter to make nut-free

1 cup (120g) whole-wheat flour or unbleached all-purpose flour (or Gluten-Free Flour Blend [page 231] to make gluten-free), divided

1/4 teaspoon salt

1/4 teaspoon baking soda

1/4 teaspoon ground cinnamon, or more to taste

1/2 cup (120g) plus 2 tablespoons (20g) nondairy semisweet chocolate chips, divided

1. Preheat the oven to 350°F (180°C). Line an 8 x 8-inch (20 x 20cm) baking pan with parchment paper, making sure to leave some paper hanging over the edges of the pan. Warm the milk in a small saucepan over medium heat until it is hot (alternatively, heat the milk in a small microwave-safe bowl in the microwave). Transfer the milk to a large bowl. Add the maple syrup, sugar, flax seed, vanilla, and almond butter and stir until smooth. (It will take a minute or so for the nut butter to mix in. If desired, warm the nut butter before adding so it mixes in quickly.)

2. In a small bowl, combine 3/4 cup (90g) of the flour with the salt, baking soda, cinnamon, and 1/2 cup (120g) of the chocolate chips. Add this mixture to the wet mixture and stir to combine. Add the remaining 1/4 cup (30g) flour 1 to 2 tablespoons at a time to make a stiff batter. (Depending on the nut butter and flour used, you may not need all of the flour.)

3. Drop the batter into the baking pan. Spread it out into an even layer using oiled hands or a spatula. Sprinkle the remaining 2 tablespoons (20g) chocolate chips on top and press them into the batter gently. Bake for 22 to 24 minutes, or until a toothpick inserted 1 inch (3cm) from the edge of the pan comes out almost clean. Bake less time for gooey blondies and more time for drier. Cool the blondies for 15 minutes, then remove them from the pan by pulling up on the parchment paper. Cool for another few minutes before slicing. Store on the counter for a few days.

Per single serving at 6 servings: Calories 470, Total Fat 24g, Saturated Fat 5g, Sodium 167mg, Total Carbs 60g, Fiber 9g, Sugars 31g, Protein 12g

Blender Peanut Butter Cake

This is the easiest cake you will ever make. Everything, including the flour, goes in the blender! And it bakes up beautifully, just like a regular cake or sheet cake. This is a simple, moist cake that works as a base for all kinds of creamy frostings. This cake also makes great a birthday cake. Bake it in two cake pans and add the frosting of your choice.

Prep time: 15 minutes
Active time: 15 minutes
Inactive time: 19 to 24 minutes
soy-free, nut-free option
Serves 8

Cake

1 1/2 cups (360ml) nondairy milk

3/4 cup (150g) coconut sugar (plus 2 tablespoons for a sweeter cake, if desired)

2 tablespoons maple syrup

1 1/2 teaspoons vanilla extract

1/2 heaping cup (180g) smooth peanut butter (or sunflower seed butter to make nut-free)

3 tablespoons (45ml) organic safflower or other neutral oil

1 cup (120g) whole-wheat flour or spelt flour plus 1 cup (120g) unbleached all-purpose flour

1/4 to 1/2 teaspoon salt (see note)

2 teaspoons baking powder

1/4 teaspoon baking soda

Glaze

1/2 heaping cup (135g) nondairy semi-sweet chocolate chips

1/4 cup (60g) nondairy dark chocolate chips

2 teaspoons solid refined coconut oil (optional)

1/4 cup (60ml) nondairy milk

2 tablespoons (32g) smooth peanut butter or almond butter

1 tablespoon sugar (optional)

Optional Garnish: Shaved nondairy chocolate, unsweetened cocoa powder, shredded unsweetened coconut

1. Preheat the oven to 350°F (180°C). Grease a 9 x 9-inch (23 x 23cm) brownie pan or a 9 x 13-inch (23 x 33cm) quarter sheet cake pan.

2. Cake: In a blender, combine the milk, sugar, maple syrup, vanilla, peanut butter, and oil and blend until the sugar has dissolved and the mixture is smooth. Add the flour, salt, baking powder, and baking soda and pulse for 2 to 3 seconds to create a smooth batter. (Alternatively, combine the flour, salt, baking powder, and baking soda in a large bowl and add the milk mixture. Stir to make a smooth batter.)

3. Pour the blended batter into the prepared pan. Tap the bottom of the pan against the work surface to even out the batter. Bake for 19 minutes if using a sheet cake pan and 22 to 24 minutes if using a brownie pan, or until a toothpick inserted in the center comes out clean. Cool the cake for 10 minutes, then remove it from the pan and cool it on a wire rack for 15 minutes.

4. Glaze: Combine the semisweet chocolate chips, dark chocolate chips, oil, and milk in a small saucepan over medium-low heat. Stir frequently, until most of the chocolate starts melting. Take the saucepan off the heat and stir until smooth. Add the peanut butter and sugar (if using) to the warm mixture and stir until smooth. (It will take a minute to thoroughly combine.) Pour the glaze over the cake and spread it using a spatula. Garnish with the shaved chocolate, cocoa, or coconut (if using). Cool for 10 minutes.

Note: If the peanut butter is unsalted, add a bit more salt to compensate.

Per serving: Calories 483, Total Fat 26g, Saturated Fat 8g, Sodium 280mg, Total Carbs 58g, Fiber 5g, Sugars 33g, Protein 11g

Peanut Butter Chocolate Marble Cake

1. Preheat the oven to 350°F (180°C). Line a 9 x 5-inch (23 x 13cm) loaf pan with parchment paper. Transfer half the peanut butter batter from the blender to a small bowl. Add 3 tablespoons (21g) unsweetened cocoa powder and 1 tablespoon water to the batter and stir until well combined to make a chocolate batter.

2. Pour half of the chocolate batter into the pan, then half of the peanut butter batter, then the remaining chocolate batter, and then the final layer of the peanut butter batter. Top with 2 to 3 tablespoons (20 to 30g) nondairy semisweet chocolate chips.

3. Bake the cake for 60 minutes, or until a toothpick inserted in the center comes out almost clean. Cool the cake for 15 minutes, then remove it from the pan. Let the cake cool completely before slicing.

Almond Butter Cheesecake Brownie Bars

These bars are a two-in-one dessert. The nut butter cheesecake layer is smooth and creamy and the brownie layer is chocolatey. The serving size makes a loaf pan that helps portion control. The brownies, when baked a bit longer than done, bake up cakey but get fudgy during the chilling time. Double the recipe to make a larger pan or make just the cheesecake layer and bake it into your favorite pie crust.

Prep time: 15 minutes
Active time: 15 minutes
Inactive time: 25 minutes
soy-free, gluten-free option
Serves 6

Brownies

1/4 cup (60ml) **maple syrup**

2 to 3 tablespoons (24 to 36g) **coconut sugar or other sugar**

3 tablespoons (48g) **smooth almond butter**

1/4 cup (60ml) **almond milk or other nondairy milk**

1/2 teaspoon **vanilla extract**

1/4 teaspoon **baking soda**

1 teaspoon **ground flax seed (optional)**

1/2 cup (60g) **oat flour or unbleached all purpose flour**

2 tablespoons (14g) **unsweetened cocoa powder**

Pinch salt

2 to 3 tablespoons (20 to 30g) **nondairy semisweet chocolate chips**

Cheesecake

2/3 cup (160ml) **nondairy yogurt (see note)**

1/4 cup (65g) **smooth almond butter**

1/2 teaspoon **vanilla extract**

2 to 3 teaspoons **fresh lime juice or lemon juice**

1 tablespoon **cornstarch**

1/8 teaspoon **salt**

3 tablespoons (36g) **coconut sugar**

2 tablespoons (20g) **nondairy semi-sweet chocolate chips**

1. Preheat the oven to 350°F (180°C). Grease a 9 x 5-inch (23 x 13cm) loaf pan (or line it with parchment paper).

2. Brownies: In a medium bowl, combine the maple syrup, sugar, almond butter, milk, vanilla, baking soda, flax seed (if using), flour, cocoa, and salt, stirring to combine. Pour the brownie batter into the loaf pan. Sprinkle the top of the batter with the chocolate chips. Bake for 11 to 13 minutes, or until the center is set.

3. Cheesecake: In another medium bowl, combine the yogurt, almond butter, vanilla, lime juice, cornstarch, salt, and sugar. Taste and add more lime juice and sugar if needed (keep in mind that the lime juice will taste stronger after baking).

4. Take the brownies out of the oven and pour the cheesecake mixture over the brownies. Sprinkle the top of the cheesecake with the chocolate chips. Bake for 25 minutes, or until the center of the cheesecake is set. Cool completely and chill for at least 30 minutes. Slice and serve.

Note: I use Kite Hill plain almond yogurt, but vanilla will work as well.

Per serving: Calories 312, Total Fat 15g, Saturated Fat 3g, Sodium 94mg, Total Carbs 41g, Fiber 5g, Sugars 25g, Protein 7g

One-Hour Cinnamon Rolls

These cinnamon rolls use aquafaba to help them retain additional moisture, resulting in soft and amazing rolls. Make them now or make them ahead. If you have time, use the two-rise method to make the rolls even fluffier and softer (see sidebar). Add ground cardamom, chai spice, or nutmeg for variation.

Prep time: 15 minutes
Active time: 45 minutes
Inactive time: 20 minutes
soy-free, nut-free
Serves 9

Cinnamon Rolls

3/4 cup (180ml) 110°F (43°C) water
1/4 cup (60ml) **unsalted aquafaba, room-temperature nondairy yogurt, or 1 1/2 tablespoons ground flax seed combined with 1/4 cup (60ml) full-fat coconut milk**
1 tablespoon **sugar**
1 tablespoon **maple syrup**
1 (0.25-ounce [7g]) packet **active dry yeast or 2 1/2 teaspoons active dry yeast**
2 tablespoons (30ml) **organic safflower or other neutral oil**
2 1/2 cups (300g) **unbleached all-purpose flour or 1 1/2 cups (180g) unbleached all-purpose flour plus 1 cup (120g) whole-wheat flour, divided, or more as needed**
1/4 teaspoon **salt**

Filling

1 to 2 tablespoons **organic safflower oil or melted nondairy butter, or more as needed**
1/3 cup (65g) **coconut sugar or brown sugar, or more to taste**
2 1/2 teaspoons **ground cinnamon**
1/4 teaspoon **salt**

1. Cinnamon Rolls: Line an 8 x 8-inch (20 x 20cm) baking pan or 9-inch (23cm) pie pan with parchment paper. In a large bowl, combine the water, aquafaba, sugar, maple syrup, and yeast, stirring until the sugar has dissolved. Let this mixture sit for 1 minute for the yeast to activate.

2. Add the oil and stir to combine. Add 2 cups (240g) of the flour and salt and knead. Add the remaining 1/2 cup (60g) flour, a few tablespoons at a time, and continue kneading to make a soft, somewhat smooth dough, 4 to 6 minutes. Transfer the dough to a lightly floured work surface. Roll the dough out using additional flour into a 10 x 14-inch (25 x 35cm) rectangle.

3. Filling: Spray or brush the oil on the dough. Sprinkle the sugar, cinnamon, and salt evenly over the oil. Roll the dough tightly along the longer edge to make a cylinder.

4. Using a pizza cutter or kitchen string, slice the dough into 3/4-inch (2cm) thick slices. Place the slices in the baking pan, working from the center of the pan to the edges and being sure not to overcrowd the rolls. Spray or brush additional oil on top of the rolls. Cover them lightly with a towel. Preheat the oven to 350°F (180°C). Let the pan sit near the warming oven for 15 to 25 minutes, or until the cinnamon rolls have almost doubled in size. Remove the towel.

5. Bake the cinnamon rolls for 21 to 23 minutes, or until golden on some edges. Let the rolls sit for a few minutes while you make the simple glaze.

6. Simple Glaze: In a small bowl, combine the confectioners' sugar, cinnamon (if using), and lemon juice or milk. Whisk until the glaze is smooth. Drizzle the glaze immediately on the cinnamon rolls. (If the glaze hardens before you use it all, heat it in the microwave, add a bit more milk, and use.)

Note: When arranging the sliced rolls prior to baking, start from the center of the pan and move outward so the center is not too packed. The center roll takes the longest to cook—overcrowding the center might lead to doughy rolls.

Per serving: Calories 248, Total Fat 5g, Saturated Fat 0.4g, Sodium 171mg, Total Carbs 49g, Fiber 1g, Sugars 24g, Protein 4g

Simple Glaze

1 cup (120g) confectioners' sugar

1/4 teaspoon ground cinnamon (optional)

1 tablespoon fresh lemon juice (optional) or nondairy milk

The Two-Rise Method and Make-Ahead Cinnamon Rolls

Two-Rise Method: After you have kneaded the dough, cover it and let it rise for 1 to 1 1/2 hours, or until it has doubled in size. Lightly punch it down and proceed with the directions.

Make-Ahead Cinnamon Rolls: Make the dough and let it rise for 1 hour. Lightly punch it down to remove excess air and proceed with the directions, but instead of baking the rolls after brushing them with additional oil, cover them with plastic wrap and refrigerate for up to 1 day. Bring to room temperature (about 1 hour), then bake at 350°F (180°C) for 21 to 23 minutes, or until the rolls are golden on some edges.

Richa's Brownies

These brownies are so fudgy and perfect. This recipe works amazingly with most flours and my Gluten-Free Flour Blend (page 231) as well. These brownies go from underdone to done to overdone and chewy really quickly. You want to err on the side of underbaking. I use palm oil–free chocolate in these brownies. (Pictured are the gluten-free version.)

Prep time: 10 minutes
Active time: 15 minutes
Inactive time: 30 to 32 minutes
soy-free, gluten-free option, nut-free option
Makes 9 brownies

Wet Ingredients

1/2 cup (120ml) nondairy milk

3/4 cup (150g) plus 2 tablespoons (24g) raw sugar

2/3 cup (160g) mixture of nondairy dark and semisweet chocolate chips

1/4 cup (60ml) organic safflower or other neutral oil

1 tablespoon ground flaxseed

1/4 cup (22g) unsweetened cocoa powder

1/4 teaspoon fine sea salt

1 teaspoon vanilla extract

Dry Ingredients

1 cup (120g) plus 2 tablespoons (16g) spelt or whole-wheat flour combined with 1 tablespoon cornstarch, or 1 1/4 cups (150g) Gluten-Free Flour Blend (page 231)

1/8 teaspoon baking powder

1/8 teaspoon baking soda

4 tablespoons (40g) nondairy semi-sweet chocolate chips, divided

1. Preheat the oven to 350°F (180°C). Line an 8 x 8-inch (20 x 20cm) baking pan with parchment paper (or grease it well).

2. **Wet Ingredients:** In a medium microwave-safe bowl, heat the milk to almost boiling in the microwave (alternatively, heat the milk in a medium saucepan over medium heat). Add the sugar and whisk until combined. Add the chocolate chips, let the mixture sit for 1 minute, then whisk to melt the chocolate, about 1 minute. Add the oil, flaxseed, cocoa, salt, and vanilla and whisk well.

3. **Dry Ingredients:** In another medium bowl, whisk together the flour, baking powder, and baking soda. Add the flour mixture to the milk mixture, stirring to combine. Add 3 tablespoons (30g) of the chocolate chips. Transfer the batter to the baking pan and spread it out evenly. Add the remaining 1 tablespoon chocolate chips on top.

4. Bake the brownies for 30 to 32 minutes, or until a toothpick inserted 1 inch (3cm) from the side of the pan comes out almost clean. The center should have a dry top but it might be battery underneath. Do not over bake. If a toothpick inserted in the center comes out clean, the brownies are overbaked and might be chewy. If the brownies are overly chewy, crumble them and use them in parfaits, cookies, or ice cream. Store the brownies in an airtight container for 2 days or refrigerated in an airtight container for up to 1 week. Warm and serve.

Variation: Swirl in 1/3 cup (87g) softened peanut butter or almond butter into the batter in the pan before baking. Add some walnuts to the batter.

Per serving: Calories 344, Total Fat 15g, Saturated Fat 6g, Sodium 98mg, Total Carbs 49g, Fiber 4g, Sugars 33g, Protein 4g

Tiramisu Fudge Bars

These fudgy, creamy bars have a vanilla cashew layer with a mascarpone-like tang and a creamy cocoa-coffee layer. They're like tiramisu in ice cream fudge form. Don't like coffee? Just make a vanilla and chocolate version. But make it.

Prep time: 15 minutes
Active time: 20 minutes
Inactive time: 2 hours
soy-free, gluten-free
Serves 6

Mascarpone Cream Filling

3/4 cup (90g) raw cashews, soaked for 1 hour and drained

1/2 cup (120ml) water

3/4 teaspoon apple cider vinegar or distilled white vinegar

1 teaspoon fresh lemon juice

1/4 teaspoon salt

3 tablespoons (36g) sugar or other sweetener, or to taste (see note)

3 tablespoons (45ml) melted refined coconut oil

2 drops vanilla extract

Cocoa-Coffee Layer

2 tablespoons (14g) unsweetened cocoa powder

1/4 cup (30g) oat flour (certified gluten-free if needed)

1/4 cup (30g) raw cashews, soaked for 5 minutes and drained

2 tablespoons (30ml) melted refined coconut oil

1/2 cup (120ml) water

3 tablespoons (36g) sugar or other sweetener (see note)

1/4 teaspoon salt

1/2 teaspoon instant coffee or 2 tablespoons (30ml) brewed coffee (use less water if using brewed coffee)

1 drop almond extract

1 teaspoon rum or Kahlúa (optional)

Shaved chocolate or 2 teaspoons unsweetened cocoa powder

1. Mascarpone Cream Filling: In a blender, combine the cashews, water, vinegar, lemon juice, salt, sugar, oil, and vanilla extract. Blend for 1 minute, let the mixture rest for 2 minutes, then blend again until very smooth and silky. Taste and adjust the seasonings. Transfer the mixture to a medium bowl to chill in the refrigerator.

2. Cocoa-Coffee Layer: In the same blender (no need to wash), combine the cocoa, flour, cashews, oil, water, sugar, salt, coffee, almond extract, and rum (if using). Blend for 1 minute, let the mixture rest for 2 minutes, and blend again until smooth. Taste and adjust the seasonings, adding more coffee or cocoa if desired.

3. Line a 9 x 5-inch (23 x 13cm) loaf pan with parchment paper. Pour the cocoa-coffee mixture in the pan and spread it out evenly. Freeze for 20 to 30 minutes. Pour the mascarpone mixture on top of the cocoa-coffee layer and spread it out evenly. Sprinkle the shaved chocolate on top and freeze for 2 hours or longer. Slice and store or serve after thawing for 5 minutes.

Notes:

If you are using a liquid sweetener, reduce the water by the amount of sweetener used.

To make cashew-free, use macadamia nuts or silken tofu instead of the soaked cashews. Omit the water if using silken tofu.

Per serving: Calories 470, Total Fat 24g, Saturated Fat 5g, Sodium 167mg, Total Carbs 60g, Fiber 9g, Sugars 31g, Protein 12g

One-Bowl Pumpkin Bread

This pumpkin bread needs just one bowl and makes a moist and spicy fall loaf. Use butternut squash or sweet potato puree for variations. Add other spices of your choice. You can also dress it up with a pumpkin-spice sugar glaze or a streusel topping. Be sure to use 100 percent pumpkin, not pumpkin pie mix, which has already been seasoned.

Prep time: 10 minutes
Active time: 15 minutes
Inactive time: 50 to 60 minutes
soy-free, gluten-free option, nut-free option
Serves 8

- 1 cup (120g) unbleached all-purpose flour combined with 3/4 cup (90g) whole-wheat flour
- 1/2 cup (60g) confectioners' sugar (see variation)
- 1/4 cup (50g) brown sugar or finely ground coconut sugar
- 2 1/4 teaspoons baking powder
- 1/4 teaspoon baking soda
- 1/4 teaspoon salt
- 1 tablespoon pumpkin pie spice
- 4 tablespoons (40g) chopped walnuts or pecans (omit to make nut-free)
- 1/4 cup (60g) nondairy mini semisweet chocolate chips or dried cranberries (optional)
- 1 cup (180g) plus 2 tablespoons (23g) pureed pumpkin, sweet potato, or butternut squash (see headnote)
- 1/2 cup (120ml) nondairy milk plus 1 tablespoon, if needed
- 3 tablespoons (45ml) organic safflower or other neutral oil
- 1 tablespoon molasses or maple syrup
- 1 teaspoon fresh lemon juice
- Pepitas or nondairy mini semisweet chocolate chips, for topping (optional)

1. Preheat the oven to 365°F (185°C). Grease a 9 x 5-inch (23 x 13cm) loaf pan (or line it with parchment paper).

2. In a large bowl, whisk together the flour, confectioners' sugar, brown sugar, baking powder, baking soda, salt, and pumpkin pie spice. Add the walnuts and chocolate chips (if using). Add the pureed pumpkin, milk, oil, molasses, and lemon juice and stir to combine well, about 2 minutes. Add the additional milk if needed.

3. Transfer the batter to the loaf pan. Top it with the pepitas (if using). Bake the bread for 50 to 60 minutes, or until a toothpick inserted in the center comes out almost clean. Cool the bread for 15 minutes, then remove it from the pan. Let the bread cool completely before slicing. Store it on the counter for the day or refrigerate it for up to 6 days.

Variations: For a sweeter bread, add an additional 2 tablespoons (16g) confectioners' sugar to the dry ingredients. To make muffins, transfer the batter to lined muffin pan. Bake at 400°F (200°C) for 15 minutes, reduce the temperature to 350°F (180°C) and continue to bake for 6 to 7 minutes or until a toothpick inserted in the center comes out clean.

Note: If you don't have pumpkin pie spice, use a combination of 1 1/2 teaspoons ground cinnamon, 1/2 teaspoon ground ginger, 1/4 teaspoon ground nutmeg, and 1/8 teaspoon ground cloves.

Per serving: Calories 350, Total Fat 15g, Saturated Fat 3g, Sodium 323mg, Total Carbs 53g, Fiber 5g, Sugars 25g, Protein 6g

Gluten-Free Pumpkin Muffins

To make this gluten-free, use 1 3/4 to 2 cups (210 to 240g) Gluten-Free Flour Blend (page 231) and bake into muffins. Preheat the oven to 400°F (200°C). Line a muffin pan with paper liners. Proceed with the directions and fill the muffin pan with the batter. Bake for 15 minutes, reduce the heat to 350°F (180°C), and bake for 6 to 7 minutes longer, or until a toothpick inserted in the center comes out clean.

Gluten-Free Chocolate Chip Cookies

There are many chocolate chip cookie recipes on the web and on my blog: from crunchy to gooey to classic cookies. These cookies use chickpea flour to make them chewy on the edges and soft inside. Chickpea flour has a distinct flavor profile and it gets more pronounced during baking. It can taste bitter or raw depending on how it is used. In this cookie, the maple balances the flavor into a nuttier profile. Loads of chocolate only make it better. I like these chickpea flour cookies with the added almond flour, which adds more structure and texture and makes them more like regular chocolate chip cookies. To make these nut-free, substitute the almond flour with another gluten-free flour or more chickpea flour.

Prep time: 1 hour
Active time: 15 minutes
Inactive time: 12 to 13 minutes
soy-free, gluten-free, nut-free option
Makes 8 large or 12 medium cookies

1 tablespoon ground flax seed
1 1/2 tablespoons water
2 tablespoons (30ml) maple syrup
1 tablespoon molasses (see note)
1/3 cup (65g) raw sugar
1 1/2 teaspoons vanilla extract
1/3 cup (80ml) organic canola, safflower, or extra-virgin olive oil
3/4 cup (68g) plus 1 tablespoon chickpea flour or besan, stirred before
   measuring and divided
1/2 teaspoon baking soda
2 tablespoons 12g) almond flour
Pinch salt
1/3 to 1/2 cup (80 to 120g) nondairy
   semisweet chocolate chips
Coarse salt, to taste (optional)

1. In a medium bowl, combine the flax seed and water. Let this mixture sit for 5 minutes. Add the maple syrup, molasses, sugar, vanilla, and oil and stir until the mixture is well combined. (It will take a minute or two for the oil to incorporate.) Add 3/4 cup (68g) of the chickpea flour, baking soda, almond flour, and salt and stir until the mixture forms a stiff batter. Add the chocolate chips.

2. Refrigerate the cookie dough for at least 1 hour and up to overnight to chill. Check the dough—if it is too sticky or batter-like, add the remaining 1 tablespoon chickpea flour a little at a time.

3. Line a medium baking sheet with parchment paper. Preheat the oven to 350°F (180°C). Scoop the dough out of the bowl using a large spoon and form the dough into 1 1/2-inch (4cm) balls. Place the balls on the baking sheet at least 2 inches (5cm) apart from each other. Sprinkle the coarse salt (if using) over the dough balls for salted chocolate chip cookies. Bake for 12 to 13 minutes, or until the cookies have spread and are starting to turn golden on the edges. Bake 1 minute longer for crunchier cookies.

4. Take the baking sheet out of the oven and slam it on a heat-proof work surface to release the excess air from the cookies. (If the cookies are too thick and did not spread enough during baking, use a fork to flatten them before they cool.) Cool the cookies for 10 minutes, then transfer them to a cooling rack to cool for another few minutes before serving. The cookies are softer when warm and get chewier as they cool.

Note: Molasses can be substituted with 3 tablespoons (45ml) maple syrup. Use brown sugar instead of raw sugar if omitting the molasses.

Per medium cookie: Calories 175g, Total Fat 11g, Saturated Fat 3g, Sodium 58mg, Total Carbs 19g, Fiber 2g, Sugars 14g, Protein 3g

Mango Cupcakes

These mango cupcakes taste like summer in a bite. I top them with a cashew-mango frosting, but any buttercream-style frosting works well. To make them gluten-free, use 1 3/4 cups (210g) Gluten-Free Flour Blend (page 231).

Prep time: 10 minutes
Active time: 15 minutes
Inactive time: 24 to 28 minutes
soy-free, gluten-free option
Makes 12 cupcakes

Dry Ingredients

1 cup (120g) whole-wheat flour or whole-wheat pastry flour
1/2 cup (60g) unbleached all-purpose flour
1 tablespoon cornstarch or arrowroot starch
1 1/2 teaspoons baking powder
1/2 teaspoon baking soda
1/4 teaspoon salt

Wet Ingredients

1 1/4 cups (290g) canned pureed mango or pureed ripe mango
2/3 to 3/4 cup (130 to 150g) sugar
1 teaspoon apple cider vinegar or distilled white vinegar
3 tablespoons (45ml) organic safflower or other neutral oil
1 teaspoon vanilla extract
1/2 teaspoon ground cinnamon
1/4 teaspoon ground turmeric (optional)

Cashew-Mango Frosting

3/4 cup (90g) raw cashews, soaked for 1 hour in warm water and drained
1/3 cup (80ml) melted refined coconut oil
1/3 cup (85g) pureed mango or mango nectar, or more
4 tablespoons (48g) sugar, divided
Pinch salt
Pinch ground cinnamon

1. Preheat the oven to 350°F (180°C). Line a muffin pan with paper or silicone liners.

2. **Dry Ingredients:** In a large bowl, whisk together the whole-wheat flour, all-purpose flour, cornstarch, baking powder, baking soda, and salt.

3. **Wet Ingredients:** In a blender, combine the mango, sugar, vinegar, oil, vanilla, cinnamon, and turmeric and blend until the sugar has dissolved. Add the mango mixture to the flour mixture and stir to combine. Stir for at least 15 seconds so the batter is smooth and has no lumps.

4. Fill the cupcake liners with batter and bake for 24 to 28 minutes. Cool the cupcakes for 10 minutes, then remove them from the muffin pan. Let the cupcakes cool completely.

5. **Cashew-Mango Frosting:** Combine the cashews, oil, mango, 2 tablespoons (24g) of the sugar, salt, and cinnamon. Blend for 1 minute, taste, and add additional mango and the remaining 2 tablespoons (24g) sugar if needed. Let the mixture rest for 2 minutes and blend again for 1 minute. Repeat this process until the frosting is fluffy and creamy. If the frosting is a bit runny, chill it for 15 to 20 minutes before frosting the cooled cupcakes.

Note: If you are using fresh mango, puree roughly chopped ripe mango with approximately 1 tablespoon water to make a smooth puree. Also, the amount of sugar you will need depends on how sweet the mango is. Start with 2/3 cup (130g) and increase it to 3/4 cup (150g) if needed.

Variation: Substitute ground cardamom for the cinnamon in the recipe.

Per serving: Calories 259, Total Fat 13g, Saturated Fat 6g, Sodium 164mg, Total Carbs 34g, Fiber 3g, Sugars 19g, Protein 3g

Orange Cupcakes

These fluffy and moist cupcakes are sweet and citrusy, with wonderfully caramelized tops and edges. I like to make these in a blender to reduce the number of vessels used. Blend, pour, and bake: these cupcakes cannot get any easier.

Prep time: 10 minutes
Active time: 15 minutes
Inactive time: 20 to 22 minutes
soy-free, gluten-free option, nut-free
Makes 12 cupcakes

1 cup (240ml) fresh orange juice
2 tablespoons (30ml) organic safflower or other neutral oil
Zest of 1/2 orange
1/2 cup (100g) raw sugar
1/2 teaspoon vanilla extract
1 1/4 cups (150g) unbleached all-purpose flour (or 1 1/2 cups [180g] Gluten-Free Flour Blend with xanthan gum [page 231] to make gluten-free), plus more if needed
1/4 teaspoon baking soda
2 teaspoons baking powder
1/4 teaspoon salt
1/2 to 3/4 cup (75 to 113g) finely chopped nuts or fresh or dried fruits, plus more for topping (any variety, optional)

1. Preheat the oven to 375°F (190°C). Line a muffin pan with paper or silicone liners. In a blender, combine the orange juice, oil, orange zest, sugar, and vanilla. Blend until thoroughly combined. (Alternatively, combine the ingredients in a large bowl and whisk to combine.)

2. Add the flour, baking soda, baking powder, and salt to the blender and pulse a few times to combine. (Alternatively, combine the dry ingredients in a bowl and whisk well. Add the flour mixture to the orange juice mixture and stir to combine.) The batter should be somewhat thin but not runny. If it is too runny, add more flour, 1 tablespoon at a time, and blend again. Add the dried fruit (if using) and stir gently to combine.

3. Pour the batter into the muffin liners. Top the batter with more dried fruits or nuts (if using). Bake the cupcakes for 20 to 22 minutes. Cool the cupcakes for 5 minutes in the pan, then remove them from the pan and cool a few more minutes before serving. The cupcakes can be kept, covered, on the counter for the day or refrigerated up to 5 days.

Per serving: Calories 107, Total Fat 3g, Saturated Fat 0.2g, Sodium 157g, Total Carbs 20g, Fiber 1g, Sugars 10g, Protein 2g

Orange Cake with Glaze

The Cake: Grease an 8-inch (20cm) round cake pan (or line it with parchment paper). Preheat the oven to 350°F (180°C). Follow the directions for the Orange Cupcakes and pour the batter in the cake pan. Bake for 30 to 35 minutes, or until a toothpick inserted in the center comes out clean.

The Glaze: Combine 2 to 3 tablespoons (30 to 45ml) fresh orange juice (or a combination of fresh orange juice and the liquor of your choice) with 1/3 cup (40g) confectioners' sugar. Stir to combine until the glaze is smooth. (Add additional confectioners' sugar if the glaze is too thin or the orange flavor is too strong). Drizzle the glaze over the cake, slice, and serve.

Per serving: Calories 161, Total Fat 4g, Saturated Fat 0.3g, Sodium 236mg, Total Carbs 30g, Fiber 2g, Sugars 15g, Protein 3g

Lemon Chia Coconut Muffins

These zesty, lemony bites are perfect for breakfast or as a snack. The lemon refreshes, chia fills you up, and the sweet coconut helps satisfy your sweet cravings. There is no added oil in these muffins as they have plenty fat and moisture from the coconut milk. These were a favorite among the recipe testers and their children.

Prep time: 10 minutes
Active time: 15 minutes
Inactive time: 25 minutes
soy-free, gluten-free option, nut-free
Makes 11 to 12 muffins

1 cup (240ml) full-fat coconut milk
Zest of 1 lemon
Juice of 2 lemons
1/4 cup (40g) plus 1 tablespoon chia
    seeds, divided
2/3 cup (133g) raw sugar
1/2 teaspoon ground turmeric
1/2 teaspoon vanilla extract (optional)
1 cup (120g) whole-wheat flour com-
    bined with 1/4 cup (30g) unbleached
    all-purpose flour (or 1 1/2 cups
    [180g] Gluten-Free Flour Blend
    [page 231] to make gluten-free), plus
    more if needed
3 tablespoons (15g) plus 2 tablespoons
    (10g) unsweetened dried shredded
    coconut, divided
1/2 teaspoon baking soda
1 1/2 teaspoons baking powder
1/4 teaspoon salt
Finely chopped dried fruit (any vari-
    ety), nuts (any variety), or candied
    lemon (optional)

1. Heat the coconut milk in a small saucepan over medium heat (alternatively, heat the milk in a small microwave-safe bowl in the microwave). Add the lemon zest, lemon juice, 1/4 cup (40g) chia seeds, and sugar and whisk until the sugar has dissolved. Let the mixture sit for 10 minutes to cool and for the chia seeds to hydrate. (At this point, you can also let the mixture sit overnight for the chia seeds to hydrate even more.)

2. Meanwhile, line a muffin pan with paper or silicone muffin liners. Preheat the oven to 350°F (180°C). In a large bowl, whisk together the flour, coconut, baking soda, baking powder, and salt. Whisk the milk mixture to distribute the chia seeds. Add the milk mixture to the flour mixture and whisk to combine. The batter should be somewhat thin but not runny. If it is too runny, add a few tablespoons more flour and whisk to combine. Add the dried fruit (if using) and stir gently to combine.

3. Fill the muffin liners with batter. Sprinkle the remaining coconut and 1 tablespoon chia seeds on top. Bake the muffins for 24 to 26 minutes. Cool the muffins for 5 minutes in the pan, then remove them and allow them to cool a few more minutes before serving. The muffins can be kept, covered, on the counter for up to 2 days or refrigerated for up to 5 days.

Per serving: Calories 165, Total Fat 6g, Saturated Fat 5g, Sodium 185mg, Total Carbs 26g, Fiber 3g, Sugars 13g, Protein 3g

Marble Pumpkin Chocolate Loaf

This loaf is moist and gorgeous. It is basically a marbled pumpkin loaf. With the added turmeric, the pumpkin layer is a beautiful deep yellow. (You can leave it out if you are not fond of turmeric.) This bread is also a great treat for Halloween. Tiger stripes for breakfast, anyone?

Prep time: 10 minutes
Active time: 15 minutes
Inactive time: 55 to 60 minutes
soy-free, nut-free
Serves 6

- 1 1/4 cups (300g) **pureed pumpkin, sweet potato, or butternut squash (see note)**
- 1/4 cup (60ml) **maple syrup**
- 1/2 cup (120ml) **nondairy milk, plus more as needed**
- 3 tablespoons (45ml) **organic safflower or other neutral oil**
- 1 teaspoon **fresh lime juice or lemon juice**
- 1/2 cup (100g) **raw sugar (see variation)**
- 1 1/2 cups (180g) **unbleached all-purpose flour combined with 1/4 cup (30g) whole-wheat flour and 1/4 cup (28g) almond flour**
- 2 1/2 teaspoons **baking powder**
- 1/4 teaspoon **baking soda**
- 1/4 teaspoon **salt**
- 3 teaspoons **pumpkin pie spice**
- 1 teaspoon **ground turmeric**
- 2 tablespoons (30ml) plus 1 teaspoon **warm water, divided**
- 3 tablespoons (21g) **unsweetened cocoa powder**
- 1/2 teaspoon **vanilla extract**
- 2 tablespoons (20g) **nondairy semi-sweet chocolate chips or chopped nuts (optional)**

1. Preheat the oven to 365°F (185°C). Grease a 9 x 5-inch (23 x 13cm) loaf pan (or line it with parchment paper).

2. In a medium bowl, combine the pumpkin, maple syrup, milk, oil, lime juice, and sugar and stir until the sugar is well combined.

3. In another medium bowl, combine the flour, baking powder, baking soda, salt, and pumpkin pie spice. Add the flour mixture to the pumpkin mixture and stir until well combined. The batter should be thick, a bit like muffin batter. Add more flour if it is flowy like cake batter and more milk if it is stiff. Divide the batter between 2 medium bowls.

4. To one bowl, add the turmeric and 1 teaspoon of the water and stir to combine. To the other bowl, add the cocoa, vanilla, and the remaining 2 tablespoons (30ml) of water and stir to combine.

5. Add half of the chocolate batter to the loaf pan and even it out with a spatula. Add half of the pumpkin batter and spread it out evenly. Repeat this process for the next two layers. (Alternatively, make just two layers, using all the chocolate batter for one and all the turmeric batter for the other.) Sprinkle the chocolate chips (if using) on top of the batter.

6. Bake the loaf for 55 to 60 minutes, or until a toothpick inserted in the center comes out almost clean. (Depending on the pureed pumpkin, pan, and oven, you might have to bake longer than the recommended time.) Let the loaf cool completely before slicing. Store on the counter for the day and refrigerate for up to 4 days.

Notes: Be sure to use 100 percent pumpkin, not pumpkin pie mix, which has already been seasoned. If you don't have pumpkin pie spice, use a combination of 1 1/2 teaspoons ground cinnamon, 1/2 teaspoon ground ginger, 1/4 teaspoon ground nutmeg, and 1/8 teaspoon ground cloves.

Variation: If you prefer a sweeter bread, add 2 tablespoons (24g) more raw sugar to the wet ingredients.

Per serving: Calories 335, Total Fat 8g, Saturated Fat 1g, Sodium 294mg, Total Carbs 64g, Fiber 6g, Sugars 27g, Protein 5g

Sweet Potato Chocolate Pie

This pie is so versatile. Fill the tasty no-bake crust (of which there are two equally delicious versions—the No-Bake Oat Crust with this recipe and the chocolate coconut crust on page 197) with the creamy, chocolatey filling to make a pie. Or place the filling in individual serving bowls and top it with some coconut whipped cream to create pudding parfaits. Finally, the filling can also be used as a delicious cake frosting. Keep in mind that this is a dark chocolate sweet potato pie. Use all semisweet chocolate (and reduce the amount of raw sugar) for a less bitter profile.

Prep time: 5 minutes + No-Bake Oat Crust
Active time: 12 minutes
Inactive time: 2 to 3 hours
soy-free, gluten-free, nut-free
Serves 10

1/4 cup (60ml) full-fat coconut milk or other nondairy milk

1 1/2 tablespoons (14g) cornstarch or arrowroot starch

1 1/2 cups (360g) pureed sweet potato or pumpkin puree

1/4 cup (50g) coconut sugar or finely ground raw sugar

1 teaspoon pumpkin pie spice

3 ounces (85g) nondairy 70% dark chocolate

1/2 cup (120g) nondairy semisweet chocolate chips

2 teaspoons vanilla extract (see variation)

1 recipe No-Bake Oat Crust (opposite)

1. Combine the milk and cornstarch in a medium saucepan over medium heat. Add the sweet potato, sugar, and pumpkin pie spice. Bring to a boil, stirring occasionally, 5 to 7 minutes. Turn off the heat. Add the dark chocolate and semisweet chocolate chips and let the mixture sit for 2 minutes. Stir until the chocolate is melted and the mixture is smooth.

2. Add the vanilla and stir to combine. Taste and adjust the seasonings. Pour the filling into the crust. Spread it out evenly using a spatula. Chill the pie 2 to 3 hours and serve. For clean-edged slices, chill the pie in the freezer for 30 minutes, then slice. Serve as is or with whipped coconut cream or a drizzle of salted caramel.

Note: If you don't have pumpkin pie spice, use a combination of 1 1/2 teaspoons ground cinnamon, 1/2 teaspoon ground ginger, 1/4 teaspoon ground nutmeg, and 1/8 teaspoon ground cloves.

Variation: Add 2 to 3 tablespoons (30 to 45ml) liquor of your choice when you add the vanilla extract.

No-Bake Oat Crust

2 1/4 cups (270g) oat flour (certified gluten-free if needed), plus more as needed

1/3 cup (65g) coconut sugar or finely ground raw sugar

Pinch salt

2 tablespoons (30ml) melted coconut oil or 1 tablespoon nondairy milk

1 tablespoon vanilla extract

1/3 cup (80ml) maple syrup, plus more as needed

1. In a medium bowl, combine the oat flour, sugar, salt, and oil and mix well. Add the vanilla and maple syrup and combine using your hands. The dough will come together by pressing and mixing for 1 to 2 minutes.

2. Add more flour or maple syrup as needed to help the crust hold together. Use your hands to press the dough together. Taste and adjust the seasonings. Press the dough into a 9-inch (23cm) pie pan that has been greased or lined with parchment paper.

Variation: To make a cookie dough crust, add 1/3 cup (80g) mini semisweet chocolate chips or finely chopped dark chocolate into the crust mixture once it has started to come together and use your hands to gently combine.

Per serving: Calories 360, Total Fat 13g, Saturated Fat 8g, Sodium 18mg, Total Carbs 57g, Fiber 6g, Sugars 29g, Protein 6g

10
Everyday Basics

This chapter features some of the basic ingredients called for in this book, such as seasoning blends, a gluten-free flour blend, pizza dough (regular and gluten-free), condiments, and even vegan Parmesan.

While many of the following recipes can be made easily at home, they can also be time-consuming, so plan ahead when making the recipes from this chapter.

If you are in a pinch for time, several of the items in this chapter have commercially made counterparts. If you don't have time to make them at home, feel free to purchase them. But just re-member that nothing is as satisfying as making your own food!

Chickpea Flour Tofu (page 238)

Easy Pizza Dough

This is the twenty-minute basic pizza dough that works for thin-crust or deep-dish pizzas (for deep-dish pizza, see instructions opposite). The dough just needs to come together to be a somewhat even ball. As the dough sits for fifteen minutes, it will smooth out further. Keep the dough on the softer side (i.e., slightly sticky), as softer dough can be shaped more easily and also rises well during baking. It comes out great and once you get a feel of how the dough feels and works, you can play around with other flours and reduce the time needed to prepare it. Be aware that this dough will double during baking, so roll it out fairly thin (thicker crust will yield a bready result after baking). For my Gluten-Free Pizza Crust, see page 232.

Prep time: 10 minutes
Active time: 30 minutes
Inactive time: 15 minutes
soy-free, nut-free
Serves 6 to 8
Makes 2 (12- to 14-inch [30 to 35cm])
thin-crust pizzas or 2 (8- to 9-inch
[20 to 23cm]) deep-dish pizzas

1 1/4 cups (300ml) **warm water**

1 tablespoon **active dry yeast**

1/2 teaspoon **sugar or sweetener of**
choice

2 1/2 cups (300g) **or more unbleached**
all-purpose flour, divided

3 teaspoons **extra-virgin olive oil,**
divided

1/3 cup (40g) **semolina flour or finely**
ground cornmeal combined with 3/4
teaspoon salt

1. Preheat the oven to 425°F (220°C). In a large bowl, combine the water, yeast, and sugar. Let the mixture sit for a few minutes to activate and get frothy.

2. Add 2 cups (240g) of the all-purpose flour and 2 teaspoons of the oil. Add the semolina flour mixture and stir the dough with a large spoon or spatula until well combined. Add the remaining 1/2 cup (60g) flour, 1/4 cup (30g) at a time, stirring to combine. Now, use your hands to mix and knead the dough for a few seconds to create a soft, slightly sticky dough. Add another tablespoon flour if needed. Gather the dough into a ball and let it sit for 15 to 20 minutes in a warm place or near the warming oven.

3. Drizzle the remaining 1 teaspoon oil over the risen dough and spread all over. Shape the dough into a ball. Divide it into 2 equal parts and shape each one into a smooth ball. Place 1 ball on a medium baking sheet lined with parchment paper.

4. Lightly flour the dough and use your hands to spread the dough into a 12- to 14-inch (30 to 35cm) oval. (Alternatively, roll out the dough using a rolling pin.) Keep the edges thicker than the center. Repeat this process with the other dough ball. Let the crusts sit for 5 to 10 minutes. Meanwhile, add your desired sauces and toppings.

5. Bake the crusts for 17 to 20 minutes, depending on their size and thickness. Bake longer for thicker crusts. Cool for 1 minute, slice, and serve.

Per serving: Calories 188, Total Fat 2g, Saturated Fat 0g, Sodium 224mg, Total Carbs 36g, Fiber 2g, Sugars 0.3g, Protein 6g

Dough for Deep-Dish Pizza

Follow steps 1 and 2. Once the dough has sat for 15 minutes, drizzle the oil over the pizza dough and spread it over the dough. Punch the dough down. Divide it into 2 equal pieces using a pizza cutter. Shape each into a somewhat smooth ball. Flour the work surface. Using your hands or a rolling pin and flour as needed, shape the dough into an 11-inch (28cm) diameter circle. Repeat this process with the second ball of dough. Place the rolled-out dough in the pans, making sure to pull some of the dough above the pans' edges. (Keep the bottoms thick; otherwise, the pizzas might not support the heavy toppings.) Put the crusts in the oven and bake for 5 minutes. Remove the crusts from the oven.

Add fillings and sauces of choice. Bake for 25 to 30 minutes depending on the size and fillings. Cover the edges of the pizza with foil or parchment in the last 10 minutes of baking if the edges are browning too much. Cool for 5 minutes before slicing.

Variation: For an herbed crust, mix 1 teaspoon Quick Italian Herb Blend (page 163) and 1/2 teaspoon garlic powder into the semolina flour. For a whole-grain crust, use half whole-wheat or white whole-wheat flour with half unbleached all-purpose flour. To omit the semolina flour, substitute it with 1/3 cup (40g) unbleached all-purpose flour. The result will be a softer, airier crust.

Gluten-Free Flour Blend

I use this blend for muffins, blondies, brownies, and cookies. Oat and coconut flours keep the baked results soft and moist. This blend was tested with the recipes in the book wherever it is mentioned as an option. Generally, it is a one-for-one substitute. Depending on the recipe, you might need a few tablespoons more of the blend than of wheat flour.

Prep time: 5 minutes
soy free, gluten-free
Makes 1 3/4 cups (210g) flour

1/2 cup (55g) **almond flour**
3/4 cup (90g) **oat flour (certified gluten-free if needed), sorghum flour, or rice flour**
2 tablespoons (22g) **tapioca starch**
3 tablespoons (33g) **potato starch or cornstarch**
2 tablespoons (15g) **coconut flour (see note)**
1/2 teaspoon **xanthan gum (optional, see note)**

In a medium airtight container, combine the almond flour, oat flour, tapioca starch, potato starch, coconut flour, and xanthan gum (if using).

Note: Coconut flour can be subbed with rice flour if you will be using the flour blend for cookies. Use the xanthan gum if you will be using this blend for muffins.

Per 1 3/4 cups: Calories 892, Total Fat 36g, Saturated Fat 5g, Sodium 41mg, Total Carbs 123g, Fiber 20g, Sugars 4g, Protein 25g

Gluten-Free Pizza Crust

This pizza crust comes together quickly. It uses a batter to make the crust rather than a dough. The crust comes out thin on a baking sheet, but it is sturdy and holds heavy toppings well.

Prep time: 10 minutes
Active time: 15 minutes
soy-free, gluten-free
Serves 4 to 6
Makes 2 (11-inch [28cm]) thin-crust pizzas or 2 (9-inch [23cm]) small thick-crust pizzas

---

3/4 cup (180ml) warm water, divided

1 1/2 teaspoons active dry yeast

Pinch raw sugar or 1/8 teaspoon sweetener of choice

1/2 cup (80g) white rice flour, plus more if needed

1/2 cup (55g) super-fine almond flour

1/2 cup (60g) tapioca starch

1/2 teaspoon baking powder

1/4 teaspoon garlic powder

1/4 teaspoon dried thyme or oregano

1/2 teaspoon salt

2 teaspoons extra-virgin olive oil

1. In a large bowl, whisk together 1/2 cup (120ml) of the water, yeast, and sugar. Let this mixture sit for 2 minutes.

2. In a medium bowl, whisk together the rice flour, almond flour, tapioca starch, baking powder, garlic powder, thyme, and salt. Add the flour mixture to the water mixture and whisk well. Add the oil and the remaining 1/4 cup (60ml) water and whisk into a thick batter. Cover the bowl and let the batter sit for 30 minutes.

3. Line 2 medium baking sheets with parchment paper. If the batter is too runny, mix in a few teaspoons rice flour. Using a ladle, pour half of the batter onto the parchment. Using the ladle or a large spoon, spread the batter out using a circular motion, working from the center of the batter to the outside. Repeat this process with the other half of the batter on the second baking sheet.

4. Preheat the oven to 400°F (200°C). Let the baking sheets sit near the warming oven for 10 minutes. Bake the crust for 10 minutes.

5. Add the sauces and toppings of your choice and bake the pizzas at 400°F (200°C) or 425°F (220°C) (depending on the pizza toppings, as higher heat is often required for nondairy cheese to melt) for 6 to 7 minutes. Cool for 1 minute, slice, and serve.

Per serving: Calories 230, Total Fat 10g, Saturated Fat 1g, Sodium 360mg, Total Carbs 33g, Fiber 3g, Sugars 1g, Protein 5g

Vegan Parmesan

There are several vegan Parmesan recipes on the web. Use your favorite or make this. The optional additions make a deeply flavored Parmesan.

Active time: 5 minutes
soy-free, gluten-free, nut-free option
Makes about 1/2 cup (70g)

1/3 cup (40g) raw cashews, almonds, pepitas, pecans, or walnuts
1 to 2 tablespoons nutritional yeast
1/4 teaspoon dried thyme
1/4 teaspoon dried rosemary
Dash black pepper
Pinch garlic powder
Salt, to taste
1/4 teaspoon ground mustard (optional)
Pinch fresh lime zest (optional)

In a food processor, combine the cashews, nutritional yeast, thyme, rosemary, pepper, garlic powder, salt, mustard (if using), and lime zest (if using). Pulse in 2- to 3-second intervals until the mixture forms a fine meal. Taste and adjust the seasonings. Store the Parmesan in an airtight container in the refrigerator for up to 1 month.

Per 2 tablespoons: Calories 75, Total Fat 5g, Saturated Fat 1g, Sodium 42mg, Total Carbs 5g, Fiber 1g, Sugars 0g, Protein 4g

Whole-Grain Rolls

These rolls use a tangzhong starter, which is is a roux made with flour and water that is added to yeast-bread recipes for additional moisture and softer results. These can be made with 100 percent whole-grain flour or a combination of flours. Buns are more flexible than a whole loaf as they don't have to hold an entire loaf's dome.

Prep time: 15 minutes
Active time: 25 minutes
Inactive time: 1 1/2 hours rising time + 40 minutes baking time
soy-free, nut-free
Makes 12 rolls

Tangzhong
1/4 scant cup (30g) whole-wheat flour
1/2 cup (120ml) water

Sponge
1 cup (120g) whole-wheat flour
1 cup (240ml) warm water (see variation)
2 1/2 tablespoons (38ml) maple syrup or other sweetener of choice
1 tablespoon active dry yeast

Rolls
2 cups (240g) whole-wheat flour or 1 cup (120g) whole-wheat flour combined with 1 cup (120g) whole-spelt flour, plus more if needed
1 teaspoon salt
3 tablespoons (45ml) extra-virgin olive oil
1 teaspoon fresh lemon juice
1/4 teaspoon almond extract (optional)
Extra-virgin olive oil or melted non-dairy butter, for brushing

1. Tangzhong: In a small saucepan over medium heat, combine the flour and water. Cook until the mixture is gel-like—smooth and slightly shiny—stirring frequently. Set aside.

2. Sponge: In a large bowl, combine the flour, water, maple syrup, and yeast. Stir with a large spoon for 2 minutes, until the batter is very smooth and the gluten is starting to develop. Let the bowl sit, covered, for 1 hour in a warm place. In a stand mixer, combine the sponge and tangzhong.

3. Rolls: Combine the flour and salt in a medium bowl. Add this mixture to the stand mixer. Start kneading (I knead at setting 2 on my KitchenAid stand mixer). Add the oil, lemon juice, and almond extract (if using) and continue kneading for 5 minutes. Let the dough rest for 2 minutes. Check the dough to see if it needs more flour or water (it should be soft and smooth, not stiff and not sticky). Add more flour, 1 tablespoon at a time, if needed.

4. Knead for another 5 to 7 minutes. The dough should not break immediately when a small portion is pulled out. You can let the dough rest for 15 to 20 minutes at this point. Divide the dough into 12 equal balls. Flatten each ball into an oval, then roll it up like a jelly roll (see variation). Place the dough seam-side down in a 9 x 9-inch (23 x 23cm) baking pan. Repeat this process for all the dough balls. Brush oil on top of the rolls.

5. If you are making these rolls ahead, they can be refrigerated or frozen until you are ready to use them. To refrigerate them, cover the pan with plastic wrap and refrigerate overnight. Let the pan sit on the counter for 1 hour before baking. To freeze them, let the rolls rise for 15 minutes before freezing the pan. Freeze the pan in a large zip-top plastic bag or wrapped in plastic wrap. Thaw the rolls and let them rise for 1 to 1 1/2 hours before baking. If you are not making the rolls ahead, cover the pan with a towel and let the rolls rise for 25 to 40 minutes, or until the rolls double in size.

6. Preheat the oven to 375°F (190°C). Bake the rolls for 20 to 22 minutes. Remove the pan from the oven and brush more oil on top of the rolls. Remove the rolls from the pan after 10 minutes. Wait for another 5 minutes before serving the warm rolls with olive oil or nondairy butter or as a side with anything. Store leftover rolls in a bread container on the counter for up to 2 days or refrigerate them for up to 1 week.

Variation: When making the sponge, substitute the water with 1/4 cup

(60ml) aquafaba combined with 3/4 cup (180ml) water. To make burger buns, shape the rolls into an oval, then lightly roll them into balls. Place the buns at least 2 inches (5cm) apart on a large baking sheet lined with parchment paper. Proceed with the directions.

Per serving: Calories 155, Total Fat 4g, Saturated Fat 2g, Sodium 106mg, Total Carbs 26g, Fiber 4g, Sugars 3g, Protein 5g

Wheat Flatbread

This is a simple flatbread or tortilla to serve with curries and soups or to make tacos or wraps. I use boiling water to keep these soft. Make a bunch and freeze them for future use. For a gluten-free version, see page 237.

Prep time: 10 minutes
Active time: 35 minutes
Inactive time: 30 minutes
soy-free, nut-free
Serves 4

1 cup (120g) whole-wheat flour
1 cup (120g) unbleached all-purpose flour, plus more as needed
1 tablespoon organic safflower or other neutral oil, plus more as needed
1/2 teaspoon salt
1 cup (240ml) boiling water, divided
Melted nondairy butter or extra-virgin olive oil, as needed

1. In a medium bowl, combine the whole-wheat flour, all-purpose flour, oil, and salt. (Mix the oil into the flour using a spoon or your hands to distribute it evenly.) Add 1/2 cup (120ml) of the water and stir to combine. Add the remaining 1/2 cup (120ml) water, 2 tablespoons (30ml) at a time, and stir to combine.

2. As soon as the mixture starts to stick together but is still a bit floury, use your hands or a large spoon to press it together a couple of times to form a dough. Once the dough comes together (it does not need to be very smooth), even it out, brush it with butter, and let it sit, covered, for 1 hour.

3. Lightly flour a work surface and knead the dough until it is smooth, 2 to 3 minutes. Divide the dough into 8 to 9 smooth balls, using some flour if the dough is too sticky. Lightly flour the work surface again and roll each ball out into a 7-inch (18cm) circle.

4. Heat a medium skillet over medium-high heat. Add a flatbread and cook for 1 to 2 minutes. Flip and cook the other side of the flatbread for 1 to 2 minutes. Brush the flatbread lightly with butter and continue to cook until both sides have a few golden-brown spots. (Alternatively, you can cook the flatbread over a direct flame. Place the flatbread over a direct gas flame. Move and flip the flatbread to cook on the flame until some brown spots appear, 5 to 10 seconds at a time.) Brush the flatbread with more butter and store it wrapped in a kitchen towel for the day (see note). Repeat this process for all the flatbreads. To reheat, fold the flatbreads in a paper towel and microwave for 10 seconds. Alternatively, reheat them in a skillet or over a direct flame.

Note: Flatbreads can be made ahead and stored in the refrigerator for up to 4 days. They can also be frozen in an airtight container (uncooked or cooked) for months. I prefer uncooked frozen flatbreads to make fresh flatbreads when needed.

Per serving: Calories 245, Total Fat 5g, Saturated Fat 1g, Sodium 298mg, Total Carbs 45g, Fiber 4g, Sugars 1g, Protein 7g

Gluten-Free Flatbread

These sturdy gluten-free flatbreads are perfect to use as tortillas, to make wraps, and to use with burgers. They don't crack or break easily. These flatbreads puff easily on a gas flame and can be used like pita breads. Powder the psyllium husk by processing it in a blender, and use any gluten-free flour that you prefer.

Prep time: 5 minutes
Active time: 30 minutes
soy-free, gluten-free, nut-free
Serves 4

2 tablespoons (16g) powdered psyllium husk

3/4 cup (180ml) hot water

1/2 cup (60g) buckwheat flour, amaranth flour, sorghum flour, or chickpea flour, plus more if needed

2 tablespoons (18g) cornstarch or tapioca starch

1/4 teaspoon baking powder

1/4 teaspoon salt

1/2 teaspoon herbs of choice (optional)

1/4 teaspoon garlic powder (optional)

1 teaspoon organic safflower or other neutral oil, plus more for brushing

Rice flour, for dusting

1. In a medium bowl, combine the psyllium husk and water. Let this mixture sit for 2 minutes. The mixture will become a gel.

2. In another medium bowl, whisk together the flour, cornstarch, baking powder, salt, herbs (if using), and garlic powder (if using). Add the flour mixture to the psyllium husk mixture. Add the oil and stir until well combined. Using your hands, press the flour into the gel. It will take about 30 seconds for the dough to start coming together. It may seem too dry in the beginning. Mix and knead until the dough is well formed.

3. If the dough starts to get very sticky, add more flour, 1 tablespoon at a time, until a soft, slightly sticky dough is formed. Spray or brush oil on the dough ball. Let the dough sit, covered, for 5 to 10 minutes.

4. Divide the dough into 7 to 8 equal balls. Lightly dust the balls with rice flour and roll them between your palms to create a smooth surface on the balls. Generously dust a work surface with rice flour to roll the balls out into 6- to 7-inch (15- to 18cm) flatbreads.

5. Heat a medium skillet over medium-high heat. Dust the excess flour off a flatbread and place it in the skillet. Cook for 30 to 45 seconds, or until small bubbles start to appear. Flip and cook the other side until the bubbles start to get bigger. At this point, you can continue to cook it in the skillet until both sides have golden spots. Alternatively, you can place the flatbread over a gas flame. Move it every 2 to 4 seconds to puff and brown. Brush oil over the flatbread. Cover the flatbread and set aside. Repeat this process for all the flatbreads. Store the flatbreads on the counter for the day or refrigerated for up to 3 days.

Per serving: Calories 92, Total Fat 2g, Saturated Fat 0g, Sodium 180mg, Total Carbs 18g, Fiber 4g, Sugars 0g, Protein 2g

Chickpea Flour Tofu

This chickpea flour tofu is a good substitute for soy tofu. It works well in stir-fries, sauces, and curries. Toss the chickpea flour cubes in 1 tablespoon cornstarch before adding them to stir-fries or making my Crisped Tofu (page 243). For dishes that require longer cooking times, add the chickpea tofu later in the recipe.

Prep time: 5 minutes
Active time: 10 minutes
soy-free, gluten-free, nut-free
Serves 4

1 cup (90g) chickpea flour or 1 1/4 cups (113g) besan
1/2 to 3/4 teaspoon salt
1/4 teaspoon garlic powder
1/4 teaspoon ground turmeric (optional)
1/4 teaspoon ground cumin or Garam Masala (page 244, optional)
1 3/4 cups (420ml) water (see variation)

Variation: Use vegetable stock instead of water. Add 1 tablespoon nutritional yeast for a cheesy flavor or 1 teaspoon additional herbs or spices of your choice.

1. Grease a 9 x 5-inch (23 x 13cm) loaf pan (or line it with parchment paper) and set aside. In a medium bowl, whisk together the chickpea flour, salt, garlic powder, turmeric (if using), cumin (if using), and water until there are no lumps, or, alternatively, you can combine the ingredients in a blender and process until smooth. Pour the chickpea flour mixture into a deep saucepan over medium heat and cook, stirring continuously, 4 to 5 minutes. The mixture will start to get lumpy as the saucepan heats up and then thicken evenly and considerably.

2. Once the mixture is evenly thick and stiff, keep cooking for another 2 to 3 minutes so the chickpea flour gets cooked through. Be sure to occasionally tap the spoon or spatula to return any of the mixture stuck on it to the saucepan. If the mixture is starting to brown, reduce the heat to medium-low. Carefully taste the mixture to ensure that there is no raw chickpea flour flavor and adjust the seasonings if needed.

3. Pour the mixture into the prepared loaf pan and even it out using a spatula. Let it cool, then refrigerate it for at least 1 hour to set. Remove the set slab from the pan. Slice into cubes. Store the tofu in an airtight container in the refrigerator for up to 4 days. The tofu can leak some moisture while it sits; if so, drain it and use.

Per serving: Calories 111, Total Fat 2g, Saturated Fat 0g, Sodium 447mg, Total Carbs 18g, Fiber 5g, Sugars 3g, Protein 6g

Samosa Potatoes

These should be your all-purpose mashed potatoes. Serve as a side with a chutney of your choice. Make patties of the potatoes, coat them in panko, pan-fry the patties, and serve them with sauces or chutneys. Make pinwheels by rolling the potatoes in a large tortilla, baking it for 12 to 14 minutes, and serving it with Tamarind Chutney (page 240). Finally, stuff them into puff pastry sheets, seal the sheets, and bake them until they are golden for snack samosa puffs. Use whatever spices you have and adjust the flavors to your preference.

Prep time: 10 minutes + boiling time
Active time: 15 minutes
soy-free, gluten-free, nut-free
Serves 4

- 2 large or 3 medium Yukon gold or white potatoes, scrubbed
- 1 to 1 1/2 teaspoons ground roasted cumin
- 1 1/2 to 2 teaspoons ground coriander
- 1/2 teaspoon cayenne
- 3/4 teaspoon salt, or more to taste
- 1/4 to 1/2 teaspoon ground turmeric
- 1/2 teaspoon garlic powder
- 1/2 teaspoon amchur (dried mango powder) or 1/2 teaspoon chaat masala
- 1/2 teaspoon chaat masala or 1/8 teaspoon kala namak (Indian sulphur black salt), or to taste
- 1 teaspoon organic safflower or other neutral oil
- 1/4 teaspoon coarsely crushed or whole cumin seeds
- 1/2 teaspoon coarsely crushed or whole coriander seeds
- 3/4 cup (115g) fresh or thawed frozen green peas (optional)
- 3 tablespoons (9g) chopped fresh mint
- 2 tablespoons (6g) chopped fresh cilantro
- 1 teaspoon fresh lemon juice
- 1 (1/2-inch [1cm]) knob fresh ginger, peeled and coarsely chopped

1. If you will be pressure-cooking the potatoes, cut them in half and add them to a pressure cooker or Instant Pot with enough water to cover them. Cook on high pressure manual for 5 minutes. Let the pressure release naturally.

2. If you will be boiling the potatoes, peel and quarter the potatoes. Add them to a medium saucepan and cover them by at least 1 inch (3cm) of cold water. Turn on the heat to high and bring the water to a boil. Reduce the heat to low to maintain a simmer and cover the saucepan. Cook for 15 to 20 minutes, or until the potatoes are easily pierced with a fork.

3. Drain the potatoes and transfer them to a medium bowl. Mash the potatoes really well. Add the ground cumin, ground coriander, cayenne, salt, turmeric, garlic powder, dried mango powder, and chaat masala and stir to combine. Heat the oil in a medium skillet over medium heat. Add the cumin seeds and coriander seeds and cook for 1 minute, or until they change color. Add the peas (if using) and a pinch salt and cook for 2 minutes. Add this mixture to the potato mixture.

4. Pulse the mint, cilantro, lemon juice, and ginger in a small blender. (Alternatively, put the mint and cilantro in a small bowl. Add the lemon juice. Mince the ginger and add it to the mint mixture, stirring to combine.) Add the mint mixture to the potato mixture and stir to combine. Taste and adjust the seasonings if needed.

Variation: To make Quick Samosa Pinwheels, press some of the samosa-potato mixture onto a large tortilla and drizzle with tamarind chutney. Roll up the tortilla, slice, and serve.

Per serving: Calories 175, Total Fat 1.8g, Saturated Fat 0g, Sodium 470mg, Total Carbs 35g, Fiber 5.7g, Sugars 3g, Protein 6g

Tamarind Chutney

This is a super quick chutney to use with the Samosa Sliders with Tamarind Chutney and Mango (page 108) or with Samosa Potatoes (page 239). And, of course, this is a wonderful dip for the Zucchini, Carrot, and Chickpea Fritters (page 185) and Baked Vegetable Pakoras (page 181).

Prep time: 10 minutes
Active time: 10 minutes
soy-free, gluten-free, nut-free
Makes about 1/2 cup (120ml)

2 tablespoons (32g) tamarind paste or
    concentrate
1/4 cup (60ml) maple syrup or agave
2 tablespoons (16g) confectioners'
    sugar
1/4 teaspoon salt, or more to taste
1/2 teaspoon roasted ground cumin
1/2 teaspoon cayenne
1/2 teaspoon chaat masala or 1/8 tea-
    spoon kala namak (Indian sulphur
    black salt)
1/4 cup (60ml) water
Fresh lemon juice (optional)

In a medium saucepan over medium heat, combine the tamarind paste, maple syrup, confectioners' sugar, salt, cumin, cayenne, chaat masala, and water. Bring to a boil. Carefully taste and adjust the seasonings, adding some lemon juice for additional tang, if needed. Remove the saucepan from the heat, let the chutney cool, then transfer it to an airtight container and refrigerate for up to 1 week.

Variation: Add the paste of 4 soaked dates to the saucepan with the other ingredients and proceed with the directions.

Per 2 tablespoons: Calories 85, Total Fat 0g, Saturated Fat 0g, Sodium 250mg, Total Carbs 22g, Fiber 0g, Sugars 20g, Protein 0g

Barbecue Sauce

I like this barbecue sauce for the deep flavor, which is not overly sweet or dominated by the ketchup. This recipe seems to call for a lot of ingredients, but many are just spices to add the complex flavor. It benefits from chilling for a few hours for the flavors to meld well and get stronger. Use with the Quinoa Carrot Barbecue Burgers (page 113), the Barbecue Pizza with Jerk Beans and Vegetables (page 160), or the Buddha Bowl with Nacho-Spiced Sweet Potatoes (page 136).

Prep time: 10 minutes
Active time: 10 minutes
soy-free option, gluten-free, nut-free
Makes 2/3 cup (160ml)

1/4 cup (60ml) **maple syrup**

1/4 cup (60ml) **ketchup or 3 table-spoons (48g) tomato paste**

2 teaspoons **molasses**

1 tablespoon plus 1 teaspoon **dis-tilled white vinegar or apple cider vinegar**

1/2 teaspoon **fresh lemon juice**

1 teaspoon **tamarind paste or 2 tea-spoons vegan Worcestershire sauce (see note)**

1/4 to 1/2 teaspoon **liquid smoke**

1/2 teaspoon **smoked paprika**

1/4 teaspoon **garlic powder**

1/4 teaspoon **ground ginger**

1/4 teaspoon **onion powder**

1/4 teaspoon **cayenne**

1/4 teaspoon **black pepper**

1/4 teaspoon **ground mustard**

1/4 teaspoon **ground cumin**

1/4 teaspoon **ground allspice**

1/4 teaspoon **salt**

1. In a medium bowl, whisk together the maple syrup, ketchup, molasses, vinegar, lemon juice, tamarind past, liquid smoke, paprika, garlic powder, ginger, onion powder, cayenne, pepper, mustard, cumin, allspice, and salt.

2. Taste and adjust the seasonings. The sauce gets stronger as it sits. Store in the refrigerator in a clean jar for up to 1 month.

Note: If you choose to use vegan Worcestershire sauce, please note that the recipe will no longer be soy-free.

Per 2/3 cup: Calories 325, Total Fat 1g, Saturated Fat 0g, Sodium 615mg, Total Carbs 84g, Fiber 2g, Sugars 71g, Protein 2g

Caramelized Onions

These easy caramelized onions make a great topping on a burger patty or bowl. Unlike many caramelized onion recipes, these don't take hours. Keep some of these ready in the refrigerator for adding to all your bean-based dishes.

Prep time: 10 minutes
Active time: 15 minutes
soy-free, gluten-free, nut-free
Serves 4

2 teaspoons organic safflower or other neutral oil
1 large red onion, sliced paper thin
1/4 teaspoon salt
1/4 teaspoon sugar
1/2 to 1 teaspoon molasses

1. Heat the oil in a large skillet over medium heat. Add the onion and stir to coat it in the oil. Add the salt and sugar and cook for 4 to 5 minutes, stirring occasionally, until the onion is translucent.

2. Add the molasses and a splash water, stir, and continue cooking for another 4 to 5 minutes. If the onion starts to brown quickly at any point, reduce the heat to medium-low. You can continue to cook down the onion to your preference.

Variation: Add a combination of cayenne, smoked paprika, and balsamic vinegar to the onions. Add spice blends of your choice, like the Baharat Spice Blend (page 100), Garam Masala (page 244), or Berbere Paste (page 68).

Per serving: Calories 50, Total Fat 2g, Saturated Fat 1g, Sodium 80mg, Total Carbs 8g, Fiber 1g, Sugars 6g, Protein 1g

Flax Egg

Ground flax seed, when mixed with water, makes a gooey mixture that works well to substitute chicken eggs in baking and other recipes that need binding, such as lentil or bean burgers. It is not an exact substitute in each recipe for an egg, especially when there are multiple eggs used.

Active time: 5 minutes
Inactive time: 15 minutes
soy-free, gluten-free, nut-free
Makes 1 Flax Egg

1 tablespoon ground flax seed
2 1/2 tablespoons (38ml) water

In a small bowl, combine the flax seed and water. Let the mixture sit at room temperature or in the refrigerator for 15 minutes before using.

Variation: To make a chia seed egg, combine 1 tablespoon chia seeds or ground chia seed and 3 tablespoons (45ml) water and proceed with the directions.

Per serving: Calories 30, Total Fat 2g, Saturated Fat 0g, Sodium 4mg, Total Carbs 3g, Fiber 2g, Sugars 0g, Protein 1g

Crisped Tofu

This pan-crisped tofu works really well in most of the saucy stir-fries. The crisping step helps bolster the tofu, preventing it from breaking into a soft mess.

Prep time: 10 minutes
Active time: 15 minutes
gluten-free, nut-free
Serves 4

1 to 2 teaspoons organic safflower or other neutral oil (see variation)

14 ounces (400g) firm tofu, pressed and cubed (below)

Heat the oil in a medium skillet over medium heat. Add the tofu and cook for 9 to 10 minutes, or until some sides are golden. Stir occasionally to flip. Remove from the skillet and use.

Variation: To make baked crisped tofu, omit the oil. Preheat the oven to 400°F (200°C). Spread the cubed tofu on a medium baking sheet lined with parchment paper and bake for 20 to 30 minutes, depending on the texture you prefer—bake longer for crisper and chewier tofu.

Note: Pressing the tofu to remove excess moisture and using a well-seasoned nonstick pan, will reduce the possibility of the tofu sticking and breaking during crisping. If the tofu almost always sticks to the pan, then it's time for a new pan.

Per serving: Calories 413, Total Fat 26g, Saturated Fat 3g, Sodium 16mg, Total Carbs 9g, Fiber 3g, Sugars 1g, Protein 35g

How to Press and Cube Tofu

Firm or extra-firm tofu, when pressed to remove excess moisture, changes into pleasing and sturdy tofu—it doesn't stick or break as much and crisps up amazingly in a pan or the oven.

Wrap the tofu in paper napkins or paper towels, then wrap it in a kitchen towel. Place a heavy object on top and let it press for 10 to 15 minutes. Unwrap the tofu, chop it into cubes, and use.

You can also use a tofu press and let it press for 10 minutes.

Garam Masala

What is garam masala? *Garam* means *hot* and *masala* in this context means *a blend of spices*. Contrary to the direct meaning, the spice blend itself is not generally hot. It has black pepper but no red chiles. It can, however, feel hot once you eat some. The spices will warm you up from the inside. The flavor of garam masala is complex and strong and can be used in other cuisines as well. There are various recipes for garam masala depending on family recipes, regional recipes, chefs' recipes, and such. This is the version I generally use.

Active time: 10 minutes
soy-free, gluten-free, nut-free
Makes 2/3 cup (50g)

3 (2-inch [5cm]) cinnamon sticks or 3
   teaspoons ground cinnamon
1/2 teaspoon ground nutmeg or 1
   small nutmeg
1/4 cup (20g) coriander seeds
2 tablespoons cumin seeds
1 tablespoon black cardamom pods
   (optional)
1 tablespoon green cardamom pods
   or 1 1/2 teaspoons ground green
   cardamom
1 tablespoon whole cloves
1 to 1 1/2 tablespoons black peppercorns
10 to 12 dried Indian bay leaves (optional)

In a spice grinder, grind the cinnamon sticks and nutmeg until they are finely ground. Add the coriander seeds, cumin seeds, black cardamom (if using), green cardamom, cloves, peppercorns, and Indian bay leaves (if using) and grind to a powder. Store in an airtight container for up to 3 months.

Note: You can also roast the spices before blending. Dry-roast all the ingredients except the nutmeg in a small skillet over medium-low heat for 4 to 5 minutes, stirring occasionally. Cool completely. Grind the cinnamon sticks and nutmeg, and then add the rest of the spices, grind, and store as directed.

Per serving: Calories 156, Total Fat 8g, Saturated Fat 1g, Sodium 47mg, Total Carbs 29g, Fiber 16g, Sugars 3g, Protein 6g

Quick Garam Masala

2 tablespoons (12g) ground coriander
1 tablespoon ground cumin
2 teaspoons black pepper
3/4 teaspoon ground cloves
3/4 to 1 teaspoon ground cinnamon
1/2 teaspoon ground cardamom
1/4 teaspoon ground nutmeg

Combine the coriander, cumin, pepper, cloves, cinnamon, cardamom, and nutmeg in an airtight container. Store for up to 2 months.

Kashmiri Garam Masala

This garam masala from the state of Kashmir has different spices and makes a blend that works beautifully with creamy sauces, roasted vegetables, or chickpea curries. The spice blend has a good amount of black pepper to induce heat in the body to help it withstand the cold conditions in the hilly regions of the state.

1 tablespoon black peppercorns

1 tablespoon coriander seeds

1 teaspoon cumin seeds

1 teaspoon ground cinnamon

1 teaspoon ground cloves

3/4 teaspoon ground cardamom

1/2 teaspoon ground ginger

Blend or grind the spices together and store in an airtight container.

Makes about 3 1/2 tablespoons (21g)

Curry Powder

Contrary to popular belief, curry powder is neither a traditional Indian spice blend nor is it the same as garam masala. Curry powder has turmeric and other spice inclusions. Curry powder is a British or Western spice blend approximating the spice blends from north and south India. It works well as a handy spice blend in certain dishes.

Active time: 10 minutes
soy-free, gluten-free, nut-free
Makes about 5 1/2 tablespoons (33g)

1 recipe Quick Garam Masala (page 244)

1 tablespoon ground turmeric

1/2 teaspoon ground ginger

1/2 teaspoon ground mustard

1/2 teaspoon cayenne, or more to taste

In an airtight container, combine the quick garam masala, turmeric, ginger, mustard, and cayenne. Store for up to 2 months.

Per 5 1/2 tablespoons: Calories 183, Total Fat 8g, Saturated Fat 1g, Sodium 50mg, Total Carbs 36g, Fiber 20g, Sugars 3g, Protein 7g

Crunchy Baked Cauliflower

This is a basic baked cauliflower recipe to use with most of the sauces in this book. The baked cauliflower bites are lightly spiced, so they work with the strong flavors of the sauces they are paired with. Broccoflower, Romanesco, or broccoli may be used instead of cauliflower. I use a batter-and-breadcrumb coating on the cauliflower, as it makes crunchy bites as well as keeps the cauliflower inside moist. These baked bites stay crunchy for a few hours and eventually soften because of the moisture in the cauliflower; toss them in your favorite sauce just before serving.

Prep time: 20 minutes
Active time: 15 minutes
Inactive time: 25 minutes
soy-free option, nut-free, gluten-free option
Serves 4

2/3 cup (80g) unbleached all-purpose flour or 1/3 cup (40g) whole-wheat flour and 1/3 cup (40g) unbleached all-purpose flour

1/3 cup (50g) cornstarch or tapioca starch

1/2 teaspoon baking powder

3/4 to 1 1/4 teaspoons salt, divided

1/4 teaspoon black pepper

1/4 teaspoon cayenne (optional)

1 teaspoon garlic powder

3/4 cup (180ml) plus 2 tablespoons (30ml) water, plus more as needed

1 teaspoon soy sauce (or coconut aminos to make it soy-free)

2 teaspoons organic safflower or other neutral oil

1 1/2 cups (120g) panko breadcrumbs or dry breadcrumbs

1 medium head cauliflower, cut into 1- to 1 1/2-inch (3- to 4cm) florets

1. Preheat the oven to 425°F (220°C). Line a large baking sheet with parchment paper.

2. In a medium bowl, combine the flour, cornstarch, baking powder, 1/2 to 3/4 teaspoon of the salt, pepper, cayenne (if using), and garlic powder. Add the water, soy sauce, and oil and stir to combine. If needed, add more water, 1 tablespoon at a time, to make a thin, pancake-type batter. (Keep the batter on the thicker side if using broccoli.)

3. In another medium bowl, combine the panko breadcrumbs and the remaining 1/4 to 1/2 teaspoon salt.

4. Dip the florets in the batter, tap them gently against the side of the bowl to remove excess batter, then dip or roll them in the breadcrumbs to coat at least half of the florets, and place them on the baking sheet. (I like to use the stems to dip and coat to avoid messy hands.) Spray oil on the florets.

5. Bake the florets for 25 to 30 minutes, or until a toothpick passes through them easily. Broil for 1 minute to brown them, if needed.

Gluten-Free Variation: Use gluten-free white rice flour instead of all-purpose flour in the batter and use gluten-free breadcrumbs to coat the vegetables.

Note: If you have leftover batter, make it into savory crepes. Heat a skillet over medium heat. Spread a half teaspoon oil over it. Add a small ladle full of batter and move the skillet to spread. Cook until the crepe is dry.

Per serving: Calories 271, Total Fat 3g, Saturated Fat 0g, Sodium 635mg, Total Carbs 54g, Fiber 4g, Sugars 3g, Protein 7g

Saucing the Cauliflower

These cauliflower bites go great with a variety of sauces:

- Manchurian Sauce (page 44)
- Sweet and Sour Sauce (page 24)
- Peanut Butter Sauce (page 2)
- Kung Pao Sauce (page 35)
- Buffalo Sauce (page 84)
- Firecracker Sauce (page 78)

Breading Stations

To make preparing breaded recipes more efficient, set up a breading station with the bowls of batter and breadcrumbs and the prepared baking sheet arranged in the order you will be using them.

If you plan to serve these bites without a sauce, add more of the spices and salt to the batter.

11
My Everyday Kitchen

For the longest while after transitioning to a vegan diet, I was cooking predominantly Indian and Indian-influenced meals because I found that I could easily veganize Indian food. When I started to experiment more with other cuisines, I was faced with trying new ingredients, sauces, and seasonings. Sometimes I would be hesitant or nervous about the new flavors. I took my time with each new ingredient, using it in many ways, and kept on cooking. You can probably notice how my ease and confidence with different ingredients grew on the blog. The blog chronicles my culinary story as I learned to cook, use new ingredients, and experiment.

I use plenty of spices and herbs—dried and fresh—for flavor. My recipes also use other flavoring ingredients, such as sauces, vinegars, condiments, and the like. The recipes also use many beans, legumes, vegetables, nuts, whole grains, and seeds.

If you have been cooking vegan food regularly, you might already have a pantry set up for the recipes in this book. If you are a beginner, this chapter goes through the ingredients and components used often throughout the book.

Split peas

Lentils, Peas, and Beans

I grew up eating Indian food, which uses a wide variety of dals and beans. To this day, I use legumes liberally in my cooking and they are the main protein in my meals. Lentils and beans are available dried or canned. Using dried lentils or beans increases the cooking and prep time as most beans need a few hours of soaking and cooking to cook through. Keep reading to learn how to cook beans in a saucepan on the stove or in a pressure cooker. (Also, see the table on page 251 for a quick-reference guide to cooking times when using a pressure cooker.) While cooking legumes from scratch may seem time-consuming, keep in mind that cooked lentils and beans can be frozen for quick use later. Freeze 1 1/2-cup (300g) portions in sealed freezer-safe containers or zip-top bags for up to three months.

Following are the most-used beans in the book:

- Black beans
- Chickpeas
- Kidney beans
- Lentils (brown, green, and red)
- Split peas

Other beans that can be used instead of the ones in the preceding list include the following:

- Beluga lentils (instead of brown, green, or red lentils)
- Black-eyed peas (instead of chickpeas or black beans)
- Cannellini beans (instead of chickpeas, kidney beans, or black beans)
- Pinto beans (instead of black beans)
- Navy beans (instead of chickpeas, kidney beans, or black beans)

Cooking Lentils in a Saucepan or Pressure Cooker

Most whole lentils–brown, green, and beluga–have similar cooking times. Use beluga lentils for recipes that need lentils that hold their shape and brown lentils for creamier results. Note that 1 heaping cup (100g) dried brown lentils will yield about 3 cups (600g) cooked lentils. Look through the lentils for any shriveled individuals or stones, soak the lentils for 10 to 15 minutes, then cook them in water or with the recipe as needed.

To cook lentils in a saucepan on the stove, combine the lentils with 3 cups (720ml) water in a medium saucepan over medium heat and cook for 20 minutes. Reduce the heat to medium-low and simmer for 15 minutes, or until the lentils reach the desired tenderness.

To pressure-cook lentils, cook the lentils with 2 cups (480ml) water for 10 to 11 minutes at high pressure (manual for 10 to 11 minutes in an Instant Pot). Let the pressure release naturally.

Cooking Beans in a Saucepan or Pressure Cooker

There are many kinds of beans. Most can be cooked ahead in a saucepan or a pressure cooker. Look through the beans to remove any shriveled individuals or stones. Rinse the beans, then cover them with water by 3 inches (8cm) for a few hours or up to overnight. Drain the beans and cook with fresh water.

To help beans be more digestible, bring the soaked beans to a boil with just enough water to cover the them, then discard that water and start with fresh water. Another option is to sprout the beans before using. After soaking them overnight, drain the beans and place them in a bowl covered with a damp towel. Rinse the beans every 8 hours, until they have sprouted, then use them in your chosen recipe. Note that kidney and cannellini beans should not be sprouted, as they contain a toxin that can be poisonous.

To cook beans in a saucepan, combine 1 cup (100g) beans with 3 to 4 cups (720 to 960ml) water and cook for 40 to 60 minutes, depending on the beans. (See table for pressure cooker or Instant Pot cooking times.)

Beans	Pressure Cook Times (Soaked)	Pressure Cook Times (Not Soaked)	Saucepan (Water Needed)	Saucepan Times (Soaked)
Black	6–8 minutes	24–28 minutes	4 cups (960ml)	60 minutes
Black-eyed peas	8–10 minutes	12 minutes	3 cups (720ml)	40–45 minutes
Cannellini	5–8 minutes	20–30 minutes	3 cups (720ml)	60 minutes
Chickpeas	25 minutes	35–40 minutes	4 cups (960ml)	60 minutes
Kidney, red	20–25 minutes	30–35 minutes	N/A	60 minutes
Lentils, beluga	6 minutes	8–10 minutes	3 cups (720ml)	30 minutes
Lentils (green, brown, or whole red)	6 minutes	10–12 minutes	3 cups (720ml)	25–30 minutes
Lentils, split red	N/A	2–3 minutes	3 cups (720ml)	12–18 minutes
Mung	10 minutes	15–20 minutes	2 1/2 cups (600ml)	45 minutes
Peas, split (yellow, green, chana dal)	4–7 minutes	10–15 minutes	4 cups (960ml)	40 minutes
Pinto	6–10 minutes	20–25 minutes	3 cups (720ml)	60 minutes

Grains and Flours

I use these flours and whole grains in the book for baking and other recipes. Following are the commonly used flours and grains in this book.

Almond Flour: Almond flour is used in gluten-free baking in this book. Gluten-free baking tends to make drier results and a higher-fat nut flour like almond helps retain more moisture and keep the baked goods soft.

Basmati Rice (White or Brown): I almost always use basmati rice wherever rice is mentioned, whether it is Indian food or another cuisine. Brown basmati rice cooks up quicker than some other types of brown rice. I cannot digest brown rice well; hence, the photos in the book show mostly white rice, which can easily be substituted with brown rice, quinoa, or another cooked grain.

Measuring Flour

Flour can get very packed or overly fluffed depending on storage. Ideally, you want to spoon the flour into the cup, then level it off using the flat edge of a knife. Errors in flour measurement can cause unwanted effects in the baked result. If the batter (or whatever you are making) doesn't end up as the recipe describes, adjust the flour or wet ingredients a bit to get to the consistency mentioned.

Besan (Gram Flour): Besan is flour made from skinned brown chickpeas (or chana dal). Besan has a nuttier flavor than white chickpea flour and is available in Indian stores and online. If you are highly sensitive to gluten, be sure to get besan that is marked gluten-free.

Chickpea Flour: Chickpea flour is made by grinding garbanzo beans (chickpeas). (In the United States, white chickpeas are commonly used.) Besan (gram flour) is flour made of skinned brown chickpeas. In most recipes, chickpea flour and besan can be used interchangeably, as the flavors are similar. Chickpea flour, however, needs more water than besan to give batter a similar consistency. Chickpea flour works better than besan in baking. The recipes specify which type of flour works best. Chickpea flour is more readily available than besan in grocery stores and online.

Coconut (Dried and Shredded): Dried shredded coconut is available in most grocery stores and online. Look for unsweetened shredded coconut.

Coconut Flour: Coconut flour is not made of regular shredded coconut but ground from dried, defatted coconut meat. It is used in this book in the Gluten-Free Flour Blend (page 231). Coconut flour absorbs a lot of moisture and cannot be used as a one-to-one substitute for other flours. It can be found online or in specialty grocery stores.

Cornstarch: Cornstarch is used as a thickener or binder in some recipes. It can be substituted for arrowroot starch.

Gluten-Free Flour Blend: The Gluten-Free Flour Blend (page 231) is a blend I often use for baking muffins, cookies, and cakes. The blend uses certified gluten-free oat flour, almond flour, coconut flour, and starch. You can use other gluten-free blends of your choice as a substitute. The blends that have xanthan or other gums will give more predictable results in recipes.

Oats (Rolled Oats and Oat Flour): I use oats in rolled and ground form in the book. They are easily available in grocery stores. If you are gluten-sensitive, look for certified gluten-free oats and oat flour.

Quinoa: Quinoa is another grain of choice in this book. Anything you can serve over rice can be served with quinoa and vice versa.

Rice Flour: Rice flour is used as a gluten-free thickener. It is used in the batter for Gluten-Free Crunchy Baked Cauliflower (page 246). Rice flour also makes an appearance in my Gluten-Free Flatbread (page 237). I prefer white rice flour as it has a neutral flavor compared to the earthy brown rice flour. It is available in grocery stores and online.

Spelt Flour: Spelt is a nutty ancient wheat. Spelt flour tends to bake less dense and less earthy-flavored results than other whole-grain flours, which is why I prefer it for whole-grain baking. It is available in grocery stores and online.

Starches: I use tapioca, potato, and cornstarch in this book. They are great thickening and binding agents. Tapioca and potato starches are used in my Gluten-Free Flour Blend (page 231) and Vegan Mozzarella (page 152) to add volume and stretchiness in addition to acting as binders.

Unbleached All-Purpose Flour: When it comes to all-purpose flour, I prefer to use unbleached and organic. It is available in grocery stores.

Whole-Wheat Flour: Whole-wheat flour is whole-grain flour made from wheat berries. Depending on the type of wheat used, it can be dark or light (e.g., white whole-wheat flour). It is available in grocery stores.

Fresh Ingredients

Many of the savory recipes in this book call for garlic, ginger, onions, zucchini, peppers, cauliflower, broccoli, carrots, tomatoes, and sweet potatoes, among other vegetables. Other fresh ingredients used in the book include fresh herbs (such as basil, cilantro, and mint) and greens (such as spinach, kale, rainbow chard, and Swiss chard). Many of the recipes get their tanginess from tamarind, vinegars, fresh lemon juice, or fresh lime juice. Here are some specific facts about some of the fresh ingredients used in these recipes.

Cilantro: Cilantro, of course, is the plant and its leaves, and coriander is the seeds from that plant. I use cilantro mostly as a garnish in this book. Sometimes it is an essential garnish, as the fresh burst of flavor balances out the spices and heat and adds color and texture to the final dish. Use fresh cilantro leaves and tender stems.

Garlic: Garlic is used in many forms and in many ways in the book—raw garlic, roasted garlic, and garlic powder are all called for in my recipes. If the fresh cloves are too small, use two for each clove listed in the recipe. If they are too big, then reduce the quantity accordingly.

Ginger: The sizes of gingerroots vary drastically. Some roots can be large and fat and some small and skinny. A 1-inch (3cm) knob fresh ginger will give you about 1 tablespoon chopped ginger. Gingerroot can range from young, juicy, and fresh to fibrous and mature or too sharp. I like to find the juiciest and least fibrous specimens, as they blend up well and are not intrusive in the dish when minced or chopped. You can peel the root first or use it unpeeled.

Green Chiles: A hot green chile is sometimes the only heat in a recipe, though green chiles may vary considerably in heat from batch to batch. Use bird's eye chiles or serrano chiles. Add cayenne to the dish later if the chiles turn out to be mild. To control the heat, remove the seeds from the chiles prior to using them in a recipe.

Jackfruit: Young green jackfruit is used in some recipes. Jackfruit is available in young or ripe, fresh or canned, in Asian stores, Indian stores, some grocery stores, and online. For the recipes in this book, get young green jackfruit. If you get it fresh, look for YouTube videos explaining how to slice it.

Mint: Fresh mint is used to make sauces or chutneys, and it's sometimes employed as a garnish.

Miso: I had not used miso until a few years into my vegan diet. Miso is a paste of fermented soybeans. (If you are avoiding soy, you can purchase soy free chickpea miso.) Miso adds umami to dishes and enhances the cheesy flavor in sauces.

Nondairy Milks: Almond milk and canned full-fat coconut milk are the nondairy milks most frequently used in this book. However, other nondairy milks—such as soy milk, hemp milk, or cashew milk—can also be used.

Nutritional Yeast: Nutritional yeast is a highly nutritious inactive yeast that is used in vegan cooking to add a cheese-like flavor to dishes. It comes in flake or powder form, and both are interchangeable in these recipes.

Onions: Red or white onions are the onions used in the book wherever they are mentioned. Onions that are used raw in a recipe are generally first soaked in water for 15 minutes to reduce the sharp flavor. Depending on the water content of the onion, the time required to cook it until translucent may vary.

Tamarind Paste: Tamarind paste is used in a few recipes (namely Thai curries and pastes). The distinct sour profile is necessarily for the authentic Asian flavor. You can use fresh tamarind pulp from dry pods that have been soaked and squeezed, but tamarind paste made of concentrated tamarind is more readily available.

Tempeh: Tempeh is made of fermented soybeans, and it makes a great meat substitute. Tempeh is found in the refrigerated section of most supermarkets. Tempeh can be made with just soybeans or soybeans in combination with grains. If you are gluten-sensitive, look for gluten-free tempeh or tempeh made with only soybeans. Soy-free tempeh is also available in some specialty stores (look for tempeh made with black-eyed peas or split peas).

Tofu: Firm tofu is used in this book and is readily available in supermarkets. Good substitutes for tofu are tempeh, soy-free tempeh, soy-free hemp seed tofu, cooked chickpeas or beans, and my Chickpea Flour Tofu (page 238).

Tomatoes: I usually use fresh, just-ripe Roma tomatoes. They are firm, not too sweet, and just tart enough. I also use canned crushed tomatoes. Finally, I also use tomato paste and ketchup in some recipes. (The paste and ketchup can be used interchangeably.) Fresh tomatoes pick up the spices and flavors and let them shine more than canned tomatoes. If you feel like the canned tomato flavor is taking over the dish, double the spices and herbs.

Vegetable Broth: I rarely use vegetable broth in my recipes because it can often make recipes one-dimensional. The recipes have enough flavor from the spices, herbs, and cooking methods. However, if you prefer vegetable broth, feel free to substitute some or all of the water listed with vegetable broth.

Other Pantry Items

A well-stocked vegan pantry also includes ingredients that some people may consider miscellaneous ingredients. However, the following ingredients are all used in this book, and I recommend you keep them on hand.

Chipotle Chiles in Adobo Sauce: In this book, I use chipotle chiles in adobo sauce as well as dried chipotle powder or flakes. Substitute 1 chipotle chile in adobo sauce for 1/2 to 1 teaspoon chipotle powder and vice versa.

Chocolate: I use palm oil–free chocolate in this book. I recommend semisweet or dark chocolate from brands like Enjoy Life, Lulu's Chocolate, 365 Everyday Value Dark Chips from Whole Foods, Theo, and SunSpire. Brands keep changing their formulas and offerings, so always check the ingredients and labels.

Extracts: Vanilla extract is frequently used in the dessert chapter. Almond extract is used in some recipes. Both are readily available in grocery stores.

Nuts: I use raw cashews, peanuts, macadamia nuts, almonds, and walnuts in this book. Many recipes provide alternatives to use a different nut or make them nut-free.

Nut Butter: I use natural peanut butter and almond butter in the book. Both can be used interchangeably and often can be substituted by roasted sunflower seed butter.

Oils: I use extra-virgin olive oil, unrefined and refined safflower oil, unrefined and refined coconut oil, toasted sesame oil, and organic safflower or coconut oil spray in this book. For high-heat cooking, I use a small amount (1 to 2 teaspoons) organic safflower or other neutral high-heat oil. Coconut oil is often used in desserts.

Dried Red Chiles: Whole dried red chiles are used to add smoky flavor and heat. Use dried California red, Kashmiri, New Mexico, or ancho chiles for less heat and Thai, cayenne, or árbol for a spicy (hot) result. When used whole, dried red chiles do not immediately add much heat. Adjust the heat by adding more red pepper flakes or cayenne later, or break the whole chiles in two before using them so they release the heat into the dish faster. Substitute whole chiles with red pepper flakes to taste. Red pepper flakes are crushed (not ground) dried red chiles, usually a combination of more than one chile such as cayenne, ancho, bell, and other dried chiles.

Seeds: I use pepitas (shelled raw pumpkin seeds), shelled raw hemp seeds, raw sunflower seeds, chia seeds, flax seeds, and ground flax seed in the book. These are available in grocery stores or online.

Soy Sauce and Tamari: Soy sauce is used in some of the Asian and Asian-inspired recipes. To ensure a gluten-free recipe, use tamari or gluten-free soy sauce. Soy sauce and tamari have slightly different flavors. Soy sauce is available in low-sodium and other varieties, which may have slightly different flavors and salt levels. In some recipes that use larger amounts of soy sauce or tamari, start with the lower range and add more to your preference.

Sriracha Sauce and Hot Sauce: Sriracha and hot sauce are used for heat in some recipes. Both have a distinct flavor profile and are easily available in grocery stores. Some brands of sriracha can contain fish or other nonvegan ingredients. I've found that Huy Fong brand sriracha works best. For hot sauce, use any vinegar and cayenne-based hot sauce.

Sweeteners: I use coconut sugar, raw sugar (in granulated and confectioners' forms), organic cane sugar, molasses, pure maple syrup, and Medjool dates in this book. Most of these are easily available in grocery stores. Use soft, fresh Medjool dates or other soft dates for best results in recipes calling for dates.

Tahini: Tahini is just blended sesame seeds. Some brands might add additives, so check for a gluten-free label if needed. My Tahini Garlic Sauce (page 123) is a life-changing dressing you will want to eat every week.

Vinegars: I use raw apple cider vinegar, rice vinegar, and distilled white vinegar in the book. Most of these can be interchanged with one another.

Spices and Herbs

I use many spices and herbs for layers of flavor in the recipes. Spices don't always mean added heat. Most spices actually add a flavor to the overall dish. Whole spices stay fresh for years, while ground spices go stale and rancid after a few months. A good option when setting up your pantry is to invest in whole spices or small quantities of freshly ground spices and herbs. Following are the most commonly used spices and herbs. (There are a few not mentioned in the list that are used in a recipe or two—these can be omitted or substituted with a similar spice or herb.)

Allspice (ground)	Coriander (seeds and ground)	Nutmeg (ground)
Basil (dried and fresh)	Cumin (seeds and ground)	Old Bay Seasoning
Bay leaves	Curry powder	Onion powder
Black pepper (peppercorns and ground)	Dill (dried and fresh)	Oregano (dried)
Cardamom (ground)	Fennel seeds	Paprika (smoked and sweet)
Cayenne	Fenugreek leaves	Parsley (dried and fresh)
Celery seed	Garam masala	Red pepper flakes
Chipotle chile (ground and in adobo sauce)	Garlic powder	Rosemary (dried and fresh)
Cinnamon (ground)	Ginger (ground)	Thyme (dried and fresh)
Cloves (ground)	Kala namak (Indian sulphur black salt)	Turmeric (fresh and ground)
	Mustard (seeds and ground)	

Homemade Nut Butter

To make your own nut butter, add 2 to 3 cups (160 to 240g) nuts to a food processor and process until smooth. You might need to scrape down the sides of the processor once in a while. Let the processor rest after 3 to 4 minutes to cool and process again. You can add a bit of oil to move things along faster.

Pantry List

Following is a pantry list of the ingredients used in this book that can be helpful when making your shopping list.

Legumes
Black beans
Chickpeas
Kidney beans
Lentils (brown, green, red, and beluga)
Split peas

Grains and Flours
Almond flour
Basmati rice (white or brown)
Besan (gram flour)
Chickpea flour
Coconut (dried and shredded)
Coconut flour
Cornstarch
Oats (rolled oats and oat flour)
Quinoa
Rice flour
Spelt flour
Starches
Unbleached all-purpose flour
Whole-wheat flour

Other Pantry Items
Chocolate
Extracts (vanilla and almond)
Miso paste
Nutritional yeast
Nuts (raw cashews, peanuts, macadamia nuts, almonds, and walnuts)
Nut butter (peanut butter and almond butter)
Oils (extra-virgin olive oil, unrefined and refined safflower oil, unrefined and refined coconut oil, toasted sesame oil, safflower or coconut oil spray)
Seeds (pepita seeds [shelled raw pumpkin seeds], shelled raw hemp seeds, chia seeds, flax seeds, and ground flax seed)
Soy sauce and tamari
Sriracha sauce and hot sauce
Sweeteners (coconut sugar, raw sugar [granulated and confectioners'],

organic cane sugar, molasses, pure maple syrup, Medjool dates)
Tahini
Tamarind paste
Vegetable broth
Vinegars (raw apple cider vinegar, rice vinegar, and distilled white vinegar)

Spices and Herbs
(See list on page 255.)

Fresh Ingredients
Fresh herbs
Fresh produce
Garlic
Ginger
Green chiles
Jackfruit
Nondairy milk
Tempeh
Tofu

Tools of the Trade

I use the following equipment in my kitchen to prepare many of the recipes in this book.

Blender: Blenders are frequently used in the book. I use my NutriBullet (a small blender with blending and grinding blades) for all the dry or wet spice grinding and sauce blending. I also use the blender to make desserts, like my Blender Peanut Butter Cake (page 206). It makes the cleanup easy and mixing faster. I also use a high-powered blender for larger-quantity sauces and to break the nuts or grains down for sauces and batters. If you use soaked nuts, the Nutribullet can make a smooth and creamy consistency, eliminating the need for a larger high-powered blender.

Food Processor (Mini or Full Size): Food processors are like blenders but with more blades and options (like grating, shredding, or chopping). I use my KitchenAid mini food processor more than the full-size food processor. It reduces the chopping time considerably for some recipes. A food processor is a convenience, but it is not essential to make the recipes in this book. Vegetables can be shredded by using a large grater or by chopping them into thin slices.

Skillets and Saucepans: Medium to large (10- to 12-inch [25 to 30cm]) skillets with lids and medium (2-, 3-, 4-quart) saucepans are frequently called for in the book. There are several types of cookware and stoves that can affect the cooking times. For example, it can take anywhere from 30 seconds (when using steel cookware) to 3 minutes (when using ceramic cookware) for the oil to heat up to make Crisped Tofu (page 243). If tofu or sauces are sticking to the pan, it is time for a new one. Adjust the heat and cooking times accordingly. I use PFOA- and PFOE-free nonstick, hard anodized or ceramic cookware and cast iron skillets. Thick-bottom or cast iron pans work well for crisping up burgers. A cast iron grill pan adds grill marks without the fear of the patties or vegetables falling through a grill grate.

Pressure Cooker: Pressure cookers are great for cooking whole grains and beans that would otherwise take hours to become tender. I use pressure cookers generally for Indian food because of the beans, split peas, and lentils needed in many of the meals. Instant Pot is an electric pressure cooker with many other functions. With the popularity of the Instant Pot, many people now have one or another brand of pressure cooker. Some recipes that can benefit from pressure-cooking have times mentioned for the Instant Pot. Use the same time for any electric pressure cooker. Also see page 251 for cooking times for beans and lentils.

Knives: A sharp, high-quality chef's knife makes all the chopping typical of Indian food much easier. Find one that works for you. I have 2 (5-inch [8cm]) santoku knives with different types of handles and an 8-inch (20cm) Kramer knife. My mom prefers a smaller 4-inch (10cm) knife with a thin blade. Use the knives that work best for you.

Strainers and Bowls: Large strainers are needed for washing lentils, beans, and vegetables and to act as bowls to hold vegetables after chopping. A selection of bowls in various sizes make mixing and serving easy.

Baking Sheets, Pans, and Parchment Paper: Baking sheets, casserole dishes, and baking pans are used for baked recipes. I use parchment paper on the sheets and pans unless mentioned otherwise. A good quality parchment paper makes cleanup easier and faster.

Miscellaneous Equipment: In addition to the equipment just listed, other miscellaneous tools that can be helpful include spatulas for stirring and flipping, vegetable peelers, potato mashers, whisks, cutting boards, tongs, rolling pins, and pizza cutters.

Index of Recipe Groups

Gluten-Free

Gluten-Free Option

Acknowledgements

I want to thank everyone who was involved in bringing this book to life. It takes a physical and a virtual village to make a beautiful, consistent, and useful piece of work.

My gratitude goes out to the amazing recipe testers who cooked through the many variations and substitutions and to many other helpers who worked on the nutrition calculations, editing, and other tasks.

Davi and Mia, I am so happy to have you cooking along since the first book. I appreciate your work and trust your feedback and suggestions.

Sue, thank you for the support on the blog, during the publishing process, and in many other ways. Thank you for testing so much of the book.

Eve-Marie Williams, you made so much of my food, even the recipes that weren't meant to be. Thank you!

Leslie, Madeline, Lynsi, and Michelle, thank you for the consistent enthusiasm and honest notes.

Kathy and Dennis Lang, Tamar, and Hollie, thank you for coming along on this journey with me.

Nikolai and Doris, you are the sweetest.

Katharine, Noreen, Martha, thank you for the last-minute rush!

Lisa, April, and hubbs, thank you for all the conversions and nutritional calculations.

Thanks to Katie for being there to bounce ideas off of, for your excitement for the recipes, and for being you.

I want to thank each and every one of you who visits VeganRicha.com, likes what I put out there, and who bought my first book, *Vegan Richa's Indian Kitchen*. I am always amazed that you all cook my recipes and love them. I learn from you, the substitutions, the way you serve, which recipes you cook again and again. Thank you for the support, encouragement, comments, feedback, and enthusiasm.

My deepest gratitude for this book, the blog, and for so much more goes to my husband, Vivek. Without his constant support, understanding, open mind, open palate, and willingness, I would not be blogging and writing cookbooks. Sometimes I did wonder if his compliments meant that the food really *was* that good. (You know husbands.) Thank you, babe, for helping us get through all the crazy days when the kitchen looked like I had made ten things but there wasn't anything to eat (but we had an entire kitchen to clean). Thank you for eating combinations of things that didn't go together and for all the discussions, ideas, and perspectives. Thank you for cooking for me when I couldn't, for waiting patiently while I finished photographing, for all the appreciation, and thank you for being you. Thank you, Mummiji and Papaji (my in-laws), for creating and bringing up this fabulous man.

Thank you, Jon and the team at Vegan Heritage Press, for making this book happen and for the endless patience and guidance at every step.

I am grateful to Mom and Dad for being the stable foundation filled with unconditional love my life has been built on. Thank you to my sis, bro, and the fam who support and encourage me, even though they do not necessarily want me to feed them anything other than Indian food and pizza.

Thank you, Chewie, for without you I wouldn't have discovered the compassion I have for animals, I wouldn't have taken the time to think and make the connection, and I wouldn't have become vegan.

About the Author

Richa Hingle is the prolific and award-winning recipe developer, blogger, and photographer behind VeganRicha.com and author of the best-selling *Vegan Richa's Indian Kitchen*. Her instructions are easy to follow and her step-by-step photographs welcome the uninitiated into their kitchens. She loves to show people how easy it is to cook vegan Indian or other cuisines, which are allergy friendly and have gluten-free and soy-free options. Richa has been featured on Oprah.com, the Huffington Post, *Glamour*, Babble, VegNews.com, Rediff.com (as part of their top thirty Indian food blogs), The Kitchn, *Cosmopolitan*, MSN, BuzzFeed, and TreeHugger. She won a 2016 VegNews Bloggy Award, and her first book was listed as one of PETA's seven must-have vegan cookbooks and one of 2015's top cookbooks by *Vegetarian Times*.

Visit Richa at her website:

www.veganricha.com

Some of the recipes in this book will have recipe videos on Richa's YouTube channel:

www.youtube.com/veganricharecipes

Connect with Richa via social media:

Facebook – www.facebook.com/veganricha
Intagram – www.instagram.com/veganricha
Twitter – www.twitter.com/veganricha
Pinterest – www.pinterest.com/veganricha

A portion of the proceeds from the sale of this book will go toward the following organizations:

Help Animals India
https://helpanimalsindia.org/

Wildlife SOS
http://wildlifesos.org/

FOUR PAWS International
http://www.four-paws.us/

Old Dog Haven
https://olddoghaven.org/

Animal-Kind International
https://www.animal-kind.org/

Index

Metric Conversions and Equivalents

The recipes in this book have not been tested with metric measurements, so some variations may occur.

LIQUID

US	METRIC
1 tsp	5 ml
1 tbs	15 ml
2 tbs	30 ml
1/4 cup	60 ml
1/3 cup	75 ml
1/2 cup	120 ml
2/3 cup	150 ml
3/4 cup	180 ml
1 cup	240 ml
1 1/4 cups	300 ml
1 1/3 cups	325 ml
1 1/2 cups	350 ml
1 2/3 cups	375 ml
1 3/4 cups	400 ml
2 cups (1 pint)	475 ml
3 cups	720 ml
4 cups (1 quart)	945 ml

GENERAL METRIC CONVERSION FORMULAS

Ounces to grams	ounces x 28.35 = grams
Grams to ounces	grams x 0.035 = ounces
Pounds to grams	pounds x 435.5 = grams
Pounds to kilograms	pounds x 0.45 = kilograms
Cups to liters	cups x 0.24 = liters
Fahrenheit to Celsius	$(°F - 32) x 5 ÷ 9 = °C$
Celsius to Fahrenheit	$(°C x 9) ÷ 5 + 32 = °F$

WEIGHT

US	METRIC
1/2 oz	14 g
1 oz	28 g
1 1/2 oz	43 g
2 oz	57 g
2 1/2 oz	71 g
4 oz	113 g
5 oz	142 g
6 oz	170 g
7 oz	200 g
8 oz (1/2 lb)	227 g
9 oz	255 g
10 oz	284 g
11 oz	312 g
12 oz	340 g
13 oz	368 g
14 oz	400 g
15 oz	425 g
16 oz (1 lb)	454 g

OVEN TEMPERATURE

°F	Gas Mark	°C
250	1/2	120
275	1	140
300	2	150
325	3	165
350	4	180
375	5	190
400	6	200
425	7	220
450	8	230
475	9	240
500	10	260
550	Broil	290

LENGTH

US	METRIC
1/2 inch	1.25 cm
1 inch	2.5 cm
6 inches	15 cm
8 inches	20 cm
10 inches	25 cm
12 inches	30 cm